41 Seconds to Freedom

41 Seconds to Freedom

An Insider's Account of the
Lima Hostage Crisis, 1996–97

Luis Giampietri

with Bill Salisbury and Lorena Ausejo

BALLANTINE BOOKS
NEW YORK

For dramatic and narrative purposes,
this book contains re-created conversations, thoughts, and scenes.
The material facts of the hostage crisis remain unchanged.

Published in the United States by Presidio Press,
an imprint of The Random House Publishing Group,
a division of Random House, Inc., New York.

PRESIDIO PRESS and colophon are trademarks of Random House, Inc.

ISBN 978-0-89141-907-5

Printed in the United States of America

Book design by Katie Shaw

*Dedicated to all the people who lost their lives
and to all those who were so deeply affected by this tragic event*

ACKNOWLEDGMENTS

I first decided to write this account only for family and friends. I did not want the passage of time to obscure a single detail of that dreadful, hideously bizarre experience I and others suffered as terrorist captives: I wanted to leave a testament to my wife, children, grandchildren, and friends that described our time in hell at the Japanese Ambassador's residence in Lima.

When I finished the memoir, my wife and children suggested I publish it. I agreed but knew I would have to find a writer who could give literary shape to the story. I had the good fortune to count among my friends a young, talented, and enthusiastic journalist who could tell my story with style and flair: Lorena Ausejo. We worked together and prepared a Spanish language manuscript. But bureaucratic obstacles and the threat of pirated editions in Latin America convinced us we should seek a U.S. publisher for an English language edition.

Through a longtime friend, Bill Salisbury, we contacted a successful, enthusiastic agent, Charlotte Gusay, who agreed to represent us if Bill wrote an English language version of our book.

Bill had worked with me during the 1970s as a US Navy SEAL adviser to the Peruvian navy. He is now a well-known, bilingual writer in the United States on special operations and counterguerilla warfare.

Profuse thanks and gratitude of course to my wife Marcela who has been unflagging in her support throughout some very difficult times; to my children, Luis Felipe, Alessia Milagros, Sergio Martin, and Angelina who have also shared my victories and failures; to Lorena and Bill who helped make this book reality; to Charlotte Gusay who worked with three authors separated by distance, culture, and language; to Bill's son, Mark, who as a former Navy SEAL benefited the book with his knowledge of commando tactics; to Bill's wife, Maria, who read both the Spanish and English language manuscripts and contributed valuable suggestions; to our steadfast and patient editor at Presidio Press, Ron Doering; to my beloved seventy-one comrades who shared my captivity of 126 days; to all other hostages who shared any part of that terrible ordeal; to President Alberto Fujimori who defended Peruvian democracy so tenaciously; to those dedicated people who desperately sought a peaceful end to the crisis: Monsignor Juan Luis Cipriani; the late Canadian ambassador to Peru, Anthony Vincent; the Japanese ambassador to Mexico, Teruseke Terada; Peruvian minister of education, Domingo Palermo; to all those anonymous people who supported us and suffered for our freedom; to all my friends, brothers and sisters in spirit; and finally to the memory of my deceased parents, Lucho and Rosita.

Before I finish, I would like to mention that every important moment in this account is real and the way it happened. However, many of the events have been re-created based on information received from third-party accounts I didn't live though; other events have been re-created based on suppositions to give the story dramatic continuity. Also, certain details of how terrorists died are conjecture: investigations continue.

Of course I would not be here to recount my story if not for the commandos who rescued us. The selfless courage of these commandos is personified in Colonel Juan Valer and Lieutenant Colonel Raul Jiménez, who paid the ultimate price for our freedom. I must also recognize the tactical genius and leadership of the man who directed the rescue, General José Williams. General Williams and his men have my eternal gratitude.

I close these lines by giving thanks to God. He honored our secret covenant and I will always strive to do the same.

LUIS GIAMPIETRI ROJAS

CONTENTS

INTRODUCTION

Peru. Machu Picchu. Land of the Incas. Pizarro (or was it Cortés?). Atahuallpa (or was it Montezuma?). Like many gringos, this was all I knew of the country when in 1972 the US Navy ordered me to the capital of Lima as adviser for a fledgling SEAL team in the Peruvian navy. (I didn't even know Peru had a navy, let alone one with a SEAL team, submarines, cruisers, and aircraft.)

The prospect of this duty did not thrill me. Although the Vietnam War was winding down, I still hoped for a third tour before the light at the end of the tunnel flickered out.

Before I headed south, the navy sweetened the deal with six months of Spanish at the Defense Language Institute in Monterey, California, followed by a year of Latin American studies at the University of Florida.

I arrived in-country and began a four-year tour knowing somewhat more than I had when I'd started my education. Peru, I'd learned, is located below the equator in South America, which means the seasons are the reverse of ours. An intensely Catholic country, Peru celebrates Christmas beneath a sun just beginning to burn through a winter sea mist called *La Garua* that presses down upon the coast from June through November. It did not rain in Lima the entire time I was there. *La Garua* promised but never delivered.

The country is shaped like California but three times the size. Peru has a Pacific coastline of fifteen hundred miles that stretches from Ecuador in the north to Chile in the south and has some of the best surfing anywhere—

including the longest left-breaking wave in the world, near Puerto Chicama. The coast is cooled by the Humboldt Current, which wells up from the Antarctic. Water temperatures—of agonizing concern to navy SEALs—are often in the fifties and sometimes dip into the forties. Wet suits are not optional. In contrast, the coastal plain encompasses a vast desert broken by some thirty-eight rivers that flow across it to the sea from the Andes. The Andean cordillera, which separates the coastal desert from Peru's share of the Amazon jungle, has glacier-encased mountains that soar to twenty-three thousand feet.

Peru has a diverse population of twenty-eight million comprising mainly Europeans (15 percent), mixed-race mestizos (37 percent), and Indians (45 percent). Andean Indians speak Quechua—the language of the Incas—or Aymara. Coastal whites and mestizos speak Spanish.

Seventy-eight percent of Peruvians earn less than fifty-eight dollars a month. Despite this poverty, Peru is rich in natural resources. Fish meal, metals, petroleum, and sugar account for most exports. But a rudimentary infrastructure limits economic growth and social integration. Peru has only two paved roads of consequence: the Pan American Highway that runs the length of the coast from Ecuador to Chile, and the Central Highway that connects Lima with a few mountain valleys. No interstates.

Divided racially, economically, and geographically, Peru appears ripe for communist "wars of national liberation," and such wars have indeed periodically flared since the Russian Revolution in 1917.

But the Peruvian military, aided chiefly by US advisers and equipment, has not been kind to revolutionaries. It put down serious uprisings with brutal efficiency in 1932, 1947, 1962, and 1968. Then came 1980 and two communist groups the likes of which the Peruvian military had never seen: *Sendero Luminoso* ("Shining Path" or SL) and *Movimiento Revolucionario Túpac Amaru* ("Túpac Amaru Revolutionary Movement" or MRTA). These terrorists waged an unrelenting war against the government for sixteen years with atrocities that recall the Mau Mau and Khmer Rouge. The war lingers still and shows disturbing signs of intensifying.

Peru was peaceful during the 1970s when I was there. Revolution was for other places, like the dwarf nations of Central America. You could travel anywhere a road reached in Peru without fear. When I returned for a visit in 1986, you couldn't travel beyond the outskirts of Lima without risking death at the hands of terrorists.

I returned to visit an old friend who had been my counterpart and first commanding officer of the Peruvian SEALs then—Lieutenant Commander Luis "Lucho" Giampietri. Lucho was an apolitical and thoroughly professional officer—something of a rarity in Latin America.

Lucho's size alone inspired respect. He was slightly taller than six feet with a barrel chest and biceps to match. He was in terrific physical shape: He could swim and free-dive better than most US Navy SEALs I knew, and in those days I knew them all.

Lucho's SEALs were at the pointy end of the spear in 1986. His platoons operated in all regions of the country: coast, mountains, and jungle. I had sent several of these men to Basic Underwater Demolition/SEAL training in Coronado, California. They achieved the highest graduation rate of any foreign nation. Unlike many trainees from warmer climes, the Peruvians were undismayed by hypothermic temperatures off the California coast. They had trained in the frigid waters of the Humboldt Current: Cold was their meat.

During the first difficult years of the war against SL and MRTA, Lucho personally led his men in combat. Later, as the second-ranking admiral in the Peruvian navy, he was in charge of joint operations against terrorists and narcotic traffickers in the Andes and Amazon jungle. Admiral Giampietri provides a chilling inside account of the war in this book and how Peruvian SEALs, marines, and army commandos met and defeated the terrorists in a war without quarter.

But Admiral Giampietri's greatest personal triumph in the war came a few years after he had retired and settled into what he thought would be a tranquil time with his wife and four children—two of whom were SEALs. He was mistaken. The easy days would have to wait.

For the first time Admiral Giampietri reveals in this book how he and seventy other men survived 126 days at the hands of fourteen terrorists who seized the Japanese ambassador's residence in Lima a week before Christmas in 1996. He also reveals the riveting details of the key role he played in the most spectacular hostage rescue of our time.

Admiral Giampietri presently serves as a member of the Peruvian Congress and as first vice president of the country.

BILL SALISBURY

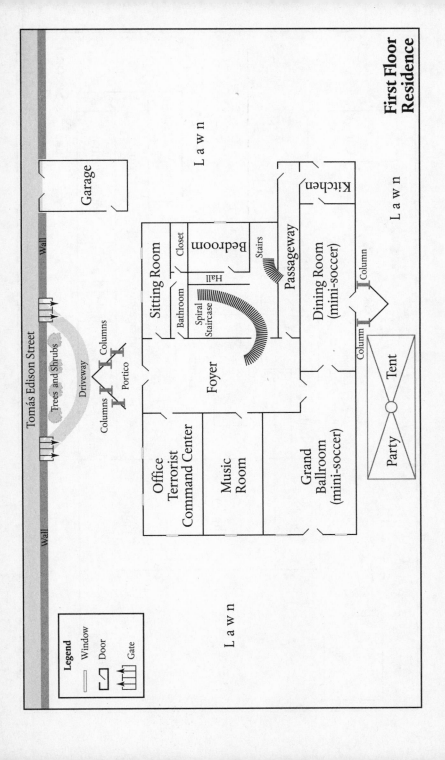

**First Floor
Residence**

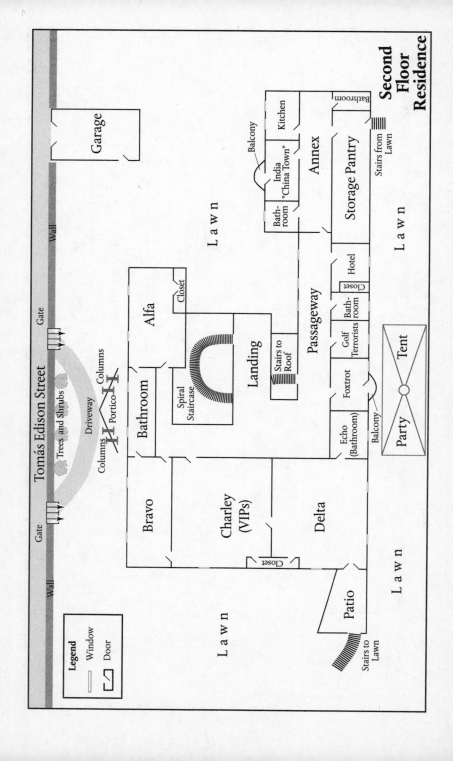

Second Floor Residence

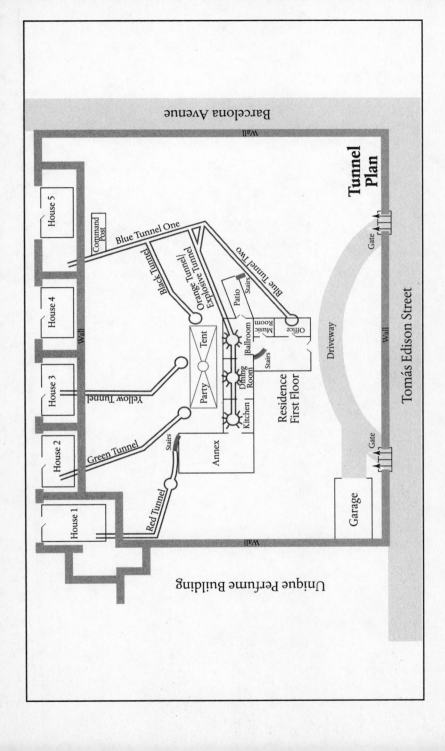

41 Seconds to Freedom

1

The Takedown

THE EXPLOSION was loud and close, as if the charge had gone high-order just outside the ambassador's residence. But we heard only the explosion; no shattering glass or even rattling windows. Much of the shock wave seemed to have bounced off the high stucco wall surrounding the residence. As with an ambushing enemy's first volley, the precise location of the blast was a mystery. I saw my wife, Marcella, flinch and suspected most in the crowd of nearly six hundred guests had flinched as well.

But no one panicked. Such explosions had been part of our lives during the past sixteen years of vicious warfare with terrorists determined to force a Marxist regime on Peru. We'd come to expect and endure the car bomb, the dynamited electrical pylon, the assassin's grenade.

A man nearby said, "Well, at least they didn't hit a power station. We still have lights, *gracias a Dios.*"

Marcella and I resumed our conversation with General Carlos Domínguez, former director of Peru's Counter-Terrorism Department, and Oscar Mavila, president of the Institute for Human Development—a public polling business. A photographer from *El Comercio*—the *New York Times* of Peru—had taken a photo of us talking just before the explosion. I would later see that photo published many times.

Oscar had called to us as we passed him in the grand ballroom on our way to the front door. We'd arrived some thirty minutes earlier to celebrate the emperor's birthday at a party the Japanese ambassador, Morihisa Aoki, hosted each year.

This was my first invitation to the event, and I was a reluctant guest. Since my retirement from the Peruvian navy, I'd been happily at work with my deep-sea diving company until the government convinced me I should head the Peruvian Institute of Oceanography.

My love of the sea more than money or prestige prompted me to accept the position. But while the job provided marvelous opportunities—such as working closely with Scripps Research Institute in La Jolla, California—it also brought with it social obligations I could have done without. Invitations to attend diplomatic receptions arrived endlessly in a blizzard of little white envelopes. After nearly a year I'd had enough of the blizzard and was declining most invitations.

I decided to decline the most recent invitation I'd found in the middle of my desk as I arrived to begin the day's work at the institute less than two weeks before Christmas. The invitation, addressed to my predecessor, invited the institute's president to attend the emperor's birthday party at the Japanese ambassador's residence.

I called to my secretary in the next room: "Maritza—tell the Japanese, *por favor*, that I won't be attending their celebration on the seventeenth."

"Right away, *mi almirante*, right away." Then the ever-efficient Maritza paused, and I knew what was coming. "But perhaps you should attend. Remember, the Japanese are giving us an ocean research vessel." She paused again. "And you might have a chance to talk with President Fujimori about your plans for the ship."

That did it. I sighed and said, "You're right—as usual. It's just that I've also been invited that night to a party for Eric Giovannini." Eric had been my aide during the anti-terrorist campaign in the jungle.

Maritza's reminder about the research vessel doomed me, though. Like all third-world countries, Peru often had to depend on the charity of others. "But the Japanese don't even know my name."

"I've already taken care of that, *mi almirante*. A messenger is on his way from the embassy with another invitation addressed to you. And you don't have to stay at the party very long. You'll have time for fun with your friends."

I put the invitation aside and settled into the comfortable swivel chair behind my desk. *Fun with my friends*, I thought. Maritza was right—I would have fun telling and listening to war stories I'd told and heard before. Amazing how time improved the stories—like properly aged Tacama wine.

I'd also learn what my old command, *Fuerzas de Operaciones Especiales* (FOE), had been up to. The Special Operations Force had recently fought in our never-ending territorial dispute with Ecuador. I knew fresh war stories would be in the air, and I was eager to hear them.

I turned the chair and looked at the plaques on the wall behind me. My gaze lingered on two that hung side by side and set above the others I'd collected during my forty years in the navy.

Both featured seals—the kind with flippers. The seal on the plaque for our FOEs balanced a round black bomb with a sputtering fuse on its nose; the seal on the plaque for the US Navy's Sea-Air-Land Teams (SEALs) peered from beneath a beret, its whiskered face half concealed behind a flipper draped with a spy's cloak. The flipper clutched a gleaming K-Bar knife.

SEALs and FOEs—which we pronounced *FO-eighs*—had been training and operating together since the early 1970s, when I was turning a small underwater demolition team into the Special Operations Force. I modeled the force on US Navy SEALs. Peru had sent twelve men to SEAL basic training in Coronado, California, between 1973 and 1975. Eleven of those men graduated from this, the most grueling combat course in the world. The men formed the core of our FOEs. A friend of mine who was a senior SEAL officer once told me Peru had an extraordinary graduation rate. Seventy percent of US trainees, he noted, failed to complete the course; foreign trainees had an even more dismal dropout rate.

The only officer to graduate in one course was a Peruvian.

SEALs had also been coming to Peru since the 1970s to train with us. And for the last several years we had operated together searching for drug traffickers in the Amazon Basin and high valleys of the Andes. Several SEALs were in-country now, and I hoped a few would be at Eric's party.

But first the emperor's birthday. I reached for the phone to call my wife with the news of yet another invitation for the Christmas season. As I waited for Marcella to answer, I made a note to decorate our tree while we still had time.

THE JAPANESE AMBASSADOR'S residence was located in the elegant old neighborhood of San Isidro and covered nearly an acre. A guard stopped our driver less than a block from the residence and asked for our invitation. The guard glanced at the card, returned it, and waved us on without so much as checking to see who was in the backseat.

"We got off cheap," I told Marcella. "If this were the US or Israeli ambassador's place, we'd have to show three different kinds of identification, then wait while guards and dogs checked the car. After that would come the detectors for weapons and explosives. They would even confiscate cell phones and pagers."

"I don't mind the bother of good security," Marcella said. "I'd feel much safer if we were at the Israeli or US ambassador's residence."

The driver passed through an open gate and up a circular driveway. He dropped us off at the entrance, where a guard directed us through a single metal detector. The guard told us we could keep our cell phones: They were only checking for weapons. I'd left my holstered Beretta in the car.

No one would have taken my pistol at the FOE party.

After we passed through the detector, we walked beneath a high portico with Doric columns like those of antebellum mansions in the southern United States. Tara of *Gone with the Wind* fame had inspired this imposing mansion.

Only the massive open door through which we walked had a Peruvian touch: The door had been fashioned from Amazon mahogany. The door opened onto a marble foyer with a home office to our right and a music room next to that. Near the end of the foyer a winding staircase with gleaming balustrade led to the second floor. I half expected to see Clark Gable tell Vivien Leigh, "Frankly, my dear, I don't give a damn." Just beyond the staircase, doors led to a grand ballroom and dining room.

We made our way to the head of the receiving line, where Ambassador Aoki greeted us. The ambassador was a tall, spare man with white hair. He was in his late fifties and wore glasses. He shook my hand and said he hoped we would like the new research vessel. I assured him we would and that our gratitude was boundless. With fixed smiles on our faces, Marcella and I continued down the line, shaking hands and exchanging bows with the embassy staff.

Once we were through the receiving line, we walked across the ballroom and out open French doors onto an enormous lawn, where a buffet awaited beneath a red-and-white party tent. The buffet featured a bewildering array of raw seafood.

I saw many familiar faces near the buffet. One group included air force officers Orlando Denegri and Pepe Garrido, army general Carlos Domínguez, and the head of Peru's Counter-Terrorism Department, General Máximo Rivera. Walking toward the group was our foreign minister, Francisco Tudela, who was engaged in earnest conversation with Supreme Court justice Carlos Giusti at his side. Giusti was undoubtedly talking about his untiring battle to reform the country's judicial system. I hoped Giusti, a charismatic man of strong character, wasn't tilting at windmills.

I said hello and shook hands with Lieutenant Colonel Roberto Fernandez as he paused on his way to the buffet. The colonel was military aide to the president of the Peruvian Congress. He excused himself when the pager clipped to his belt beckoned.

I checked the crowd to see if any active-duty admiral senior to me was present. I saw none. I wasn't surprised: I'd heard the army, navy, and air force chiefs had to attend a reception at the Chilean embassy before they could celebrate the emperor's birthday.

Among the several ambassadors I recognized were Jorge Gumucio of Bolivia, Dennis Jett of the United States, Anthony Vincent of Canada, and Tabare Bocolandro of Uruguay. A priest whom I didn't recognize was talking to Ambassador Gumucio. Two congressmen were talking with Ambassador Vincent. The jovial Eduardo Pando was a good friend, but the very sight of Javier Diez Canseco tightened my jaw. I and others viewed Diez Canseco as an anti-military obstructionist who sympathized with those bent on turning Peru into a Marxist state.

I glanced away from Diez Canseco toward the ballroom doors and saw Ambassador Jett departing with his entourage, closely followed by the Israeli ambassador, Joel Salpak, and his bodyguards.

I began to plan our own escape. My talk with President Fujimori about the Japanese research ship would have to wait: At the last minute he'd canceled after a late return from the Andean provinces. These provinces had suffered the most devastation during our War on Terror and were not yet secure enough for people to live normal lives.

Despite the president's absence, the Fujimori family was well represented. I saw his sister, Juana, and mother seated in a secluded spot between two azalea bushes. They were chattering away in sweet oblivion.

The president's brother, Pedro, was standing in the buffet line. With him were the president's army and navy aides-de-camp. The aides wore dress uniforms. My civilian status at least spared me the discomfort of those high, tight collars.

The navy aide, Commander Rodolfo Reátegui, was a good friend. He saw me looking toward him and left the buffet to talk with us. We'd just started our conversation when Ambassador Aoki appeared in the doorway to the garden. The blessed moment had arrived.

Marcella kissed Rodolfo on the cheek, and I gave him an *abrazo*. Then we moved toward the ever-growing knot of people around the ambassador. We were not the only guests eager to leave.

When our turn arrived, we said our good-byes to Aoki and his wife. As we were walking through the ballroom toward the front door, Oscar Mavila called to us. He was standing only a few feet away with General Domínguez.

We joined the two men out of politeness and had just started talking about some trivial matter when the explosion interrupted.

Within minutes we saw them sprinting in from the garden, where most guests had remained beneath the party tent. The intruders wore military field uniforms. Many guests thought they were members of the Peruvian army taking position to guard against a terrorist attack. But as I watched two of them clatter with their boots across the marble floor of the foyer into the ballroom, I knew they were not here to protect us.

Red-and-white bandannas covered the lower half of their faces, and bandoliers of bullets crisscrossed their chests like outlaws in a Mexican cowboy movie. But the intruders didn't carry six-shooters: They carried AKM automatic rifles, and their torsos were wrapped in bulletproof vests. Grenades and radios dangled from belts. Fighting knives protruded from sheaths fixed to shoulder harnesses.

One intruder bristling with weapons stopped no more than three feet from us and shouted, "Everybody on the floor! Now! Keep your fucking heads down, *carajo!*"

He emphasized the order with a burst of four rounds from his AKM.

We hit the deck as one, heads down. I threw an arm over Marcella and drew her to me. Whimpering then sobs filled the room. I saw a man near me weeping into the tapestry rug of the ballroom, his body trembling.

The terrorist fired another burst from his AKM. Now we heard the sound of shattering glass; shards struck those closest to the windows. People screamed. Terrorists shouted and fired their weapons. Sirens wailed from outside as police and military vehicles hurtled down quiet streets toward the residence.

From the floor I could see only the boots and uniform of the terrorist nearest me. The gear looked new—as if the Peruvian army had just issued it. It had yet to experience the jungle.

Beyond the terrorist, I spotted other uniforms and heard more boots on marble. I could hear doors slamming and windows closing: The terrorists had herded all the guests inside and were securing the residence.

Outside, a fierce firefight raged. Police and frustrated bodyguards exchanged rounds with terrorists and each other. Contradictory orders filled the air. Chaos flourished as the fog of war drifted in.

The gun battle began just as the mayor of Callao's limousine stopped at the front doors. His bodyguards, who thought they were under attack from beyond the wall, hustled the unfortunate man into the residence and slammed the door behind him. Alexander Kouri in dinner dress joined us on the ballroom floor.

Police hurled tear gas grenades through broken windows. As the suffocating smoke spread, the terrorists donned masks and returned fire. A few grabbed smoking grenades and threw them back at the police.

Hostages—for that is what we'd become in less than a minute—gasped, choked, and cried as they inhaled the gas despite futile efforts to hold their breath. People began to stand and stumble, clutching their throats. A terrorist raked the ceiling above our heads with a volley from his AKM and yelled, "Get down, huevonazos, get down! We'll tell you assholes when you can stand!" Pulverized plaster showered the hostages as they dropped to the floor.

I crawled ever so slowly to a nearby coffee table and grabbed a glass half filled with bourbon and water. I saturated a handkerchief with the reeking liquid and crawled back to Marcella.

"Here," I said, "put this over your mouth and nose." She complied, and the watered-down smell of Jack Daniels replaced the suffocating stench of gas. I saw men taking off neckties to soak in whatever liquid they could find. The lucky located water; the unlucky found sake or worse. But anything was better than the gas searing your throat and lungs and saturating your sinuses. I removed and doused my tie with the weak bourbon and covered the lower part of my face. I half closed my eyes as the tears flowed. I choked back vomit welling in my throat.

During a lull in the gas attack, one of the terrorists shouted: "Where's Aoki? Don't make me look for him!" He spoke through a battery-powered megaphone.

Ambassador Aoki stumbled through the hostages toward the man. He managed to look dignified despite the danger. The terrorist handed him the megaphone and ordered him to tell the police to cease fire.

The ambassador took the megaphone and said in an amplified voice loud enough for those outside to hear: "Please, please. Stop firing. You'll harm my guests!"

The ambassador was famous for his bad Spanish. Perhaps this is why he chose to speak in French. The police, not being linguists, intensified their fire and launched more gas canisters.

Another man appeared as if by magic at the ambassador's side. He was in his forties and had the look of a long-distance runner. He immediately began speaking flawless Spanish to the terrorist who had snatched the megaphone from Aoki.

"Por favor, señor, déme el megáfono. I'll get them to stop."

THE AMPLIFIED VOICE of Michel Minnig carried a desperate plea in Spanish to the more than three hundred armed men outside and the firing stopped. Minnig was Swiss and represented the Red Cross in Peru. He was in our country to inspect the prisons where we kept captured terrorists. He made me uneasy with his barely concealed dislike of the military. But he didn't make me feel uneasy now: he made me feel great relief.

Within minutes a terrorist shouted, "You can sit up but we'll kill the first *hijo de puta* who stands without our permission."

Then in teams of two the terrorists began to load windows and doors with demolition. I sat up with Marcella and watched as they attached what looked like *quesos rusos* of various sizes to barricade the residence and thwart any rescue attempt.

The *queso ruso* or "Russian cheese" is an improvised explosive device similar to those the Vietcong favored in Vietnam. To make a small one for throwing, you pack a metal container such as a beer or fruit can with plastic explosives—Semtex, C-4, or RDX. Use a number ten can or something larger if you want a bigger boom.

You work nails or pieces of scrap steel into the explosive. Peruvian terrorists often add human feces to the mix. You detonate the charge with time fuse and a blasting cap. You cut the fuse to whatever time delay you want.

But the terrorists weren't using time fuse: They were instead prepping the charges to fire electrically without a delay. Two wires ran from the blasting cap rather than a length of time fuse. The wires were attached to a handheld device called a "clacker" that is the firing mechanism for the Claymore mine. Squeeze the clacker to generate electricity through the wires to detonate the cap and main charge.

Two terrorists next to each window in the ballroom grasped clackers. The electrical wires ran no more than three feet from the clackers to the blasting caps. A white cord of PETN—a mega-high explosive—festooned the windows to connect the *quesos rusos* in a deadly daisy chain. I counted four charges dangling around a nearby ceiling-to-floor window. Judging from the size of the containers, I estimated the total explosive weight at about twenty kilos. *Load-heavy,* I thought.

If the terrorists squeezed the clackers, we would have a nanosecond before the explosions. Shrapnel and concussion would kill the terrorists and many hostages. The rest of us would die crushed beneath tons of collapsing concrete and steel or perish in flames. Images of Waco tormented me.

I looked into the eyes of the terrorist at the nearest window and saw an emotion I'd seen in young men many times before: fear. But this young man was a young woman. She'd removed her cap to reveal a riot of curly black hair. She couldn't have been much older than fifteen. I wondered where she had celebrated her birthday, her *quinceañero*—or if she had celebrated at all.

I prayed that fear and her youthful yearning for the years to come would stay her hand if the final moment arrived. Or that I would be close enough to kill her before she cranked the charge. And I prayed our would-be saviors outside the residence did not catch "go fever." This was a time for patience.

I checked my watch: 2230. We'd been in captivity for about two hours. Except for an occasional sob or random scream, all was quiet. The *terrorista* takedown of the residence was complete. But who were they?

2
Dead Dogs and Good Terrorists

I CONSIDERED THE QUESTION while I tried to get an accurate count of our captors and catalog their weapons, which was difficult because the terrorists were on the move throughout the house. I calculated there must be about twenty: It would take at least that number to control the nearly six hundred hostages.

As for weapons, most terrorists I saw had K-Bar knives and carried Kalashnikov 7.62 × 39mm rifles. Two were armed with Belgian FAL 7.62 × 51mm rifles, and one sported an Uzi submachine gun. Each terrorist had four grenades, a bag of *quesos rusos*, and two squad radios. A few radios were equipped with police scanners.

As for who they were, I had little doubt they were from one of the two major terrorist groups in Peru: *Sendero Luminoso* (SL), Shining Path; or *Movimiento Revolucionaro Túpac Amaru* (MRTA), Túpac Amaru Revolutionary Movement. We were on the edge of a precipice in either case. Both were ruthless, unyielding, and capable of killing us all—as well as themselves—at any moment.

SENDERO LUMINOSO HAD ANNOUNCED its presence to the good people of Lima on a cadaver-gray dawn in 1980. They awoke to a macabre sight: scores of dead dogs hanging from streetlights throughout the city. Each had a sign dangling from its twisted neck that read DENG XIAOPING, SON-OF-A-BITCH.

Imagine a similar sight assailing the eyes of early risers in San Diego or Seattle. They might well have echoed a common utterance that morning: "Holy shit! Who is this asshole Deng Xiaoping?"

The short answer: He was a revisionist Chinese leader who had challenged Mao Zedong's orthodox brand of communism. To understand why anyone in Peru would care about an ideological battle fought thousands of miles from our shores, you have to understand the phenomenon of Abimael Guzman or "Presidente Gonzalo"—the near-mystical founder and leader of SL.

Guzman had been a philosophy professor at a university in the southern city of Arequipa during the 1960s. He organized a radical group of professors and students who were disciples of Mao. On the run from authorities, Guzman sought refuge in China for two years. While there he trained diligently in the intellectual and practical aspects of how to conduct a People's War. He was a very good student. When he returned to Peru, the authorities were no longer interested in him. That would change.

Guzman began his ten-thousand-mile journey, Mao's Little Red Book in hand, at a new government university in Huamanga—a small, ancient city known mainly for its churches. This Andean city at an altitude of more than nine thousand feet is located in the department or state of Ayacucho—an Indian word in Quechua that means "corner of the dead." Several hundred miles southeast of Lima, Ayachucho is the poorest and most remote department in Peru. Soaring mountain peaks and wild, isolated valleys dominate the landscape. Some villages have existed since before the time of the Incas yet do not appear on any government map.

Guzman toiled in Ayacucho for more than a decade, preparing the ground for the seeds of Mao's communism and a People's War. There he recruited his People's Army from among the campesinos of remote villages scattered among the mountains and valleys far beyond the end of the road and government control. Loyalty to the cause was demonstrated by the murder of a policeman, with proof in the possession of the dead man's weapon.

A "holy family" of zealots, whom Guzman recruited from his university students, spent years in the villages indoctrinating the young men and women in the revolutionary thought of Mao as interpreted by Guzman. One of the basic concepts the "teachers" taught their eager students was class warfare.

Shortly after the appearance of the dead dogs, SL began calling attention to itself in an even more gruesome and deadly fashion. Villagers having been identified by the teachers as having contact with the government or any other organization that might challenge SL for control were tortured and murdered. Favorite SL targets were Catholic priests, evangelical ministers, and foreign aid workers.

Class or status could also bring a death sentence. The teachers identified people within the villages who had more money and property than their neighbors, even if the distinction was slight.

The central government at first was indifferent as isolated village after isolated village fell to SL. The government only became alarmed as SL began attacking larger villages much closer to the capital city, also called Ayacucho. These villages had small garrisons of police or national guards, and some villagers had organized themselves during the 1980s into armed *rondas* or militias initially to protect livestock from marauding bandits. The *rondas* resisted SL; some villages without them organized themselves spontaneously to throw out SL cadres. These villages paid a terrible price.

One such village was so remote its name was known only to its inhabitants and appeared on maps as a number. The village was shrouded much of the year in mountain mist; a single rope bridge over a deep ravine connected it with a path that led to a rutted dirt road more than a day's walk away. It took yet another day to reach a road where a traveler might flag down an ancient car or truck . . . if the road had not been closed, as it often was, by landslides.

But no one in the village much cared. They tended their livestock and the terraced fields of the mountain slope behind the settlement as they had since the time of the Incas. Corn with plump white kernels grew on the terraces while cattle, llamas, and sheep grazed in small pastures. No one wanted for food, but those few villagers who left seldom returned.

One day a teacher from the university crossed the bridge to teach the boys and girls how to read, write, and do their numbers. After school the teacher invited the young men and women to study sessions, where he would teach them about the world beyond the rope bridge. He told of class struggle, of how the wealthy exploited the poor, and of how their own village had a class structure that allowed the wealthy campesinos to exploit their poorer neighbors.

"Who controls your daily life?" he asked. "Who tells you when to rise, when to rest, what lands to work, what livestock to tend? Who decides how to distribute the product of your labor? Who oversees the distribution of bread from the communal oven? Who decides how much water each farmer will receive for his land? Who must you treat as if they were members of a royal family?"

The answer was obvious: the *alcalde* and council of elders. Although elected, these men controlled the economic life of the village and therefore the elections. They also decided who would be punished, although the village was practically without crime. Many of the young men and women who became disciples of the teacher were children of the elders.

Within a few months of the teacher's arrival, several men who were not from the village crossed the bridge when the sun was high in the sky and went directly to a house where the elders were meeting. The men walked through the door with machetes, knives, clubs, and a few rifles. The teacher was with them. He told the elders the men were from SL and had come to establish a new order. The *alcalde* and the elders would no longer control daily life. Committees of young people who were the teacher's disciples would now determine matters of communal concern. The ten armed strangers would remain to protect the village and punish anyone who violated the rules of SL.

The strangers then forced all villagers to assemble in the village plaza, where the teacher gave the first of many speeches about the new order of *Sendero Luminoso*. He also identified various types of punishment for crimes against the people. Execution was the ultimate sanction. To illustrate, he ordered three men armed with machetes to bring the village priest forward. The men forced the terrified victim to kneel. They cut off his ears, nose, and tongue. The priest was still screaming with blood flowing from his wounds when a terrorist decapitated him and held up the head for all to see.

The villagers submitted to the new order. What choice did they have? After two months the armed men departed, leaving two of their number behind with the teacher. This was the moment the villagers had been awaiting. Several men seized the teacher and his bodyguards as they were distributing bread from the huge communal oven at one end of the plaza. They tied the teacher and bodyguards to stunted trees in the plaza and whipped them with nail-studded leather straps. Then they forced the bleeding men across the bridge with a warning that the men would be killed if they returned.

Reprisal was swift and awful. An SL column of sixty men, women, and teenagers descended on the village after bombarding it with sticks of dynamite launched from slingshots. The teacher was in the column. The villagers resisted, and SL killed several outright. When SL had seized the village, they ordered everyone to assemble on the plaza in front of the oven.

This adobe oven was the pride of the village. It was large enough for two people to stand inside and remove freshly baked loaves of bread from shelves. The oven had been built a few feet off the ground. The villagers had built a deep trench beneath; to bake the bread, they stacked wood in the trench and lit it.

When everyone had assembled before the oven, the teacher pointed out the elders and *alcalde*. Men, women, and boys seized the men and packed them into the oven. SL closed and bolted the heavy iron door. The teacher identified family members of the doomed men, and SL forced them to fill the trench with wood. An SL woman threw gasoline from a can onto the wood and set it ablaze. As the heat intensified, the villagers could see the air above the roof vents shimmer.

The men inside the kiln screamed for almost an hour before they fell silent. A few villagers could not stand the sound and covered their ears, but not for long. SL beat them bloody with clubs.

After the men had been baked alive, SL rounded up the village livestock. They cut the throats of goats, pigs, sheep, cows, and llamas with machetes. The object lesson taught, SL departed. The next day the villagers abandoned their homes and crops, crossed the rope bridge, and burned it behind them.

As the decade advanced, SL became a force in nearly all Peruvian departments. Terror was the tool of conquest. SL tortured and massacred thousands in the most horrible fashion. The government dispatched armed forces in strength to crush a rebellion that now threatened the state itself. Ayacucho in particular became a vast killing field.

Prisons throughout the country swelled with SL prisoners. Poorly paid prison guards were either unwilling or unable to control the prisoners, who turned their cellblocks into SL indoctrination centers for common criminals. They painted slogans and posted drawings of Presidente Gonzalo on walls; they marched across exercise yards waving red flags and shouting songs to celebrate Maoist triumphs. Anyone who refused to participate was beaten senseless. Suspected informers suffered a far worse fate.

During the winter of 1986 SL had seized complete control of the prisons in Lima. The situation was intolerable, and the military moved against the prisons of Lurigancho, Santa Barbara, and El Frontón. Lurigancho was in Lima, Santa Barbara in Lima's port of Callao, and El Frontón on an island in the Pacific at the entrance to the harbor of Callao. The army and Republican Guard attacked Lurigancho and Santa Barbara; Peruvian marines and SEALs took down El Frontón. After battles waged without quarter hundreds of *senderistas* lay dead in the smoldering ruins of their cellblocks. The attackers also suffered casualties but had far fewer dead. The Red Cross and other humanitarian organizations descended on Peru; the government reluctantly allowed the Red Cross to inspect the country's prisons. But SL was no longer the festering sore it had been in Lurigancho, Santa Barbara, and El Frontón.

Undeterred, SL infiltrated the shantytowns surrounding Lima and brought sabotage and butchery to the capital. Car bombs, dynamited electrical pylons, and assassinations became commonplace.

Many inhabitants of the shantytowns resisted. In one of the largest settlements, Villa El Salvador, María Elena Moyano led the resistance. Moyano was thirty-three years old and the mother of two boys, aged eleven and twelve. She was a dynamic organizer of the poor. She led a grassroots committee of women who carried out several projects: soup kitchens, food distribution centers, elementary education, and income-generating work. She lobbied the government tirelessly for health care, a reliable water system, and security for Villa El Salvador. She opposed SL attempts to recruit members from the shantytown. Terrorists responded with death threats.

In 1991 SL murdered a woman who was coordinator of a food distribution program and left a dead dog beside her body. Moyano led demonstrations against such savagery and urged townspeople to denounce the terrorists to authorities. The national press recognized Moyano's leadership and courage by nominating her as Person of the Year. Citizens of the municipality elected her vice mayor. She repeatedly condemned the bloody methods of SL despite great danger to herself.

On February 15, 1991, María Elena Moyano led a march against SL protesting its demand that workers throughout Lima hold a general strike. SL ambushed the parade and shot Moyano several times. As she lay dying, a terrorist shoved a stick of dynamite into her vagina. After the explosion, the terrorist took what remained of her head and placed it on what remained of her torso. Her two young sons witnessed the horror.

Within a year of Moyano's murder the government, now headed by Alberto Fujimori, dealt SL a devastating blow. During an operation brilliant in concept and execution, police seized Abimael Guzman without incident. He had been hiding in an apartment above a Lima dance studio.

SL paid the price for the hierarchical structure and cult of personality that had turned Guzman into the god-like Presidente Gonzalo. Within two years the group had ceased to be a serious threat—government troops had captured or killed most of its leaders. The terrorists were forced back into the mountains of Ayacucho. By that time more than twenty-five thousand men, women, and children had died during a sixteen-year war that cost Peru twenty-five billion dollars in ruined infrastructure. If SL had been at work in the United States, the per capita loss would have been nearly three hundred thousand deaths.

WHILE SL WAGED its savage, unrelenting war, another smaller but equally brutal group of terrorists labored in the shadows of the larger conflict, stacking wood for what they hoped would be the winter of Peru's discontent. In 1982 the Túpac Amaru Revolutionary Movement (MRTA) began a campaign—mainly in the cities—of assassinations, bank robberies, car bombings, and kidnapping for ransom. The terrorists named themselves for an Inca emperor, Túpac Amaru, who had led the last Indian uprising against the Spaniards in 1781. The Spanish crushed the rebellion, captured Túpac Amaru, and had him drawn and quartered in the central plaza of Cuzco.

The roots of MRTA reached far deeper into Peruvian political history than did those of SL. The group was an offshoot of the largest political party in Peru, *Alianza Popular Revolucionaria Americana* or APRA. Founded during the 1920s, APRA challenged dictatorial governments of the time and offered the country a democratic socialist alternative. When the government refused to hold elections or rigged those it did hold, armed APRA militias took to the streets of major Peruvian cities. Thousands died during the 1930s in violent confrontations with the army.

But in the 1950s the APRA leadership began to seek accommodation with the military dictatorship of General Manuel Odría. In return for APRA support, Odría stopped military action against the party and even shared some power.

Young, radical members of APRA were outraged. They saw the accommodation with Odría as a betrayal of the party's revolutionary origins. They also saw the successful guerrilla war of Fidel Castro in Cuba as a model for armed resistance in Peru. These men split with the party and formed what they called *APRA Rebelde*.

The leader of *APRA Rebelde* was Luis de la Puente, a lawyer from the coastal city of Trujillo. In 1965 he and his followers took to high, jungled hills not far from the tourist mecca of Machu Picchu in the department of Cuzco. De la Puente called his group *Movimiento de Izquierda Revolucionaria* (MIR).

De la Puente hoped to exploit what he incorrectly believed was a seething Indian resentment against *hacendados*, large landowners, who exploited their Indian peons. In fact, the Indians did not need a coastal lawyer to lead them: In the decade prior to de la Puente's misguided and short-lived war, the Indians themselves had organized into *sindicatos*, unions, and imposed land reform from below. In massive numbers they invaded and seized idle *hacendado* lands or lands the Indians had worked as tenant farmers. The Indian campesinos wanted land, not improved working conditions. And they had pretty much achieved their objective before de la Puente arrived. Many campesinos in fact resented de la Puente and his war because it disrupted farming.

De la Puente's choice of military strategy was worse than his choice of cause. He selected that strategy from the Cuban example of the *foco*—a guerrilla base in an area thought to be inaccessible to government forces. In Cuba, Castro established his *foco* in the Sierra Maestra; de la Puente chose a forbidding ridge called Mesa Pelada, Bald Mountain.

The ridge was thirty-seven miles long and twelve wide. It was anything but bald, covered as it was with dense upland jungle. Within six months the army had isolated a sickly de la Puente and called in air strikes. De la Puente and his men died drenched in flaming napalm.

MRTA is the direct ideological descendant of MIR, but did not follow its ruinous military strategy. In the early 1980s MRTA organized military training camps in the high jungle bordering the southern Amazon Basin. MRTA built clandestine training sites primarily in the Upper Huallaga Valley. This choice may well have been driven in part because the valley was the center of the coca trade. The terrorists benefited financially from large sums that drug traffickers paid for "protection." This drug money subsidized MRTA.

But the terrorists wanted more. They began a series of bank robberies and kidnappings for ransom in Lima. A terrorist who wanted to line his pockets would choose MRTA over SL.

If a ransom were not paid, MRTA would execute its hostages. The group also began a decade-long campaign of assassinating high-ranking military officers.

As SL savagery escalated, MRTA took advantage of growing public rage against the Maoists to portray itself as a humanitarian alternative. To project a Robin Hood image, MRTA would hijack trucks loaded with food and distribute it in the shantytowns. The terrorists would sometimes distribute money from their bank robberies to the poor. The national and international press began to call MRTA the "good terrorists."

But the good terrorists had it in for the United States. They attempted to kill the US ambassador with a car bomb and destroyed a Kentucky Fried Chicken restaurant in Lima.

MRTA did not deceive the left-leaning novelist and politician Mario Vargas Llosa. In a magazine article, Vargas Llosa expressed his contempt for the "good terrorists" and the media that portrayed them as such. "This distinction between good and bad terrorists," Vargas Llosa wrote, "is false . . . a close friend was a victim of MRTA, the 'good terrorists.' They kept this elderly man for months in a small cave—a so-called people's jail—where he could not stand, could not see, and had only rats and roaches for company. MRTA tortured his family with daily phone calls and tape recordings to destroy their nerves and extort their savings.

"If these are the actions of 'good terrorists,' what could be those of bad? *Sendero Luminoso* works on a grander scale, but the number of terrorist crimes doesn't determine their vileness, especially for each victim and his family."

The government captured MRTA leader Victor Polay, but in 1990 he and several of his followers managed to tunnel out of Canto Grande prison. In 1992 luck and a three-hundred-thousand-dollar reward sent Polay to a newer and much more secure prison at the navy base in Callao. Peruvian SEALs, many trained in the United States, became his jailers. No more escapes.

An hour had passed, and the murmur of whispered conversations grew louder throughout the residence. A few men began shouting for the terrorists to release the women. Others pleaded to use the toilet. The terrorists ignored them. If head calls were not permitted soon, I thought, the stench of urine and feces would add to our discomfort.

From my sitting position beside Marcella on the floor of the grand ballroom, I could see the curving staircase through the wide door that opened onto the foyer. Three terrorists were at the bottom of the staircase talking. The Red Cross hostage, Michel Minnig, was with them. The terrorists had their weapons slung over their shoulders. Red-and-white bandannas still covered their faces. The bandannas had black writing and some sort of symbol on them; I could decipher neither.

I looked through the open double doors of the formal dining room directly across from me. Hostages littered the floor. Two terrorists with weapons at the ready stood on either side of the ballroom door to the foyer. I saw two more at the entrance to the dining room. A terrorist moved in and out of my view down the foyer toward the barricaded front door. The door was undoubtedly mined as well, and two terrorists loitered near the *quesos rusos* that festooned the picture windows of the ballroom. They apparently felt secure enough that they no longer grasped the clackers, though they did remain close to the draped windows. Ten terrorists in all. There must be more.

The man Minnig was talking to left the group and climbed the stairs until he was high above everyone. He held the battery-powered megaphone. We were about to learn the identity of our captors.

3

Houdinis

THE TERRORIST pulled his bandanna down to reveal his face and I instantly recognized him from my time battling the insurgency. He was Nestor Cerpa. We had gotten two terrorists for the price of one: He'd been a member first of SL and then of MRTA.

Cerpa began his deadly career in the 1970s as a militant labor leader. He specialized in organizing worker takeovers of factories and their management. His game was to hold owners and supervisors hostage until they agreed to increase pay and improve conditions in the factories. In 1977–78 he and other workers occupied a textile plant on the outskirts of Lima for more than a year. (*We could be in for a long haul,* I thought.)

When police finally raided the plant, they lost two men in a shootout but killed four workers. The government imprisoned Cerpa for ten months—he must have had friends in high places. Not uncommon for terrorists in Peru.

He joined SL in the early 1980s because it was the only game in town. He left the madmen three years later and joined MRTA, preferring its urban worker-oriented strategy. The thought of fighting a People's War in the mountains of Ayacucho did not appeal to him.

Early in his MRTA career Cerpa went to Colombia, where he trained and operated with the guerrillas of M-19. I recalled with discomfort how these terrorists had seized the Palace of Justice in Bogotá. When the Colombian army launched a rescue attempt, the terrorists detonated explosives they'd rigged throughout the massive building. Part of the building collapsed, and fire raged through what remained. Over one hundred died in the conflagration.

Cerpa spoke to us through the megaphone: "You are prisoners of the Túpac Amaru Revolutionary Movement. You may call me Commander Huertas."

Why the phony name? I wondered. Cerpa was notorious; certainly those of us who had fought terrorism for sixteen years knew him well.

As if in answer to my question, Cerpa told us he had taken as his nom de guerre the name of a cherished comrade who had given his life when police stormed the textile factory.

A sentimental terrorist.

Cerpa assured us that we would be treated as prisoners of war. "We are soldiers in battle against the Fujimori dictatorship," he announced. "We serve the people of Peru. Unlike *Sendero Luminoso,* we do not kill and maim for the sake of terror." Cerpa paused, and I half expected him to say MRTA were the good terrorists. Instead he said, "You must call us *guerilleros,* not terrorists. *Sendero Luminoso* are terrorists. But do not think we will hesitate to kill if you do not follow our orders."

Cerpa then told us why we'd been seized. "You will be held until Fujimori releases our comrades from prison." He held up several sheets of paper and told us they contained more than four hundred names of MRTA "soldiers" whom the president must release if we were to be freed. Cerpa began an interminable reading of names. I lost interest after the first three: MRTA founder and leader Victor Polay, Cerpa's common-law wife Nancy Gilvonio, and US citizen Lori Berenson.

As Cerpa droned on, I considered the strange case of Lori Berenson, who at this point was in her late twenties. I doubt she looked as good now as when she'd entered prison in the Andes a year ago.

Berenson was an MIT dropout and dedicated "freedom fighter." She'd begun her revolutionary odyssey a few years earlier in Nicaragua, where she gave aid and comfort to the Sandinistas. From Nicaragua she'd crossed the border to El Salvador and taken up housekeeping with the communist FMLN. She married an FMLN leader but apparently tired of him and left for Peru and MRTA. She'd passed herself off with forged documents as a journalist and rented a safe house in Lima for her MRTA *compañeros.*

We'd captured her after she'd entered the congressional palace in downtown Lima claiming to be a magazine writer. We'd seized Nancy Gilvonio along with her. Gilvonio was posing as a news photographer to illustrate Berenson's phantom article.

The two had drawings of the building concealed in their bras along with notes on congressional security measures. It seems MRTA was planning to seize the Congress just as Sandinistas had done in Managua more than twenty years earlier. Using the Sandinista model revealed another difference between MRTA and SL. SL wanted nothing to do with outsiders, but MRTA had links with the alphabet soup of terrorist movements throughout Latin America that included FMLN (El Salvador), M-19 and FARC (Colombia), and MIR (Chile). I would not be surprised if one or more foreign terrorists were in the gang that was holding us.

Cerpa finally finished reading the names of the imprisoned terrorists and shouted a slogan that was to become gratingly familiar in the months to come: "¡Patria o muerte! ¡Venceremos!" Fatherland or death! We shall overcome! Fidel would have been pleased.

Cerpa descended the stairs and joined two other terrorists in the foyer. As I watched through the open door of the ballroom I saw Michel Minnig of the International Red Cross approach Cerpa. The two began an earnest conversation. Both men were in their early forties, but there the similarity ended. Minnig was slender with thinning, straw-colored hair and a decidedly Nordic aspect. He was from Switzerland and had represented the Red Cross for the past several years in such dangerous places as Iraq, Lebanon, Nicaragua, and Bosnia. He held several degrees, including one in Asian studies from the University of California–Berkeley.

Cerpa, on the other hand, would never be mistaken for Swiss. He was moon-faced with dark eyes, black hair, and brown skin—a typical mestizo with more Indian showing through than Spaniard. Born the son of working-class parents in Lima, Cerpa's graduate education had been on-the-job training as a militant union organizer. He was not, however, unfamiliar with Europe. He, along with his mother, wife, and children, had spent time in France protected by that nation's socialist government. His mother lived there still.

When Cerpa and Minnig finished talking, I noted a curious gesture: The two shook hands before Cerpa once more mounted the stairs, megaphone in hand. I braced for another diatribe. Instead Cerpa told us in a conciliatory tone that he had decided to gradually release the women, elderly, and sick.

Scattered applause. Cerpa gave a slight bow. Although I did not join the clapping, I was greatly relieved that Marcella would soon depart this horror show. I squeezed her hand.

Cerpa directed the release from his perch on the stairs. The terrorists went room to room and selected fifteen or twenty women. They would repeat this selection process many times until they had freed all women.

Among the first group to leave was an elderly Japanese woman who had difficulty making her way through the crowd. Cerpa walked down the stairs and took her gently by the arm. He guided her to the head of the line at the open front door. A younger Japanese woman walked behind her. Cerpa exchanged bows with both women and returned to the stairs.

Hard to believe, I thought. The terrorist leader had just released the mother of all bargaining chips: the mother of Alberto Fujimori. He'd also allowed the president's sister to leave. Did he know what he was doing? Perhaps this was just another ploy to show how different MRTA was from SL. I had to admit SL probably would have sent Fujimori his mother's head on one of Ambassador Aoki's silver serving trays.

But I had no illusions about what motivated Cerpa's seemingly magnanimous gesture. Although I had been unable to get an exact number, I'd counted at least ten terrorists since the takedown. I was certain at least another two were upstairs and two more were guarding the back of the residence. Assuming I had underestimated the number of terrorists elsewhere, Cerpa still could not have had more than sixteen or seventeen in his gang. He would be lucky if he could control one hundred, let alone six hundred, hostages, especially as the hours dragged on and people became increasingly desperate. Cerpa had to drastically reduce the number of people he must guard, and soon.

More than two hours passed before the last woman walked through the front door. Cerpa took full advantage of the drawn-out episode for propaganda. He'd called a local TV station on a cell phone to tell them of the pending release. He said he would allow a single cameraman through the front gate to film the women as they walked to freedom. The security force allowed the cameraman to position himself beneath a small tree near the gate, where he would remain throughout the night.

Shortly after the women departed, Cerpa began to release white-jacketed waiters and household servants. The TV camera recorded the event for the viewing pleasure of millions around the world. We were on our way to becoming celebrities, but only in the worst possible way.

After the first few waiters walked through the front door, the TV audience got a bonus. A man wearing only a plaid shirt and clutching a white tablecloth around his waist broke from the music room into the foyer. He knocked over waiters like a bowling ball striking pins. As he sprinted through the door past two startled terrorists, the tablecloth slipped to reveal his backside. The man didn't bother to cover his nakedness: He ran through the open gate like a sprinter straining for the finish line. The terrorists at the front door raised their AKMs, took aim, but did not fire. The running man tripped on his makeshift toga and collapsed on the street. Two policemen dragged him away from the gate.

The man was my good friend Commander Rodolfo Reátegui, who had somehow managed to shed his summer dress white uniform including underwear, socks, and shoes. He was determined to hide his military status from the terrorists, if not his naked backside. I was relieved to see him escape, but he had put us all at great risk. If the terrorists had fired, the armed men outside the residence would certainly have attacked through the open door—with disastrous results for the hostages. But I understood Rodolfo's motivation and would not criticize . . . especially since his escape was successful. I was sure he would be debriefed by agents of the *Servicio de Inteligencia Nacional*—SIN. The acronym was more menacing in English than Spanish.

Two terrorists grabbed hostages and, using them as shields, slammed the front gate closed. They made their way back to the residence holding their human shields by the neck. Once inside, the terrorists flung the hostages to the floor, then closed and bolted the front door.

Cerpa was furious. He shouted that he could have had the madman killed but chose not to. He warned that the MRTA would kill the next fool "with rabbit in him."

Among the millions who watched Reátegui's midnight dash to freedom was Senora Andrade, wife of the Miraflores mayor, Fernando Andrade. Miraflores was a tony if aging suburb of Lima. Just before Reátegui's escape, the mayor had succeeded in gaining the terrorists' permission to visit an upstairs bathroom. The mayor entered the bathroom and closed and locked the door behind him. He prayed God would tell him what to do at this agonizing moment.

The cell phone in his pocket vibrated. Was the Almighty about to counsel him? He flipped the phone open, put it to his ear, and heard his wife say,

"*Mi amor,* you must get out of that dreadful place." She told him of Reátegui's escape and in a trembling voice pleaded with her husband to do the same. He tried to comfort his wife and promised he would be home before sunrise.

The mayor closed the cell phone and glanced at his watch: 0145.

He'd already been inside the bathroom long enough to relieve himself. He tapped a roll of toilet paper on a wooden spool attached to the wall until the spool rattled. He wondered how much time the *cojudo* outside would give him to wipe his ass.

The mayor eyed a small window above the tiled vanity across from the toilet. He might be skinny enough to make it, he thought. He flushed the toilet and pressed himself onto the vanity. The window was open and within reach. He leaned forward, grabbed the frame, and pulled himself to a seated position on the sill, his legs dangling outside. He heard someone trying the doorknob. The mayor calculated the distance from his second-story perch to the ground, crossed himself, and jumped.

The ground rushed up to meet him. He felt an ankle give way and a sharp pain send a wave of nausea through his body. But adrenaline kicked in and the pain eased. He crept along a hedge to where the sidewall of the residence joined the front. As he peered around the corner, he found himself staring into a TV camera aimed at him from the far side of the driveway. The mayor waved frantically and pointed to his left. The camera swung around until it was once more focused on the front door.

Unknown to Andrade, another camera was following his progress from the roof of an adjacent house. The Japanese network NHK had paid the owner of the house thousands of dollars to place a night-vision camera there. A global audience watched in fascination as the red-and-green-tinted figure crawled on his hands and knees from the shrubbery to a detached garage that opened onto the street in front of the residence. The figure disappeared through an unlocked side door and within seconds the camera picked him up again as he collapsed into the arms of police in front of the garage.

An astonished Cerpa was among the millions watching the mayor's escape on TV. The residence had several TVs and the terrorists had turned them all on to gauge the media coverage of their attack. Furious once more, Cerpa rushed into the foyer but didn't bother to use a megaphone for his message. In a voice powered by rage he shouted: "If one more of you motherfuckers tries to escape, I will begin killing hostages!"

No more Houdinis. I was relieved.

4
The Census:
"I Am Admiral Giampietri of Callao"

INCLUDING THE WOMEN AND STAFF, Cerpa had freed some 150 hostages, but several hundred of us remained carpeting the floors of downstairs rooms and hallways. There were still too many hostages to control; Cerpa needed to get things organized or his operation would become the goat fuck the two escapes foreshadowed. I for one wanted Cerpa to get his shit together and stave off chaos with all that signified when you had men with guns everywhere.

Cerpa dispatched terrorists to each room, where they ordered us to stand in lines and wait to be summoned. We would walk one by one to the spiral staircase and stop in front of a scowling terrorist seated on the fourth step. The man held a child's school notebook and pencil.

My fellow prisoners trudged forward one after the other to be interrogated. The interrogator with his child's notebook wore a black scarf wrapped tightly around his head. A braided pigtail dangled down his neck from beneath the scarf. All the man needed was a parrot perched on his shoulder to complete the pirate look. His name was Rolly Rojas, but his comrades called him El Arabe. To them he looked like an Arab in a burnoose. I thought of a derogatory term I'd heard US Navy SEALs utter for such a sight: raghead.

As the Arab finished with each hostage, a terrorist would take the man and lead him to either an upstairs or a downstairs room. The more important hostages headed to the second floor: Among these were Ambassador

Aoki; Foreign Minister Tudela; General Máximo Rivera, current head of the police agency charged with fighting terrorism; General Carlos Domínguez, Rivera's predecessor; Ambassador Jorge Gumucio of Bolivia; and Ambassador Tabare Bocalandro of Uruguay. These latter two men were important for the terrorists because MRTA comrades languished in Bolivian and Uruguayan prisons.

Also marching topside were ambassadors from other countries: Guatemala, Cuba, Venezuela, Argentina, Panama, Canada, Germany, Austria, Greece, Malaysia. Seven Supreme Court justices—including my friend Carlos Giusti—joined the parade, as did several Japanese diplomats and businessmen. Peruvian diplomats and businessmen made their way up the stairs. Quite a haul.

I saw the slender priest with glasses whom I hadn't recognized at the reception walk from the stairs into the music room off the foyer. The godless Cerpa would quite likely release the man of God. Irony was in the air.

After about two hours I reached the head of the line to be summoned before the Arab. My watch read 0230. A terrorist standing at the bottom of the stairs motioned me forward.

While waiting to be called, I had seriously considered using my civilian voter registration card to conceal my military connection. Men close by whispered that I should use the card. They offered to dispose of my military identification card even if they had to eat it. I decided not to hide my status. Neither pride nor courage motivated my decision; instead I feared what the terrorists would do when they discovered the lie. And I was sure the media sooner or later would blare this tidbit to the world.

I stepped in front of the Arab, looked him in the eye, and said, "I am Admiral Luis Giampietri of Callao."

The man saw my civilian attire and asked if I was on active duty or retired.

I said I was retired and handed him my military identification card. I told him I was president of the civilian Institute of Oceanography.

The Arab glanced at the card and said: "All you fuckers are the same. You'll go with the generals and colonels." A terrorist grabbed my arm and hustled me topside.

We reached a broad landing, turned right, and stopped. Hostages were lined up with their handlers while they waited to enter two rooms at the end of the landing. I mentally designated these rooms "Alpha" and "Bravo." The rooms flanked the Doric columns of the residence and overlooked the circular driveway and street beyond the front wall. That street was Avenida Thomas Edison. Peru had a tradition of naming streets for famous people regardless of nationality.

With the terrorist holding my right arm, I glanced over my left shoulder and saw an open door to yet another room—"Charley"—with men lined up to enter. Beyond this room behind me I could see the opening to a long passageway extending away from the landing toward the back of the mansion. I assumed other rooms opened onto this passageway.

The terrorist broke my concentration when he grabbed the back of my neck in a vise-like grip and growled, "Let's go, Popeye." As he shoved me forward I resisted ever so slightly; the terrorist dug his fingers into my neck. I gritted my teeth against the pain, determined not to show what I felt. When we got to the doorway of Alpha, the terrorist released his hold on my neck and I felt a hard blow between my shoulder blades. The man had struck me with the butt of his AKM. For an instant my spine burned as if on fire. I fell into the room and landed atop a man sitting on the floor. He'd drawn his knees up to his chest and clasped them with his arms. The force of my fall knocked him sideways, but he continued to clutch his knees.

"*Discúlpame,*" I said and immediately realized the absurdity of asking the man to excuse me in these circumstances. Still, I was glad I had retained a civilized instinct. That would change.

"*No hay ningún problema, mi almirante.*"

I saw it was army colonel Roberto Fernandez, military aide to the president of the Peruvian Congress. I'd talked with Fernandez at the reception just before the attack. I remembered that our conversation was brief because he had to answer a message on his pager. I whispered in his ear: "Do you still have your pager?" He nodded. "Good. Keep it well hidden."

Fernandez nodded again and scooted over a few inches. This gave me enough room to force my way between bodies to my left and front. The open door was behind me. A terrorist stood in the doorway. The small room was filled with smelly, sweating bodies. Some men stood, while others sat in the same fashion as the colonel and I. We were packed assholes-to-elbows and bathed in the weak light of an overhead fixture with a single bulb.

We were in what appeared to be a child's bedroom that could have measured no more than three meters by four. A pair of windows took up the front wall to my right. The windows were closed, which added to the suffocating atmosphere. One of the windows had an air conditioner attached to it, but the machine was either broken or turned off. The heat of the Peruvian summer would hit us full force when the sun rose. And the temperature would be several degrees higher than normal. Peru was in the grip of a warm-water Pacific current called *El Niño*, a condition that would last more than a year and wreak havoc on world weather.

The windows overlooked the street beyond the wall and freedom, but wire mesh and padlocked grating obscured the view. I noted that the windows were also booby-trapped with *quesos rusos*—probably fifteen kilos in all. The explosives were rigged with trip wires made of monofilament fishing line. So much for freedom.

To my great delight, I saw a bathroom entrance to my left. But a terrorist stood guard and ignored a mixture of pathetic and demanding cries to use the toilet. Perhaps, I thought, the terrorists intended to humiliate us even more by forcing us to shit ourselves.

A closet with sliding doors took up most of the wall to my right. One of the doors was open, and I looked into the face of the leftist congressman Javier Diez Canseco. What, I wondered, was this man doing here? Shortly after the MRTA assault, I'd seen one terrorist greet Diez Canseco, pat him on the back, and say, "*Hola, Javier.*"

"Javier's" place in the closet was twice the size of the scrap of floor each of us outside the closet occupied. And he could lean back against the wall, I realized, as my spine throbbed.

I heard boots behind me and turned to see Cerpa in the doorway. He noticed me looking at him and said, "Why are you looking at me, Popeye? Are you in love with me?" I looked away but not before I saw him motioning for Diez Canseco to come forward. Cerpa also called the congressman by his first name. *Asshole buddies*, I thought.

Diez Canseco stumbled from the closet. When he reached me, he grabbed my shoulder to keep his balance.

I said, "*Cuidado, Javier.*" Be careful.

He gave me a startled look and said through a sappy smile, "*Gracias, amigo. Gracias.*" He had no idea who I was. Just as well. Diez Canseco walked with Cerpa into the hallway and out of sight.

I surveyed the room with its forlorn occupants. I counted heads to pass the time. Thirty-two SOBs—souls on board—most of whom were senior officers, including three police generals: Máximo Rivera, Carlos Domínguez, and Guillermo Bobbio. The terrorists referred to these men and all police as *los penes*—the pricks—because the police were the first line of attack against MRTA. The three generals might as well have had targets painted on their backs.

I estimated the terrorists had ordered around 250 hostages upstairs. Perhaps 150 or more remained downstairs. I was fairly confident from my observations that fourteen terrorists, among them two young women, held us captive. I calculated that Cerpa would have to free at least three hundred more hostages soon if he was to maintain control.

Diez Canseco returned in five minutes and began shaking hands. It seems he was leaving us. Cerpa had decided to put him in a room where the occupants were less at risk of execution. Diez Canseco was unusually cheery. He clearly approved of the move.

"Bye-bye, *Javier*," I said as he passed me.

The man looked at me and said through that same sappy smile, "*Chao, amigo.*"

Diez Canseco was barely out of the room when I made my way through and across bodies to the space he had vacated in the closet. Although I had to share the closet with three others, it was a vast improvement over my minuscule spot on the floor. I leaned against the closet wall and sighed.

I looked at my watch: 0400. What would the dawn bring? I turned away from the overhead light and closed my eyes. I was on the brink of blessed sleep when I was jolted awake by rifle fire and shouting. For an instant I flashed back to the start of the terrorist takedown. Then someone grabbed me roughly by the shirt and forced me to the floor facedown.

The terrorist shouted at me to stay the fuck down with my hands clasped behind my head or I would be a dead man. I complied. More shouts and firing. Then quiet except for a few groans.

The Arab surveyed us from the door. "Get used to it, you goddamn *perros guardianes de los ricachones.* This is a drill that will be repeated. Any rescue attempt and it won't be a drill. We'll kill you all." The Arab switched off the light and followed the other terrorists into the hallway.

Trembling, I crawled into the closet. My nerves were shot. Just as I was drifting into a shallow sleep, the Arab returned with his underlings, who once again put we "guard dogs of the wealthy" through the drill. This would go on every fifteen minutes or so until dawn. Just like Hell Week in SEAL training.

THE TERRORISTS had closed every curtain in the residence, and dawn announced itself with feeble light that seeped around the drapes. The gloomy atmosphere suited us well. The room was filled with the sounds of snoring men who slept without further harassment. Yet barely an hour had passed when someone turned on the light and pounded the butt of an AKM on the floor. We tensed for another drill.

Instead of screams and shouts we heard the voice of Cerpa, who spoke in a conversational tone. "Please do not be alarmed," he said. "We run the drills only as a precaution. No one need worry for his safety provided the police do nothing foolish. We have no wish to harm you. And as I have told your president, we will release you to rejoin your families when Fujimori frees our comrades."

I groaned. *Fat chance,* I thought. Fujimori was tough as nails.

Cerpa told us that as a sign of his trust and goodwill, he would allow us to roam about upstairs and talk to one another. He warned us not to congregate on the landing at the top of the stairs. We were welcome, he said, to use the toilets—but no closed doors. The terrorist seemed to have Mayor Andrade in mind.

Cerpa left, and several men stumbled into the hallway behind him. A few began exercising with feeble jumping jacks. I joined the line forming in front of the head. When my turn came, the toilet was still functioning and the smell bearable. That would change. I had not eaten much at the buffet and only needed to piss.

As I stood before the toilet, I peered through a doorway into Bravo. The bathroom connected the two rooms. An important fact. People in Alpha and Bravo had access to each other without having to cross the landing.

The men in Bravo were mostly military officers of lower rank. I recognized a young navy officer, Commander Alberto Heredia.

A good deed had brought Heredia to the reception. Because of his rank he normally would not have attended. But he lived near the residence, and Ambassador Aoki had invited him as a neighborly gesture. No good deed goes unpunished.

Heredia was a cheerful man who struggled with a weight problem. He was constantly trying to shed pounds to meet navy standards. Given his chubby appearance now, he wasn't having much success. He saw me and saluted. I returned his salute and gave him a thumbs-up. He grinned and returned the gesture with enthusiasm. How could he be so jolly? But I knew I could count on Alberto when the time came.

I finished and held back an urge to take a drink of water. Drinking from the faucet meant risking a debilitating case of the shits. Only fools and the impoverished would drink anything but bottled water in Lima.

I zipped up and headed for the hallway. I joined more than a hundred hostages milling about. Many smoked. I had kicked the habit years ago. The heat had begun to rise, and many hostages were now shirtless.

I decided to work my way past Charley down the passageway to the back of the residence. I saw four doors that opened to the right off the passageway. Before visiting those rooms I maneuvered through the crowd into Charley.

I concluded from its size and furniture that Charley was the master bedroom. The terrorists had removed the ambassador's bed, but two comfortable couches remained against the wall opposite me. I noticed that the door opening onto the landing was armored. Another armored door was near where the bed had been. This door was closed, but I was certain that it connected Charley with Bravo. Another armored door, this one open, led to a sitting room.

Ambassador Aoki was stretched out on one of the couches across from me watching a small TV on an end table. I recognized the teenage terrorist standing guard beside Aoki as the girl with a clacker for *quesos rusos* in the ballroom. Her name was Giovanna Vilas but the *tucos* called her La Gringa. She was armed with an AKM, a couple of pineapple grenades on her web belt, and a holstered sidearm. As I studied the latter, my stomach tightened. Dangling above the holster was a ring certainly attached to a fuse lighter. Under her body armor she wore a suicide vest.

I nodded to her and said in a friendly tone, *"Buenos días, señorita. ¿Cómo está?"* She frowned and looked at me as if I were something foul on the bottom of her boot.

I shrugged and moved past her into the sitting room. I saw a large bolted door to my right front. The door was armored and barricaded with what looked like a massive sea chest. The door did not seem to be booby-trapped—at least not from the inside. I walked over and ever so slightly pushed back the curtain covering a window next to the door. No booby traps. The few men seated on the floor ignored me.

Through the usual wire mesh and padlocked grates, I saw an upstairs patio surrounded by a low concrete wall. An opening in the wall on the far side of the patio revealed the top of what may have been a stairway to the lawn. The red-and-white party tent was still proudly in place above the buffet now rotting in the hot summer sun.

I withdrew my hand from the curtain. Ambassador Aoki's quarters with armored doors and closets was plainly the *panic room*. Perhaps it was that car bomb and Molotov cocktail attack a few years ago that had led to all the security . . .

We never learned who was responsible for the attack, but suspected MRTA. They liked to blow stuff up in front of places where ambassadors lived. MRTA had twice detonated explosives strong enough to blow out all the windows of the US ambassador's residence.

I walked to an open door in the back wall a few paces away. I peered into a spacious bathroom that I called "Echo." Two men sat talking on the edge of a bathtub while they smoked *puros*. The sharp smell of cigar smoke permeated the room. One man was the Cuban ambassador, whose name I couldn't recall. The other was the Uruguayan ambassador, Tabare Bocolandro. If I were Bocolandro, I'd stay close to the Cuban.

I brightened as I saw an old friend through the haze of *puro* smoke. The Bolivian ambassador, Jorge Gumucia, sat on the toilet reading a newspaper. Jorge was in his early sixties but looked younger despite the thinning hair on his head. Gray flecked his mustache and sideburns. He looked at me through horn-rimmed glasses beneath dark eyebrows. Jorge had a *panza* but was not fat.

I greeted the ambassador: "*Hola, compadre. ¿Cómo estás?*"

Jorge replied in a weary voice, "*Jodido, Lucho, y no muy contento, ¿y tú?*" Fucked up and not very happy, Lucho, and you?

"I've known better times."

"Haven't we all." Jorge got to his feet, shook my hand, and gave me an *abrazo*. He sat back down and I asked what paper he was reading.

"*La República*. A little pink for me. Would you like to read it?"

"No thanks. What does it have to say about our predicament?"

"*Nada*. It's the edition from day before yesterday. Found it in a wastebasket."

The Cuban and Bocolandro stood, nodded to me, and departed, still puffing on their *puros*.

Jorge looked somewhat wan, and I remembered he was diabetic. I asked if he had his medicine.

"Enough for a few days. I always carry some lemon drops but I'm just about out. I don't have my glucometer but I'm sure the numbers are low. If we don't eat soon, I'll cheat the *terrucos*." He smiled wearily. Our nickname for the terrorists was *terrucos* or simply *tucos*.

I said without much conviction: "*No te preocupas, compadre*. We'll take care of you." I made a mental note to check with the hostages for candy or snacks of any kind.

We made our good-byes, and I walked through the door between the master bedroom and sitting room toward the door to the landing. I felt a hand on my arm. It was Ambassador Aoki.

"How are you doing, Admiral?" he asked in English with an anxious, caring look. The poor man was a worrier; during the next four months he would make daily visits to the remaining hostages to apologize and ask what he could do for them.

I told him in English I was okay considering the circumstances and asked after his health.

"I'm fine, just fine. A little hungry and thirsty but I'm sure we'll get food and water soon. I've already complained to Señor Cerpa."

I thanked him, we exchanged short bows, and I walked out to the landing.

On my right the passageway extended toward the back of the residence. A staircase opening on the left of the passage directly across from me led to the roof. Three curtained windows were in the wall down from the staircase. Four doors opened on rooms across from the windows. A door barricaded with an ornate trunk was at the end of the passageway. I would learn the trunk contained Señora Aoki's kimono collection valued at more than a hundred thousand dollars.

I glanced up the staircase and saw a terrorist at work loading the door to the roof with plastic explosives. Probably Semtex from Russia by way of Cuba. Our captors had certainly rigged the residence with a lot of demo. I hoped they knew how to handle it. Demo was unforgiving.

I turned from the stairs and walked through the open door to the first room on the right-hand side of the passageway: "Foxtrot." Three men were in the center of the room talking. Two were Japanese and the third was my friend, Javier Diez Canseco. Javier had done all right for himself. No Peruvian *pene* or other *perro guardian de los ricachones* was in sight. Only young Japanese businessmen. Unlikely targets. I didn't understand why they weren't on the first floor.

Diez Canseco dominated the conversation. Beyond the men I saw a window and small balcony that overlooked the lawn. A closed, sliding glass door did not appear to be booby-trapped but was adorned with the usual wire mesh and padlocked grating. I walked to the door unnoticed.

Through the mesh and grating I had a better view of the patio than I had from Charley. Too bad the patio was beyond safe jumping distance for anyone over forty. But if a hostage could make it onto the balcony, odds were good he could jump the four meters to the lawn without breaking a leg. Maybe an ankle but not a leg. The problem was the locked wire mesh and grating.

I was also able to see into what was indeed a stairwell on the far side of the patio. Anyone who made it to the stairs would have cover all the way to the lawn.

Movement near the back wall of the residence caught my eye. I looked left and saw a *tuco* digging a shallow hole while a comrade stood nearby. They seemed to be gardening, but instead of planting roses they were planting anti-personnel mines. One of the men looked up and I turned away.

I walked past the Japanese still listening to Diez Canseco and out the door. I turned to enter the next room: "Golf."

A metallic roar engulfed me as I stepped across the threshold. I pitched forward onto my hands and knees. Through the clanging in my ears I heard shouts I could not understand. The burned smell of cordite filled my nostrils. Cordite and something else. Semtex? I gasped and shook my head to clear it. The shouts took on meaning: "Everyone back to rooms . . . Everyone back to the rooms!"

I groped my way through smoke and dust toward what I hoped was the landing. I had stumbled no more than a few steps when rough hands grabbed me and flung me through the faint outline of a doorway. I hit the floor, and there I remained until my head cleared. I saw an armored door. I was in Charley. Rough hands once more. Someone threw me against a window and pinned me there. I was a human shield.

5

The Foreign Minister Calls the President

AFTER WHAT SEEMED AN ETERNITY but was probably no more than a few minutes, the *tuco* released his hold. As he did, he shoved me so violently that a shard from the smashed windowpane nearly penetrated my eye. After the man left I tapped the shard with my fist and broke it off at the frame.

One benefit of the broken window was that we now had some ventilation; the smoke and dust from the explosion had completely dissipated. I saw no structural damage or even cracked plaster. I suspected the explosives on the door to the roof had gone high-order. If the *tuco* I'd seen booby-trapping the door had accidentally triggered the detonation, we would now have only thirteen of his comrades to worry about.

My immediate concern was for ambassadors Aoki and Gumucio. I checked the bathroom. Several men were milling about or sitting on the floor. Neither Jorge or Aoki was among them.

I made my way from the sitting room into the bedroom. I saw no more than ten or fifteen men, most of whom were in animated conversation. I heard sounds of cleanup from the passageway and wondered if there were casualties.

Someone called my name. I turned and saw Foreign Minister Francisco Tudela seated on a couch in front of the TV. He motioned for me to join him, getting to his feet as I approached. We shook hands, exchanged *abrazos*, and sat down. The TV was showing a commercial for baby food that reminded me of my hunger.

Tudela looked as if he hadn't slept in days. His eyes were red and had dark circles beneath them. He was a slender, balding man who looked younger than his forty-one years. He continued to wear his tie loosely around the collar of his white dress shirt. I had discarded my tie long ago after I'd used it as a gas filter during the takedown.

The foreign minister and I had met many times at diplomatic receptions and conferences about the Japanese research vessel. I liked the man and his easy manner. He did not suffer from the self-importance of others in high office. He also had a strong inner resolve he would display throughout our captivity.

"Do you know what happened, Lucho?" he asked.

"I think someone accidentally tripped a booby trap on the door to the roof."

"Anyone hurt?"

"I don't know. Where's Ambassador Aoki?"

"He just left to check on the others."

I noticed men were leaving and entering the room. The *tucos* had lifted the quarantine. Things couldn't be too bad. At least the military and police forces outside the residence had kept cool and not reacted to the explosion with an assault, guns blazing.

Tudela asked how I was.

"Not bad, sir." I decided to lighten the mood. "At least the assholes haven't broken any bones or cut my nuts off."

He laughed. "That's good news. They haven't done anything serious to me, either."

As senior man among the hostages, Tudela received a great deal of unwanted attention. But I saw no signs of any abuse.

Other men had crowded around us as the TV began showing scenes of the residence from the night before. Three terrorists including La Gringa were in the crowd. Several hostages laughed and applauded as we saw Commander Reátegui and Mayor Andrade dash to freedom.

Then we saw Cerpa, bandanna in place, standing beneath the Doric columns of the entrance, flanked by two armed subordinates. TV lights illuminated the scene.

Cerpa was delivering an ultimatum: "*Señor Presidente,* if you do not answer our demands to release our comrades, we will charge you our first victim—Foreign Minister Francisco Tudela." No one laughed. Tudela grew pale. I whispered in his ear: "Don't worry, sir. Cerpa won't kill anyone important because he knows Fujimori would order an immediate assault." Tudela nodded but did not reply.

Cerpa's image was replaced by a fat-faced commentator in a studio. "This just in," he said, reading from a teleprompter. "Reliable sources including released hostages tell us the terrorists infiltrated the residence dressed as waiters. They had concealed their weapons in floral arrangements and a huge birthday cake. One woman who had been a hostage said she suspected the men were not waiters because they did not know how to serve food and drink."

We erupted in laughter. The *tucos* laughed loudest of all. This fantasy would be earnestly reported around the world.

President Fujimori appeared on the screen. His face and voice were without emotion. He was colder than the Humboldt Current as he rejected Cerpa's demands. Fujimori was ready to fight to the last hostage.

Suddenly I was frustrated and angry. We were at the mercy of these two hardheaded men and helpless to do anything about it. A miscalculation on the part of one about what the other would do and we could all die. I was ambivalent about Fujimori's stand. As a military professional I understood his intransigence. Negotiate with terrorists and you invited more of the same. There would be no end to it. But as a son, husband, and father, my heart felt as if it had a hole in it.

The *tucos* were not pleased with Fujimori. La Gringa abruptly changed the channel to a *telenovela*.

We all drifted away. The foreign minister and I went into the sitting room, where we found two vacant chairs against the back wall next to the armored door leading to the patio. The door remained bolted and barricaded.

We sat down, and Tudela pulled a cell phone from his shirt pocket. I was surprised. After Mayor Andrade's escape I assumed the *tucos* would confiscate all phones. Then I recalled Colonel Fernandez with his pager. Cerpa had made a big mistake. Hostages could still communicate with the outside.

"Who are you calling?" I asked.

"The president. I have his private number."

Tudela punched in the number and put the phone to his ear. A minute or more passed. Nothing. Tudela sighed, closed the phone, and returned it to his pocket.

"No luck, huh?"

"I haven't had any luck reaching the president for the past six hours. I don't know how many times I've called, but the battery is almost gone."

"You've never gotten through?"

"Once," Tudela said in a voice freighted with resignation as much as disappointment.

"What did you tell him?"

"I told him how desperate our situation was. I told him about all the weapons and explosives. I said conditions were deplorable and urged him to begin negotiations if for no other reason than to get us food, water, and portable toilets."

"What did he say?"

"He thanked me for the call and hung up. Now he refuses to take my calls. No one answers."

No one speaks to the foreign minister anymore. Not a good sign, I thought, with a growing sense that we had been abandoned and a military solution was at hand.

I remained awhile with Minister Tudela for moral support. He was clearly worried, with good reason.

Another hostage came over, Dante Cordova, who had been the minister of education during Fujimori's first term. The top of Dante's head was as hairless and smooth as an egg; jet-black hair flanked the baldness.

He greeted us with *abrazos*. I offered him my chair and excused myself. I wanted to complete the recon.

The passageway had been swept clean of glass and plaster. The charred walls of the stairwell told me the explosion had been at the door or perhaps on the roof if the door had been open.

I entered Golf and saw a broken window. Chunks of plaster littered the floor. The stairwell had shaped the direction of the blast. Foxtrot, Golf, and—to a lesser extent—Charley and Delta had borne the brunt of the explosion. But the damage was not great, and I suffered no lasting effect. Probably a quarter-pound block of Semtex. Perhaps more but not much. *Gracias a Dios* there had been no sympathetic detonations.

Golf was a small room and half filled with people I recognized as middle-rank civil servants and businessmen. I saw Alfredo Torres, director of a public polling firm called Apoyo. I asked what he was doing to pass the time.

"I'm thinking about polling the hostages. Ask them a series of questions about how they are being treated, what do they think of most. Things like that."

I wished him luck and wondered if he had a slate of questions for the *tucos*. Well, the man was in the polling business. Why let captivity change that? Anything to pass the time.

I next visited "Hotel," which was no bigger than Golf. I recognized several justices of the Supreme Court. As I scanned the room looking for my friend Carlos Giusti, a solitary figure standing by a window staring out at the garden caught my eye. It was Pedro Fujimori, the president's younger brother. I started toward him, then thought better of it. Cerpa obviously did not know Pedro was in his grasp or Pedro would not be in this room.

I saw Giusti slumped against a wall. I went over and helped him to his feet. We shook hands and embraced. I stepped back and was immediately struck by how flushed his face was beneath his head full of white hair. High blood pressure. How many other hostages were suffering chronic illnesses with no medicine, or very little?

Then another thought struck me. I'd seen no Americans, and apart from my brief conversation with Ambassador Aoki I'd heard no English spoken. The gringos must be downstairs. I could understand Cerpa's decision to release them. He had enough on his plate and knew that if MRTA harmed an American it would all be over. Army Delta Force and navy SEALs were probably already in-country planning a rescue, calculating how many hostages would be wounded and killed. If they liked the numbers, they would attack. But as long as the gringos were unharmed, we were safe.

I heard someone yell from the landing that there was food: "*Hay comida!*"

Others picked up the cry, and people poured from the rooms. Once in the passageway they did a curious thing. Instead of pushing each other away in a mad rush for the stairs, they began to form a line. The line snaked down one side of the passageway and up the other across the landing to the staircase. Two hostages were on the top step handing out quarter slices of bread from loaves they had found in the kitchen. Those not in line stayed in their rooms to await their turn. Very orderly. We hadn't become a mob yet.

It was a meager meal, but we were happy for even this morsel. Each man took his share as if he were accepting the Eucharist at Holy Communion.

The bread ran out before all hostages had been served. Others who had not eaten their scrap shared it with the less fortunate in a touching show of solidarity.

This would be our last meal for more than forty hours.

ALBERTO FUJIMORI was in his office at the presidential palace when he heard of the takedown. His first thought was how close he had come to being a hostage. If a mechanical problem had not delayed his plane in Ayacucho, he would have attended the reception. But his relief was short-lived—he remembered that his mother, sister, and brother had planned to attend. He hoped against hope they had changed their minds or had left before the assault. He would not learn the truth for more than two hours, when Cerpa released the women.

Fujimori coolly banished thoughts of his family for the moment and reached for the red phone on his desk. No need to dial numbers, he put the phone to his ear and immediately heard the staccato rings.

Vladimir Ilyich Montesinos—named by his communist parents for Lenin—answered. Montesinos was the *eminencia gris*, the Rasputin of the administration, and Fujimori's right-hand man. He was also de facto chief of the powerful National Intelligence Service, SIN. Fujimori asked Montesinos what he knew of the situation at the residence.

Montesinos said he was at that moment with his staff evaluating contradictory situation reports. He added that he had an open line to his on-scene commander.

How, Fujimori demanded, had fourteen terrorists—some apparently teenagers from the jungle—managed to elude security and capture more than six hundred people, including generals, ambassadors, members of his cabinet, Supreme Court justices, and wealthy businessmen?

Montesinos said that they had entered the neighborhood just after sunset in an ambulance. Indifferent policemen at a security barrier had allowed the ambulance to pass without searching it. But a woman became suspicious when she saw the vehicle circling her block several times. She called Clave Medico, whose logo was on the ambulance, to ask about the suspicious activity. A dispatcher checked and told her the company had no vehicles in her neighborhood. A company official looked into the situation, but by the time he called police it was too late.

The ambulance parked in front of a house that shared the back wall of the residence. Two terrorists dressed as emergency medical technicians knocked on the door. They knew the building housed a German business rather than a family.

A night watchman answered the door and at first blocked their way. He said no one had called an ambulance.

The terrorists asked the watchman if he would sign a statement stating that the ambulance had been to the house. The man took a pen and began to sign a statement on a clipboard.

Then one terrorist seized the startled man while the other shoved a pistol in his face. They hustled him inside, secured his hands and feet with flex cuffs, and gagged him with a roll of gauze.

The rest of the terrorists emerged from the ambulance and within seconds were in the house with their weapons and explosives. They emplaced the charge on the back wall, retreated to the house, and detonated it. After that it was just "hey diddle diddle right up the middle."

"They didn't enter disguised as waiters?"

Montesinos chuckled. "No, Mr. President. That's just the usual media bullshit."

Fujimori told the spy chief he would be over shortly and hung up.

During the conversation Fujimori's fifteen-year-old son, Kenji, entered the room. He was plainly frightened. His father tried to ease his fears. Fujimori told Kenji not to worry. For every problem there was a solution. The president spared the boy the knowledge that his grandmother, aunt, and uncle were in the hands of terrorists.

THE FUJIMORI FAMILY were Japanese immigrants. Alberto Fujimori was born in Peru on July 28, 1938, Peru's Independence Day. Fujimori's father held various jobs: He picked cotton, was a tenant farmer, worked as a tailor, and started a tire repair shop in Lima. The family never had much money. The land they rented proved unproductive, and the worldwide Depression destroyed the tailor trade. The tire repair shop in Lima, however, flourished. Then came Pearl Harbor, and the United States pressured the Peruvian government to confiscate Japanese property and businesses. The tire shop was seized.

The family never fully recovered. Alberto grew up poor and suffered the usual racial slurs. Intellectually gifted and having won several scholarships for academic excellence, though, Fujimori began a successful but not spectacular academic career. He eventually became dean of the science faculty at the Agrarian University. He was also rector of the university and president of the National Assembly of University Presidents.

Fujimori gained national fame during the late 1980s as a TV talk-show host. His program, *Getting Together*, displayed his knowledge of national politics and made his name and face known throughout the country.

In 1990 Fujimori started a political party, *Cambio* (Change) 90. Incredibly, he won the presidential election. His populist approach and even his Japanese ancestry carried the day among Peru's Indians, mestizos, blacks, and Asians.

As president he confronted twin evils tearing the country apart: runaway inflation that had reached a staggering annual rate of 7,000 percent, and a ten-year insurrection that had killed thousands and left a third of the country in rebel hands.

Fujimori became the darling of the International Monetary Fund. Fujimori completely privatized the economy as well. His program was so drastic it became known as "Fuji-Shock."

Money for investment began to flow into the country, and inflation was soon on its way down to single digits.

But the War on Terror continued to go badly. Fujimori and his indispensable adviser, Vladimir Montesinos, blamed a recalcitrant Congress and corrupt judiciary for the lack of progress. In 1992 he dissolved Congress, suspended the Peruvian Constitution, and dismissed scores of judges including thirteen of twenty-three Supreme Court justices. These actions came to be known as the *autogolpe*—self-coup.

A hue and cry went up from the Western world that Fujimori had destroyed Peruvian democracy. He defended the policy by pointing out that unless the terrorists were defeated, democracy would cease to exist in any event. Peru would become a killing field just as Cambodia experienced under Pol Pot and his Khmer Rouge.

But later that year the extraordinary capture of Abimael Guzman and his leading lieutenants signaled the beginning of the end for SL as an effective force.

Victor Polay and several hundred of his MRTA followers suffered the same fate. With terrorism seemingly defeated, Fujimori held new congressional elections and established a commission to rewrite the Constitution with terms favorable for a strong executive. He ran for a second term in 1996 and won by a huge margin.

His first year in office was off to a good start when terrorism once again became front-page news. The hostage crisis was not the worst of his career, but it was certainly the most visible and could have caused the fall of his presidency.

Vladimir Montesinos was a smallish man in his early fifties and had a soft look about him that belied the steel within. He had a dangerous past. Twenty years earlier he had been an army major until the army caught him passing state secrets to the CIA. He was court-martialed and sent to prison for a year.

Montesinos began the study of law while incarcerated and earned his degree a few years after his release. He became wealthy by successfully defending cocaine lords as well as the general officers accused of ordering massacres in the SL stronghold of Ayacucho.

Montesinos's most important client, however, had been Fujimori. The man who would become president had been accused of tax evasion during the 1990 campaign. Montesinos aggressively and successfully defended him. Fujimori was impressed with Montesinos's inside knowledge of what went on in the government. Montesinos obtained most of his information from his well-connected and wealthy clients.

After the election Fujimori made no important decision without first discussing it with Montesinos. Appointed head of SIN, Montesinos was a perfect fit and soon employed the agency to spy on Fujimori's rivals as much as SL and MRTA.

MONTESINOS MET FUJIMORI at SIN headquarters, and the two men walked through the building's dimly lit halls. SIN agents rushed about going in and out of offices. Then Montesinos opened a back door onto a small parking lot. The men walked across the lot toward a windowless annex with a high flat roof. A forest of antennae sprouted from the roof along with parabolic dishes of different sizes pointed toward the heavens. Montesinos punched numbers into a keypad on a heavy steel door and followed Fujimori into a room that would become the command center throughout the crisis.

Charts covered with acetate were on the walls, a conference table dominated the center of the room, and cell phones littered the table. A TV with picture but no sound stood in a corner. Doors led to other rooms.

Six men were in the room: two SIN agents, three army generals, and an army colonel. Fujimori recognized and shook hands with the generals: José William Zapata, Luis Alatrista, and Jaime Patiño. Montesinos introduced the colonel, who commanded a special forces brigade trained for hostage rescue. The man appeared almost preternaturally fit; his face seemed to be carved from ironwood.

When Fujimori spoke, the president left no doubt he wanted a military solution and fast.

However, Montesinos had a problem. He didn't know much about the situation inside the residence, and without more intel, a premature rescue attempt could become a bloodbath for the hostages.

A telephone rang on the table. "Excuse me," Montesinos said. "This is my commander outside the residence."

He listened for a minute or so, nodding as if in agreement, issued curt instructions, and hung up.

"They're going to start releasing the women hostages within a few minutes." The men crowded around the TV. A SIN agent turned up the volume.

An image of the massive door between the Doric columns filled the screen. An off-camera announcer said he expected the women to be released at any moment.

As if on cue, the door swung open—and Cerpa stepped forward. His face was uncovered. He said he had decided to release all women as a humane measure and proof of MRTA goodwill. He urged President Fujimori to reciprocate by beginning to release the MRTA prisoners on a list he held in his hand. He would release more hostages, he added, if Fujimori freed his comrades.

Cerpa ended his speech with the usual terrorist slogan: "¡Patria o Muerte! ¡Venceremos!" Fatherland or death! We shall prevail! Then he went back into the residence and women began walking through the door. Many shielded their eyes from the harsh TV lights.

Fujimori immediately recognized his mother and sister. Montesinos squeezed his shoulder and the other men applauded. Fujimori smiled. Now his decisions would not be influenced by irrational emotion. His first such decision was to reject Cerpa's demand.

6

Papá Noel

As we chewed our bread trying to make it last longer, we heard Cerpa's amplified voice from the ground floor. He was standing in the open front door and speaking through the megaphone. His message was chilling: "Mr. President, you have ignored my repeated offer of a prisoner exchange. I am at the end of my patience. For the last time, release fifty prisoners as a sign of your good faith. I have already sent you a list through the Red Cross. If you do not free the prisoners on the list within thirty minutes, I will begin executing a hostage every five minutes until you do. Tudela and Aoki will be the first to die. Their blood will be on your hands."

Another bluff. At the sound of the first gunshot, an overwhelming force would storm the residence. Many of us would die, including most if not all of the terrorists. But was it a bluff? Cerpa's gang of zealots had killed before. Why wouldn't they kill again and join the growing list of MRTA martyrs? Fujimori was gambling with our lives.

With that troubling thought in mind I returned to Alpha. The room became stifling while sweating men filled it. The air conditioner was silent, but as I fell mercifully asleep in the closet I heard it clatter to life.

I awoke four hours later, shivering. The air conditioner was on full blast, and the room felt like a meat locker. I was hungry, thirsty, and cold. I yelled for someone to turn down the fucking air conditioner. To my surprise the noisy monster dropped to a soothing idle. But the battle would continue for the next two days between those of us who were too cold and those who were too hot. The struggle ended when the government cut off the electricity, but by then it was too late: I had contracted a vicious case of bronchitis, which would plague me throughout our incarceration.

WHEN FUJIMORI ignored Cerpa's threat, instead of killing us the terrorist decided to form a "delegation" of hostages to personally deliver his demands that the president free MRTA prisoners. Shortly after dark on Wednesday Cerpa released the ambassadors from Canada, Germany, and Greece to meet with Fujimori. The French cultural attaché joined them.

The media swarmed the men as they walked through the gates into the street. The Canadian ambassador, Anthony Vincent, dutifully read a statement from Cerpa that was little more than a rehash of his seemingly intransigent position.

After Vincent read the statement, SIN agents took the four men to the presidential palace, where Fujimori made them wait for five hours before he sent his minister of education, Domingo Palermo, to greet them. Nothing of consequence followed, which greatly offended the ambassadors.

The next morning the ambassadors told the media that Fujimori had refused to meet with them and they considered their work finished. The Greek ambassador and French cultural attaché retired to their embassies. The German ambassador took the first available flight home and never returned to Peru. The Canadian ambassador, Anthony Vincent, offered to stay and act as an intermediary between the government and MRTA. Fujimori accepted.

I AWOKE shortly after sunrise on Thursday, December 19, 1996, to begin a second full day in captivity. The terrorists had again interrupted our sleep repeatedly with their drills, but the harassment was less frequent. The *tucos*, it seemed, also needed sleep.

I stumbled across bodies toward the head. An awful stench greeted me. Through use and abuse the toilet had finally failed. Dark, fetid water covered the floor. Nausea gripped me, and I added vomit to the cesspool. Then I pissed through the doorway. I was happy to be constipated. As I walked away, the sickening odor seemed to cling to me like a second skin.

I approached a young terrorist standing in the door to the landing. He shook his head and indicated that I must stay in the room. Over his shoulder

I saw other hostages milling about. Apparently Cerpa had decided the military and *penes* would no longer enjoy the privilege of leaving their rooms.

At noon Ambassador Aoki entered Alpha and inquired after our health. He once again apologized for our plight. I took the opportunity to ask if he could speak to Cerpa about the nightly drills. Aoki was surprised when I described what the *tucos* had put us through. He said they had not done the same with the dignitaries in Charley.

"All they do to us," he said, "is come in once or twice during the night, switch on the lights, and point their guns at us. Two or three hold grenades above their heads. They don't say a word. Just stand there for a minute or more then leave."

Dry runs, I thought.

Aoki must have spoken with Cerpa, though, because the drills stopped and the terrorists began to treat us like the hostages in Charley.

But the drills did not stop for the *penes*. Between alarms the terrorists would often order the police out of the room. We would hear thumps, groans, and sometimes the sound of falling bodies. The terrorists were particularly brutal with General Domínguez. Two years earlier he had provided intelligence for a force that routed MRTA near the Andean town of Los Molinos. Seventy terrorists died in vicious fighting.

I've no doubt the *tucos* would have tortured and killed Domínguez if not for his value as a bargaining chip. I marveled at how the general withstood the abuse. How could he know they wouldn't kill him? A *tuco* often placed a pistol to his head or in his mouth and dry-fired it. But throughout his ordeal General Domínguez maintained his dignity and sometimes even cursed the terrorists to their faces.

DAWN ON THURSDAY found Fujimori in the windowless room at SIN headquarters that had become his command center. He referred to the men with him as his "mini-staff." He'd already put the so-called delegation of diplomats out of his mind.

The mini-staff included the three generals and special forces colonel, who had not left since the night before. Montesinos and a new member—the minister of education, Domingo Palermo—were also present.

Fujimori had chosen Palermo to be his principal contact with the terrorists. The choice was not random. Palermo had twice dealt with MRTA when he was the general manager of a local TV station before joining the government. Ten years previously MRTA had kidnapped the president of the TV station; Palermo negotiated his release. Then, in 1993, he again negotiated with MRTA for the release of a close friend the terrorists had kidnapped and held for ransom. Palermo was disciplined, cautious, and reserved. The president knew he could rely on Palermo to accurately present the government's position during negotiations and do as he was told.

Fujimori was resigned to talks with the terrorists. Every country with an ambassador in the residence had called to urge negotiations and the release of at least some MRTA prisoners. Japan was particularly insistent. The Japanese prime minister, Ryutaro Hashimoto, had called and cautioned Fujimori not to take any military action. Apparently Hashimoto did not like the president's response: He dispatched a contingent of more than a hundred officials headed by the foreign minister, Yuhiko Ikeda. Their JAL plane was due to touch down at Jorge Chávez International Airport on the outskirts of Lima in two hours.

Japan was sure to be a pain in the ass throughout the crisis. But Fujimori had to listen. Beginning with his first term that country had given Peru more than sixty-six million dollars in aid, which made Peru a leading Latin American recipient of Japanese assistance. Certainly more money was on the way, together with increased investments by Japanese corporations. Still, listening to the Japanese did not mean doing their bidding.

President Bill Clinton had just called, and his message was reassuring: Take a hard line and above all do not release prisoners. Clinton then offered to send his hostage rescue specialists, army Delta Force and navy SEALs. Perhaps recalling Tehran and Waco, Fujimori politely declined. Nevertheless, within the next twenty-four hours special operations teams from several nations including the United States swarmed to Lima like killer bees to honey: GSG-9 (Germany); GIGN (France); GOE II (Spain); SAT (Japan); AFEU (Colombia); Sayeret Matkal Unit 269 (Israel); US Army Delta Force and Navy SEALs. But Fujimori was determined that the rescue be a strictly Peruvian operation. He didn't want to share the thrill of victory with outsiders, although he would have been glad to share the agony of defeat.

The command center was the same as the night before with one important exception. A two-by-three-yard scale model of the residence now filled the conference table. Made of plaster and without a roof, it featured the first and second floors constructed side by side. Small plastic figures were arranged throughout the residence: Red figures were terrorists, blue were hostages.

The colonel in a fresh uniform stood by the model, pointer in hand. He briefed Fujimori on a rescue plan the staff had developed during the past several hours. The plan called for men from the colonel's brigade to fire rocket-propelled grenades into the downstairs office next to the front door. Former hostages had told SIN agents this was where Cerpa and his three lieutenants slept.

During the grenade strike another group of the colonel's men would rappel onto the roof from a helicopter with a muffled engine, blow the door to the second floor, and clear it of terrorists. A third group would blast open the front door and clear the first floor. The operation was called *Papá Noel*— Father Christmas—because the planners had scheduled it for Christmas Eve when the terrorists would least expect an assault. The plan also anticipated that the terrorists would release more hostages by then, which would reduce the number of casualties.

"How many hostages are in the residence now?" Fujimori asked.

Montesinos spoke before the colonel had a chance to answer: "We calculate 381, with the most important, including Ambassador Aoki and Chancellor Tudela, on the second floor. Our commandos will be wearing night-vision goggles that will give them a great advantage over the terrorists. We believe the commandos can clear the floor in less than three minutes. We'll have a more exact time after rehearsals."

Fujimori liked the boldness of the plan. He wanted to strike fast before the terrorists became organized and hardened their defenses. But the Japanese would be furious, especially if casualties were heavy.

Fujimori asked Montesinos the crucial question: "What are estimated casualties, dead and wounded?"

"Twenty percent dead and another 40 percent wounded is the worst-case estimate."

Fujimori, the professor of mathematics, quickly converted the percentages into casualties. He did not like the results: seventy-six dead and twice that number wounded.

"Too many," he said. "Come up with another plan."

Montesinos reminded Fujimori that any plan would only be as good as the intelligence that drove it. "Our biggest problem is lack of current information about what is going on inside the residence. Where are the terrorists, hostages, booby traps? Hostages with cell phones have provided us with some information, but that source is drying up as batteries fail. Freed hostages have also given us useful information, but that becomes stale quickly."

Fujimori thought a moment. "What about getting some insects from your friends in the CIA?"

"You mean bugs?" Montesinos informed the president that the police already possessed miniaturized microphones given to them by the US Drug Enforcement Agency. They could be concealed in any nondisposable item that entered the residence. Their means of delivery could be through the Red Cross. Technicians in the United States embassy were already monitoring virtually every radio transmission and phone conversation in Peru—including theirs—and would pass along whatever the CIA believed important.

"Good. I want another plan in two days." Fujimori thought a moment. "And cut off electricity to the residence."

THURSDAY AFTERNOON the Arab appeared in the doorway to our room and asked if anyone wanted to see a doctor. The terrorists had given permission for two Red Cross doctors to examine and treat sick hostages. Sick call would be in the foyer.

Several hands went up, including mine. The Arab told us to go downstairs.

I went below, got in line, and said hello to Carlos Giusti. I was surprised not to see Gumucio, Aoki, or Tudela in line. Perhaps the VIPs got house calls.

When my turn came, I told the doctor I believed I was coming down with bronchitis. He checked my throat and poked a thermometer in my mouth. He withdrew the thermometer, frowned, and told me my temperature was just slightly elevated. He put a stethoscope to my chest, listened for several seconds, and gave me a small bottle of cough medicine laced with codeine. No antibiotics.

Hostages were not the only ones needing medical attention. Cerpa had twisted an ankle during the assault, that a doctor wrapped with an Ace bandage. The doctor also gave him aspirin and codeine for pain.

Another *tuco*, Tito, presented a more serious problem. He'd shot himself in the leg during the takedown. He'd stopped the bleeding with a pressure bandage; an MRTA bandanna secured the bandage tightly to his leg. He claimed he needed no medical attention, but Cerpa ordered a doctor to check him.

The doctor examined Tito and said the man had been shot between the tibia and fibula in the lower leg. The bullet seemed to have lodged between the two bones, but the doctor needed X-rays for an accurate diagnosis.

Cerpa told Minnig he needed surgical supplies and an X-ray machine. Within the hour a Red Cross nurse wheeled in a machine and took X-rays of Tito's leg. A doctor at a nearby clinic examined the images and concluded that it would be too dangerous to remove the bullet. Tito spent the next fifty days in a walking cast.

I thought I would see at least one terrorist being treated for wounds received when the booby trap had detonated yesterday. But none appeared, and fourteen *tucos* still guarded us. Divine intervention is the only explanation I could come up with. God takes care of drunks and *tucos*.

An hour after sick call the Arab ordered the hostages in Alpha to stand in line outside the door. We were joined by the men in Bravo. The terrorists had finally realized it would be prudent to confiscate cell phones and pagers. I looked down the line and saw Colonel Fernandez. He winked at me. He was certainly more at ease than I was.

Two terrorists searched us. They tossed pagers and cell phones they discovered into a black plastic bag. We returned to our room, and hostages from other rooms stepped out to form a line. I immediately went to Fernandez and asked in a whisper if they had found the pager.

He grinned. "No, senor. I had it well hidden . . . beneath my balls. The *tuco* patted me down but stayed away from the crotch. I guess he didn't want me to think he was a *maricón*."

What a relief. At least we still had hope for limited communication with the outside world. I asked Fernandez if he had received any messages.

"Only from my contacts in Congress. The pager is on a single frequency that connects me only with those people. I hope I don't get too many messages. Nothing I can do now with the *celulares* gone—and messages eat up power. I'm not sure how much longer the pager will function."

Another frustration. Where could we get replacement batteries?

Friday morning brought unwelcome news the government had cut off electricity to the residence. The water pump shut down and any hope the toilets could be unclogged vanished. A diesel emergency generator kicked in, but we knew it would be a matter of days, if not hours, before it ran out of fuel. Cerpa would have to convince the government to provide more. Perhaps he could trade hostages for this vital commodity.

Cerpa passed a note to Domingo Palermo through Michel Minnig that appealed to Fujimori's sense of fair play. Instead of threats, Cerpa pointed out he had released all the women and elderly. He asked Fujimori to reciprocate and free some of the MRTA prisoners. He again named fifty he wanted released. The list was headed by Victor Polay and Cerpa's wife, Nancy.

Fujimori sent a curt reply: "If you really want to give a sign of good faith, liberate more people."

Cerpa drew up a list of thirty-eight hostages he would release that afternoon. He was happy to free these men because they were of little value as bargaining chips. Cerpa also knew he had to reduce the numbers if he was to maintain control. He would soon release many more.

Javier Diez Canseco and Alejandro Toledo were on the list. Toledo would later become president of Peru.

Before he left, Diez Canseco went from room to room pressuring hostages to sign a petition he had written with considerable direction from Cerpa. The petition called on President Fujimori to negotiate a peaceful end to the crisis and urged him to release at least some MRTA prisoners. Not everyone gave in to Diez Canseco, but he succeeded in convincing the top two men on Cerpa's death list, Ambassador Aoki and Chancellor Tudela, to sign.

Several commentators in the media and even high-ranking members of the government condemned Tudela for signing. I wonder how these people would have responded if they had spent the past forty-eight hours with AKMs at their heads and death threats in their thoughts?

Diez Canseco made a second visit to the rooms in case any hostages had changed their minds. None had. The congressman also made a little speech telling us how much he would miss us and how he would do all in his power to gain our release. He also promised to return the next day at 1:00 PM. Of course he never set foot in the residence again. This led to a running joke that lasted throughout our incarceration. Often as one o'clock approached someone would shout: "What time is it?" Someone else would yell, "One PM!" Then a chorus of hostages would cry: "Has Javier returned yet?"

7

Merry Christmas

WITH EACH HOSTAGE DEPARTURE we were saddened to see our friends leave—and not to be leaving with them. But those who were on their way to freedom did smuggle out notes we'd written to our loved ones.

A curious incident occurred as a Peruvian businessman walked toward the door. He stopped and offered one of the young terrorists he'd come to know a job in his factory "after all this has ended." The teenager was too startled to reply.

Alfredo Torres, director of the polling firm Apoyo, was among the lucky ones who walked from the gloom of our prison into the sunlight of a Peruvian summer. True to his word, Alfredo had passed his time inside the residence by taking a survey among hostages. Questions and responses included:

How would you rate the treatment you've received from MRTA?
Very good: 0%
Good: 78%
Average: 21%
Bad: 0%
Very bad: 0%
Undecided: 1%

What troubles you most about the situation?
The uncertainty: 80%

Living conditions: 8%
Lack of communication with family: 3%
Condition of the bathrooms: 7%
Food: 2%

What do you think the government should do?
Negotiate: 95%
Attack: 0%
Undecided: 5%

Do you think MRTA is a terrorist or guerrilla movement?
Terrorist: 50%
Guerrilla: 41%
Undecided: 9%

Several hostages chose not to participate, which of course disappointed Alfredo.

I found the survey insightful—although I suspected several answers may have been skewed by our peculiar and menacing situation. Cerpa was intrigued by Alfredo's profession. At one point he approached Alfredo and, after some discussion of methodology, asked the pollster what the Peruvian public thought of MRTA as opposed to SL.

Alfredo had a quick mind. He told the terrorist that polls he had conducted revealed that people did not differentiate between MRTA and SL.

Cerpa frowned. Alfredo continued, "But you now have a wonderful opportunity to demonstrate not only for the people of Peru but of the entire world that MRTA is very different from the butchers of SL. Millions will learn MRTA commandos are military professionals who follow civilized rules of warfare and do not torture or execute prisoners."

Cerpa smiled and nodded in agreement. Alfredo had in fact never conducted an opinion poll regarding MRTA and SL. But he reinforced a belief Cerpa already held: If MRTA treated the hostages humanely, the group would gain national and international stature as "good terrorists" or even *guerilleros*, rather than murderous thugs like SL.

Cerpa demonstrated his warmth for Alfredo by placing him among the first male hostages to be freed. Alfredo further endeared himself to Cerpa by asking the terrorist—along with several other hostages—for his autograph.

Cerpa gladly obliged and signed a piece of cardboard from a carton that had contained a Japanese beer called Fuji. The terrorist signed just below the brand name. Irony was truly in the air.

ALTHOUGH OUR NUMBERS had been reduced somewhat, nothing had changed in Alpha. We were as crowded and miserable as ever, but had become accustomed to the foul odors emanating from the bathroom. My main worry focused on the booby-trapped windows, and how the *tucos* were less than expert at handling explosives. A mishap in Alpha would, unlike the previous day's detonation, kill or maim us all.

That evening when Ambassador Aoki made his usual visit, I told him of my fears. He agreed and said neither Charley nor Delta was booby-trapped. When Aoki asked Cerpa to dismantle the explosives in Alpha, the terrorist refused. Aoki then moved in with us and spent three or four nights until Cerpa disarmed the explosives. He apparently did not want to risk losing his most valuable captive in a careless moment.

This was but one of Ambassador Aoki's many gestures of solidarity with the hostages. We remained his guests and are forever indebted to him for making our situation more tolerable. But a time would come when the ambassador and I would have an angry confrontation over a matter of life or death.

That night around 1900 the Red Cross brought five hundred boxed rations—our first true meal since the takedown. The fare was meager: bologna-and-cheese sandwiches, tepid bottled water, thermoses of hot coffee and hot water for tea. A few complained, but not many.

The *tucos* demanded and received double portions. They also took two thermoses of coffee—complete with hidden listening devices—into the downstairs office that had become their operations center. They always ate after the hostages in case the food or drink was drugged.

The *tucos* apparently believed the extra rations they demanded would confuse the government about their true numbers. But even after the government had an accurate count, the *tucos* continued to demand and receive extra food. Over time this gluttony would make the terrorists fat and lethargic: they would no longer be the lean, mean *guerilleros* they'd been when they assaulted the residence.

Conditions reached a new high on Saturday, the twenty-first. The Red

Cross brought us three meals, including a more substantial evening meal. The Western hostages received cold french fries and two pieces of cold roast chicken. The Japanese ate sushi and rice. All enjoyed oranges, apples, and bananas. We also had Cokes and Inca Kola—a delicious Peruvian soft drink. We drank coffee and tea from the bugged thermoses, as did the unsuspecting *tucos*.

The police and terrorists both carefully inspected the food before allowing us to eat. The process took time; hot food arrived cold. Our greater concern was that food waiting in the summer heat could spoil. We conducted our own careful inspections including sniff tests and sometimes refused to eat. Many Western hostages began asking for the Japanese ration that was meant to be eaten cold.

Also that day the Red Cross brought in nine, five-hundred-liter tanks filled with potable water they would refill every forty-eight hours along with ten portable toilets, which were placed in the residence. We cleaned the filthy bathrooms with the water. Morale improved.

After the evening meal on Saturday, Cerpa sent word to Fujimori through Palermo that he was ready to release more hostages if the president would reciprocate with MRTA prisoners. Fujimori of course refused but then told Palermo: "Don't encourage him to release more hostages. We want to keep the numbers up, so that he'll have problems of control." The hostages remained blissfully unaware of Fujimori's attitude. ·

We found ways to pass the time. Ambassador Aoki located packs of cards, a chess set, mah-jongg board, and a game of Go with its polished black and white stones. The stones and Go board quickly disappeared into a room filled with Japanese.

Aoki also located a board for checkers, but the game lacked pieces. Hostages substituted small squares of cardboard. At the beginning players had trouble keeping the squares from drifting off the board, until someone thought of putting gum on one side as an adhesive. The hostages would demonstrate many more examples of ingenuity as time passed—several much less frivolous than checkers.

After lunch several hostages gathered on the landing and in the passageway for the first of what they described as "mini-CADEs." The acronym stood for *Conferencia Anual de Ejecutivos*—Annual Conference of Executives—a gathering each year of business, government, and academic leaders to discuss the socioeconomic and political issues of the moment. We certainly had plenty of representatives from these groups in the residence and did not lack for issues of the moment. If they were not hostages, the men would have been participants in the real conference that year. They did the next best thing: organized and participated in their own CADE.

Speeches were made, and lively discussions followed. Those of us in Alpha were not permitted to participate. We had to remain where we were. We even had to eat in the room.

Themes of the mini-CADEs included the virtues and vices of a free-market economy, the need for universal education as the best means to make Peru's painfully diverse society more homogeneous, and the need for full employment to eradicate poverty. The last theme was one we often heard the *tucos* speak of, although their policy—when stripped of its revolutionary rhetoric—was simply to take from those with money and give to those without. But I never doubted the fundamental reason the *tuco* leaders sought to overthrow the government: to seize power for themselves.

I had no use for any economic theory espoused by the murderous thugs who held us captive. But for years I and many others like me had despaired of the terrible poverty many citizens suffered.

The speeches on poverty filled the air with depressing figures: 55 percent of Peruvians live in poverty; the annual per capita income is $750; Lima has one doctor for every four hundred inhabitants, while Andean departments such as Ayacucho have one for every twelve thousand; the infant mortality rate is eighty per thousand live births—only Bolivia and Haiti have worse rates in the Americas. But dry figures did not touch me with my country's poverty as powerfully as what I saw every day.

I lived in a substantial house with a substantial wall around it in a desirable neighborhood: paved streets with no potholes; cooling breezes fresh off the Pacific; flower beds and lawns tended daily by gardeners; regular garbage collection; running water and a reliable sewage system; security provided by private guards in addition to regular police patrols.

Yet no more than twenty minutes from my neighborhood festered a sprawling shantytown in conditions that would have made Charles Dickens blanch.

Naked children played in dust swirling around huts made of reed mats, bamboo poles, twine, and cardboard. Some were too exhausted to do anything but sit and stare with the dull eyes of the malnourished.

The smell of poverty, the nauseating smell of feces, urine, and rotting garbage, was everywhere. Chicken pox, measles, mumps, minor cases of flu—common childhood ailments of passing concern in developed countries were often fatal in our shantytowns and among the rural poor.

What to do? One administration years ago hit upon a solution: build a high wall around shantytowns along the road from the airport to downtown Lima, so that tourists would not be offended by what the wall concealed. One president—who touted himself as a social reformer—sought to mask the problem by calling the shantytowns *"pueblos jóvenes,"* young towns.

Most administrations were less cynical, but for reasons of inefficiency, lack of money, or corruption their programs also made little headway. The challenge was monumental, but we ignored it at our peril. Terrorism fed on poverty. SL and MRTA could easily convince hopeless people that revolution was the only way out of their miserable, subhuman condition. The nation's security and very existence demanded an effective war on poverty as well as terror.

ALTHOUGH HIS GENUINE CONCERN for the poor had helped elect Alberto Fujimori, he did not at this moment have poverty on his mind. He was consumed with thoughts of an armed solution to the growing crisis that threatened his presidency. The Japanese chancellor had made it clear before leaving Peru that his country would not take kindly to any military adventure that cost lives. The chancellor pressed for a negotiated, peaceful solution.

Fujimori saw negotiations as harmful to his image as a give-no-quarter fighter in the War on Terror. A samurai. He was the man who had brought SL to heel and imprisoned all but one important MRTA leader. If he showed weakness now, the political advantage he had gained as a strong leader would vanish. On the other hand, if he moved boldly his advantage would flourish. Unfortunately, his advisers kept presenting clumsy schemes that risked killing more hostages than they saved.

One such scheme called for a silenced helicopter to hover above the residence and drop a powerful bomb through an opaque skylight. The bomb would plummet to the foyer, where it would explode and stun or kill everyone on the first floor. Commandos would then attack through the hole in the roof and through the shattered front door. Fujimori knew these so-called silenced helicopters were at best merely muffled—everyone in the residence would hear it. And no one could tell him with certainty what kind of material covered the skylight. Would it detonate the bomb on impact and kill all the hostages on the second floor?

Yet another fantasy was for SIN agents to somehow secretly infiltrate the residence with concealed weapons. They would mingle with the hostages, contact the military and police officers, and together assault the terrorists. Fujimori's staff gave the plan a fifty–fifty chance of success. Fujimori gave it less than one shot in ten.

Saturday afternoon the emergency generator failed. Cerpa asked the Red Cross to bring more fuel, but the government refused. Fujimori clearly intended to isolate the terrorists . . . and the hostages. The president ordered cell phone service throughout the neighborhood ended and telephone lines to the residence cut. The terrorists were reduced to radio communication with the outside world, which would stop when their batteries failed. Without a functioning generator, the terrorists could not recharge their batteries. Or so we thought.

When Minnig gave the bad news about the fuel to Cerpa, the terrorist immediately contacted a local TV station with his shortwave radio. The station agreed to relay yet another demand for Fujimori to negotiate. Cerpa then ordered Aoki and Tudela to speak. Both men pleaded with Fujimori to do as the terrorist demanded.

Tudela said: "Everyone here is searching for a peaceful solution to this crisis and urges the government to seriously consider the MRTA proposals. We also believe it essential to have an open line of communication between those who control the residence and the government." Tudela expressed great frustration that he could not speak with authorities because the phone lines from outside the residence had been cut and cell service ended.

High-ranking members of the government condemned Tudela's speech. One of the ministers, Victor Joy Way, said in a voice heavy with sarcasm: "Now we are without a foreign minister. And to think, he was the best minister we had." Few recognized the harsh treatment Tudela received at the hands of MRTA. How easy to criticize when you don't have an AKM in your face or knife at your throat.

Fujimori had drafted a hard-line speech he intended to deliver on Christmas but decided to use it now as a response to Tudela. The speech was energetic and lacked even a hint of compromise: Fujimori demanded the terrorists lay down their weapons and release all hostages immediately. "The

MRTA has committed an act of terror—a violation of human rights," he said. "This is the same MRTA that has sown death and destruction throughout Peru during the past decade. This is the same MRTA that now wants a dialogue while it threatens the hostages with rifles and explosives. We will have nothing to do with those who use terror as their main argument."

Fujimori added that freedom for those who had perpetrated assassinations and terrorist assaults was unacceptable under the law and under principles of national security.

This intractable position was a nightmare for the hostages. We suffered reprisals for Fujimori's harsh words: slaps, punches, kicks, the dreaded night drills, and AKM butt strokes. Fujimori also failed to realize that by personally responding to Cerpa he fed the terrorist's towering ego: Cerpa believed Fujimori considered him an equal. But Cerpa continued to dangerously underestimate the president's iron will.

SUNDAY, DECEMBER 22. On the first Sunday of our captivity Father Wicht— the priest I had not recognized at the reception—celebrated Mass with materials the Red Cross brought to the residence: wafers and wine for Holy Communion. SIN agents had seen to it that a chalice and crucifix had a secular as well as religious purpose.

Father Wicht placed the altar halfway up the staircase on a small landing. The ceremony was very emotional even with armed terrorists standing guard. This would be the first of many Masses that strengthened our faith in moments of despair and filled our hearts with peace rather than hopelessness.

After the noon meal Cerpa announced he would free hostages who had no connection with the government or were of no value for negotiations. The terrorists had developed a list of 225 men who would walk through the front door. A very big holiday gift indeed. Merry Christmas!

At that moment, in an extraordinary act of selflessness, Father Wicht stepped forward and urged Cerpa to let him stay in place of Oscar Mavila, a businessman who owned several car dealerships. The priest said his place was with the hostages as their spiritual adviser. After a moment's thought, Cerpa allowed the swap. Perhaps he had Marx's famous dictum in mind: Religion is the opiate of the masses. Keep them on their knees and they're less likely to make mischief. But when Cerpa learned later how much Mavila was worth, the consummate kidnapper for ransom deeply regretted his decision.

Our doctors were among those to be freed. We would miss them. They had little medicine but could diagnose ailments and show us how to avoid further suffering. They also acted as our advocates with the Red Cross doctors, who seldom took a personal interest in us as patients.

Still, the hostages were not left completely without a sympathetic ear and at least a modicum of medical knowledge. Congressman Eduardo Pando—who had been assisting the doctors—became our paramedic. He had no formal training but was totally committed to the healing arts. Playing doctor had surely been Eduardo's favorite childhood game.

He had the doctors give him a list of ill hostages along with their ailments, treatments, and prognoses. The doctors left their meager medicine chest with Eduardo and sent him a *Physician's Desk Reference* through the Red Cross.

Eduardo was in constant motion among us treating real and imagined illnesses. His seemingly boundless energy earned him the nickname "Duracell." He set himself the task of memorizing the *PDR* and his speech soon filled with medical terms that baffled the rest of us. We began to call him "Dr. McCoy" from the *Star Trek* series.

Eduardo did not limit his healing efforts to what he found in *PDR*. He also practiced what might be called "the laying on of hands" to treat the afflicted. He came by this skill honestly: He was an active member of a mystical group of faith healers known as the Majicari.

A few of us dismissed Eduardo as a *brujo*—witch doctor—but there was no denying at times he seemed to achieve fantastic cures. Perhaps this was nothing more than the power of suggestion at work, but who knows? No one could doubt the man's selfless concern for us all. I certainly appreciated Eduardo, although I was too much the cynic to participate in his more unorthodox treatments.

If I had been less of a cynic, perhaps Eduardo could have laid hands on me to cure my bronchitis, which worsened with each passing day. My hacking cough became so bad that a fellow hostage, Dante Cordova, urged Cerpa to move me from Alpha to the ambassador's master bedroom in Charley and get me antibiotics. Dante, the former minister of education, knew I would not ask Cerpa for anything. He told the terrorist that Charley was much better ventilated than Alpha, and I would be less contagious there.

Cerpa allowed me to go to Charley but refused to ask for medicine. As a result, I managed to pass on the malady to several of my new roommates, including the consul general of Argentina, Juan Ibáñez.

The massive release of hostages was a time of great celebration both for friends and families and for the millions around the world who were praying for a peaceful end to the crisis. Those of us left behind could only imagine the joy they felt, and although such imaginings were accompanied by sadness and despair, we at least gained more space in the residence. Our numbers had been reduced to 106. Shorter lines to use the toilet and shorter waits for food. *No hay mal que por bien no venga.* Nothing bad happens that doesn't bring a little good.

On the day before Christmas the Uruguayan government caved in to the terrorists' demands that it release two of their *compadres* imprisoned in Montevideo for kidnapping a businessman. Peru recalled its ambassador to Uruguay in protest. MRTA then freed the Uruguayan ambassador, Tabare Bocalandro, who practically ran from the residence without any farewells.

Unlike Uruguay, Bolivia refused to release the four MRTA thugs it held on kidnapping charges. Our captors immediately retaliated against Ambassador Gumucio. They slapped him around and administered AKM butt strokes to various tender parts of his anatomy; they menaced him with grenades. He remained stoic and uncomplaining throughout assaults that would later become so vicious, we feared for his life.

As night fell on Christmas Eve, the terrorists drew back the curtains of upstairs windows and we saw a marvelous tree aglimmer with holiday lights. A local TV station had erected the tree in the street outside the residence. A priest celebrated midnight Mass by the Christmas tree. Several family members attended, carrying lighted candles and displaying placards with holiday greetings. We could hear them sing carols and pray. A group of reporters shouted, "Merry Christmas, brothers!"

Perhaps taken by all the good cheer, Cerpa allowed us to hang a banner from Alpha that read: THANK YOU BROTHERS. MERRY CHRISTMAS! As the midnight hour came upon us, we rose as one in the darkness and embraced one another.

CHRISTMAS DAY brought the most magnificent meal of our captivity. The president's daughter, Keiko, arrived with eight roast turkeys and all the trimmings. We didn't mind that the food was cold, as usual.

After the holiday feast, Monsignor Juan Luis Cipriani arrived at the residence with Minnig to celebrate Mass. Afterward Cipriani spent more than seven hours talking with Cerpa, Tito, Salvador, and the Arab.

Monsignor Cipriani, archbishop of Ayacucho, was one of the best-known and most controversial priests in Peru. A tall man in his early fifties, he moved with the coordinated ease of the professional basketball player he had once been. He had paid his way through engineering school with his basketball earnings and was a member of the national selection.

Although they differed in so many ways, Cerpa and Monsignor Cipriani shared one quality: a fierce devotion to their chosen religion. As a young man Cipriani joined the rigorous, unyielding Opus Dei—a conservative Catholic movement that for centuries has acted as protector of the True Religion. He continued the affiliation during his priesthood. As archbishop for the terrorist-infested department of Ayacucho, he took a hard line against *Sendero Luminoso.* He had little use for priests who practiced so-called liberation theology, viewing them as dupes of leftist renegades. He did his best to develop a priesthood in Ayacucho that would do battle with SL for the souls of the campesinos. Several priests died in the effort.

When Minnig first suggested to Cerpa that Cipriani conduct the Christmas Mass, the terrorist replied, "Of course! I'd like nothing better to have him stand before me." However, when Minnig pressed Cerpa to accept the archbishop as a member of the negotiating team, Cerpa's response was immediate: "That reactionary son-of-a-bitch? Absolutely not. Anybody but him."

Nevertheless, after Mass, Cerpa and his lieutenants spent hours in often contentious debate with the priest. At one point the discussion became superheated when Cerpa made a coarse joke about priests and nuns and questioned Cipriani's manhood.

Cipriani rose from his chair, looked down upon the terrorist leader seated behind a desk, and said: "Careful, señor. You should keep in mind that beneath this cassock swings *un gran par de huevos.*" A big pair of balls.

By the end of the afternoon, the men were as close to becoming friends as they could ever be, and the archbishop was now a member of the negotiating team. Cerpa also allowed Cipriani to take a sick hostage with him when he left. Japanese diplomat Kenyi Huola was severely dehydrated by a persistent case of diarrhea bordering on dysentery.

That evening the Red Cross brought us the best Christmas gift possible apart from our freedom: paper and pencils to write letters. The paper was divided into vertical halves; we would write on one half and our loved ones would reply on the other. Just as with our food, the letters would be examined by the police, the Red Cross, and the terrorists. The injured Tito was Cerpa's censor, and the petty tyrant seemed to delight in delaying the letters and defacing them. A small price to pay in return for a vital link with the outside world.

8

The Tara 72

FORMAL TALKS BETWEEN the government and terrorists began on December 28. Minister Palermo and Monsignor Cipriani met with Cerpa, Tito, and the Arab in the grand ballroom. Comfortably ensconced in an overstuffed easy chair, Cerpa launched into an hour-long monologue filled with the usual revolutionary bullshit.

Afterward the parties spoke for more than three hours. At 1600 Palermo and Cipriani left the residence with twenty-three more hostages. Cerpa released a statement to the media saying he had freed the men as yet another sign of his goodwill.

Fujimori was not pleased. He told Palermo not to return for a few days. The president wanted no more hostages freed. Our number was down to eighty-three, and he believed this lessened the pressure on Cerpa. Fujimori also issued his own press release: The meeting between Cerpa and Palermo should in no way be construed as "negotiations." The president of Peru did not negotiate with terrorists. Any such meetings were nothing more than "conversations." Fujimori had chosen to follow the US–Israeli model rather than the Japanese.

On December 31 the police organized a photo opportunity for journalists, allowing them to pass in front of the residence and take photos through the open gates of the circular driveway. As the group approached the gates, a Japanese reporter dashed up the driveway into the residence. Police appeared unable to control other journalists who followed their colleague.

Cerpa was delighted. As the media mob pressed into the foyer, Cerpa ordered Aoki and Tudela brought forward. Cerpa told the two men to stand on the stairs. Cameras flashed. Both Tudela and Aoki said the hostages were in good shape and were being well treated. Tudela repeated his message that the government should negotiate. Aoki took the opportunity to apologize to his emperor and fellow citizens of Japan for all the embarrassment he had caused them for having failed to protect his guests.

Cerpa paraded a few other hostages up and down the stairs to show what good health they were in. He concluded the show with his usual demands and lectured the reporters as he'd repeatedly lectured us: MRTA, unlike *Sendero*, were *guerilleros*, not *terroristas*. Then he called upon Boris Yeltsin and Fidel Castro to act as mediators. The spectacle over, two terrorists escorted the media out the front door.

SIN agents posing as journalists had entered the residence with the crowd. The agents planted more bugs, although they did not gain access to areas beyond the foyer and staircase. One of the agents paused at the door to give Cerpa a camera, rolls of film, and a handheld radio. The agent truthfully told Cerpa he could use the radio whenever he wanted to talk with a local cable TV network. Of course the radio was set to transmit to SIN headquarters, and a microphone was planted in the camera.

On New Year's Day we had our choice of salmon or turkey; the Japanese had a dish I could not recognize apart from the rice. The salmon had a suspicious look about it. I ate turkey. After the meal, Cerpa freed nine more hostages, including two of the three remaining diplomats.

Seventy-four of us remained, including the unfortunate but courageous Jorge Gumucio. Cerpa intended to hold this number until the bitter end. Within the next two weeks, however, first one and then another hostage fell desperately ill. Police commander Luis Valencia, chief of the anti-terrorist Delta Force, developed a raging fever and became drenched in sweat. Eduardo Pando in his role as our paramedic diagnosed constipation. *Gracias a Dios,* Eduardo had no laxatives. The reality was that Commander Valencia's fever was fueled by a throat infection that threatened us all.

Perhaps this fear of contagion led Cerpa to reluctantly allow the Red Cross to carry the stricken *pene* from the residence on a stretcher—but when another *pene*, Colonel José Rivas, complained of a crushing chest pain and numb left arm, Cerpa refused to authorize his medical evacuation. He did allow Eduardo to use the megaphone and ask for a Red Cross doctor to examine Colonel Rivas.

The doctor arrived momentarily, accompanied by Minnig and Cipriani. The doctor diagnosed a probable heart attack and urged Cerpa to let him take Rivas to a hospital for tests and treatment. Cerpa refused, saying that if anyone died in the residence, his blood would be on Fujimori's hands.

The three men continued trying to persuade the terrorist until finally Cerpa agreed to discuss the matter with his lieutenants. After twenty minutes they returned. The decision had been unanimous: Rivas stayed.

Cipriani became flushed and raised his index finger as he spoke to Cerpa: "You said if anyone died in here the blood would be on the president's hands. That is wrong. The blood will be on your hands, and the world will judge you and MRTA accordingly."

Ever concerned with image, Cerpa seemed to back down. He told the priest he and his men would reconsider and within minutes allowed Rivas to be carried out on a stretcher.

When the delegation had left with the patient, Cerpa ordered us into the foyer and yelled: "If one more of you *hijos de puta* gets sick, you'll fucking die right fucking here!" Whereupon the terrorists went among us with slaps, punches, kicks, and butt strokes as they herded us back to our rooms.

We'd seen our last fellow hostage leave. We were now the Tara 72—without Scarlett or Rhett.

THE DOWNWARD DRIFT of our numbers caused Cerpa to relocate some of us. We were now all on the second floor except for a group of Japanese businessmen and diplomats who remained below. The second-floor rooms were laid out along the lines of a reverse L. The rooms overlooking the circular driveway in front of the residence—Alpha and Bravo—together with the connecting bathroom formed the base of the letter. The rooms that stretched away from the front of the residence and extended to the end of the passageway—Charley through Hotel—formed the vertical line.

Twelve high-ranking police officers continued to occupy Alpha; an equal number of lower-ranking police and military officers occupied Bravo, along with one civilian—the ex-minister Dante Cordova. In keeping with the democratic principle that civilians should control the military, those in Bravo agreed that Dante would be their leader.

Charley and Delta held the highest-ranking hostages and became known as the "VIP lounge." Pedro Fujimori, Ambassador Aoki, and Foreign Minister Tudela were among the VIPs and were atop Cerpa's list to be assassinated if the government attacked. Father Wicht, Congressman Eduardo Pando (our medic), and Ambassador Jorge Gumucio were also in the lounge. I had joined this august—and dangerous—group because of my bronchitis, which was now better but would punish me until the end. A total of eighteen men occupied Charley and Delta. A door connected Bravo and Charley, and a narrow doorway connected Charley and Delta. You entered the bathroom for the VIP lounge through a door from Delta. I had designated the bathroom Echo. The barricaded door in Delta led to the upstairs patio.

The next room down the passageway was Foxtrot, home to eleven Japanese businessmen. Foxtrot had no connecting door with Echo, but did have a small balcony that overlooked the lawn where the party tent remained. The thoroughly rotted buffet was still in place beneath the tent. A barred double door led from Foxtrot to the balcony.

The *tucos* had made Golf, the next room down the passageway, their armory. AKMs, boxes of grenades, ammunition, mines, and plastic explosives lined the walls. The door to the passageway was locked, and at least one *tuco* was inside 24/7.

A bathroom I had given no designation was between the armory and Hotel. The only entrance to the bathroom was from the passageway. It had no connecting doors with the armory or Hotel.

Hotel was the last room off the passageway before the door blocked with the kimono-filled trunk. The door led to the service annex. Carlos Giusti and five other Supreme Court justices occupied Hotel together with the vice minister of the presidency, Carlos Tsuboyama. The annex, which was off limits to us, contained servants' quarters, a kitchen, and pantry. Stairs led from the lawn behind the residence to the annex.

Although our diminished numbers made it easier for the *tucos* to control us, we were now a more cohesive group. I believed this would make it easier to organize, resist, and escape should that moment arrive. Before Cerpa had released the other hostages, the residence was a tower of Babel filled with voices that spoke English, Japanese, Greek, Italian, Spanish of varying accents, Korean, German, Malay, Portuguese, and Arabic. Of greater concern was that some hostages were sympathetic to the terrorists, such as the Cuban ambassador and—as it turned out—several Japanese hostages. Even those who were not sympathetic to the *tucos* might nevertheless oppose an escape or rescue they feared could kill them.

I suspected I would have time to sort out friend from foe and develop plans, because I was more convinced than ever with each passing day that we were in for a long siege. I knew this because Cerpa was not exactly blazing a trail for hostage taking as a tactic of Latin American terrorists. Other madmen had pointed the way before him.

In 1974 the Sandinistas had seized partygoers at a reception for the US ambassador in Managua hosted by a close friend of the dictator, Anastasio Somoza. Somoza, never too concerned about political consequences of his acts, freed fourteen Sandinistas, paid a million-dollar ransom, and guaranteed safe passage to Cuba in return for the hostages.

Four years later the infamous Sandinista Comandante Zero seized the Nicaraguan Congress and took more than one thousand people hostage at the national palace in Managua. Once again Somoza paid a hefty ransom, freed sixty prisoners, and again guaranteed safe passage for the terrorists. Another embarrassment for Somoza, but a nonviolent one I'm sure most of the hostages in their heart of hearts appreciated.

A link between the Sandinistas and MRTA was the young US citizen, Lori Berenson. After she dropped out of MIT in 1989, her odyssey as a "freedom fighter" took her to Nicaragua and the Sandinistas for a year, then to El Salvador and the *Frente Faribundo Martí de Liberación* (FMLN) for four more years, and finally to Peru.

In 1995 our police arrested her together with Cerpa's wife, Nancy, and several other MRTA *compadres*. A search of the Lima villa they were renting in Berenson's name uncovered weapons, uniforms, thousands of rounds of ammunition, and sticks of dynamite. But the most important discoveries were detailed plans for MRTA to seize the Peruvian Congress in Lima during a session at the national palace. Shades of Comandante Zero.

But Comandante Zero's opsec—operational security, or the keeping of secrets—was far superior to that of MRTA. Many of the *tucos* Cerpa wanted to exchange for us had been rolled up based on information found in the villa raid. Berenson herself was high on the list of prisoners Cerpa had given Fujimori. She was at the moment cooling her revolutionary tush in a drafty prison near the Andean city of Puno, at a toasty twelve thousand feet above sea level.

Cerpa's hostage-taking experience began in the early 1980s, when he trained and operated with the Colombian terrorist group M-19.

In what may well have served as a blueprint for the MRTA takedown, M-19 seized more than a hundred people in 1980 at a diplomatic reception in the Bogotá embassy of the Dominican Republic. Nineteen ambassadors were among the hostages, including the US representative. Just as MRTA held us to gain release of their leader, Victor Polay, M-19 had taken hostages to trade for their imprisoned leader, Jaime Bateman. M-19 proceeded to release most of its captives during the sixty-one days following the takedown. On the sixty-first day, the Colombian government allowed the terrorists and their remaining hostages to board a plane to Havana, where Castro welcomed the terrorists and sent the hostages back to Bogotá.

Would our crisis have such a tidy, nonviolent end? I would be less than candid if I were to say I fervently hoped Fujimori would continue his refusal to negotiate our release.

Sixty-one days. Two months. MRTA had now held us for about half that time. Would we be touching down in Havana within the next month, or would we suffer the fate of hostages M-19 once again seized in 1984 at the Bogotá Palace of Justice?

This time, the Colombian government took a hard line. The army launched a two-day frontal assault on the massive building. When it was over the building was rubble and more than a hundred hostages were dead, including eleven Supreme Court justices.

What would happen to us? Perhaps the best news was what had not yet happened. Despite Fujimori's intransigence, he had not ordered an attack. I suspected we had the Japanese government to thank for that.

But if there were an attack, I knew the attacking force needed accurate, timely information about the situation inside the residence. Intelligence drove operations. A commando could move, shoot, and communicate better than anyone in the world and still fail if he executed a mission with flawed intel.

And if a commando force were to launch a rescue, who would provide it?

Certainly President Fujimori would receive many offers from foreign governments for advice, supplies, and probably even commandos if properly sanitized. But I was sure national pride would dictate the president use Peruvians for the mission. Beyond that, I knew from sixteen years of fighting the *tucos* that our commandos were among the very best trained and combat-tested in the world. Why should we look to such countries as Germany and the United States for guidance? The Germans had botched the rescue of

Israeli athletes at the Munich Olympics, and of course the US hadn't even made it across the line of departure in Iran. If it came to a rescue, I wanted my life in the hands of Peruvian commandos. But I would welcome technological assistance from the US.

The best of all possible scenarios would be for my own men of the *Fuerzas de Operaciones Especiales*—the Peruvian SEALs—to lead the way. But just as the United States never has enough SEALs for the missions at hand, I feared Peru would not have enough FOEs for a hostage rescue of this magnitude. These elite commandos were already overcommitted with operations against the Ecuadorians, who yet again were trying to seize our territory in the Amazon, the *narcotraficantes* in the Upper Huallaga Valley, and the remnants of *tucos* throughout the country. In addition, the joint command had decided two years earlier that the FOEs should be targeted primarily against external threats such as Ecuador.

There were two other military units that I was confident could plan and execute a rescue. The army had several hundred members in what it called *la División de Fuerzas Especiales*—the Special Forces Division. SF if anything was more experienced than FOEs in the War on Terror. They were the eyes and ears of the army. More importantly, they organized, trained, and led campesino *rondas* or militias similar to the Montagnard units that US special forces had led in Vietnam. But we had a distinct advantage: We were fighting in our own country, and Peruvian SF could meld much easier with the *rondas* than the Americans could with their charges. When leading *rondas*, SF advisers typically traded the field jacket for a poncho.

In the Peruvian Marine Corps was another much smaller but equally well-trained special operations force called *la Unidad Especial de Combate* (UEC). UEC seldom numbered more than twenty-five men—all of whom were trained snipers and demolition experts. I couldn't imagine a rescue force without these valuable assets.

Yes, Peruvian commandos could accomplish the mission, but not without intel. I needed to get more information on the *tucos* for them—and for ourselves if we had to escape on our own. I needed *compañeros* but not too many. I had OPSEC to maintain. I selected my first *compañero*: the efficient if somewhat plump navy commander, Alberto Heredia.

9

Cumpas and *Compañeros*

As I STEPPED INTO the passageway from Charley to find Heredia, I encountered several hostages and even a few *tucos* walking up and down the corridor as part of their morning exercises. The striders were completing a circuit that started at the top of the stairs on the landing, went down the right side of the passageway and up the left. One circuit measured 110 meters. Some striders would be on the circuit for no more than five or ten minutes, while others would toil for an hour or more. I made my way through the sweating herd toward Bravo, where I found Alberto Heredia playing cards with two police officers. Alberto appeared to have already finished his brief exercises for the day. He never was a fitness freak and had no desire to change now. He saw me standing in the doorway and excused himself from the game.

"*Buenas días, mi almirante.* Did you sleep well?"

"Not bad, Alberto. The rats stayed off my face." The residence was overrun with huge rats the rotting buffet had attracted. Most nights hostages would feel cold little feet scamper up their bodies and across their faces.

Alberto frowned. "I wasn't so lucky. I slept under my blanket most of the night and sweated like a *chancho.*"

"Other than that, how have you been?"

I was surprised to hear the usually jolly officer complain. "Not so good. I got the results of my blood test yesterday and the doctor told me my cholesterol was too high."

A Red Cross doctor drew our blood once a week and tested it for triglyc-
erides, cholesterol, glucose, and disease.

"High cholesterol won't be fatal in a man your age for a long time. Did
the doctor give you medicine?"

"No, sir. He told me I would have to eat Japanese chow. High protein, low
fat. I mean, here we are surrounded by *tucos* with loaded weapons and hand
grenades ready to kill us all and the fucking doctor is worried about my fucking cholesterol."

"We live in strange times, Alberto. But I have something else to talk with
you about. Let's walk."

We stepped into the passageway and joined the herd. I spoke to Alberto
in a low voice: "*Comandante,* I'm developing a plan to get out of here but I
need intel. I want you to help."

Heredia stopped and stared at me. Others passed us.

He said in a voice too loud, "*Sí, mi almirante. ¡A sus órdenes!*"

"Keep your voice down and don't look at me. Let's keep walking."

"I'm particularly interested in *tuco* morale," I continued softly. "We need
to know if there are bad feelings among them, especially the leaders and soldiers. Also, we should identify those we have most to fear and those who
might be sympathetic."

Heredia continued to walk, head down as if afraid he might trip over his
own feet. He nodded slightly.

"Try to make friends with the *tucos.* Hang out with them. You can get
closer to them than I can, especially the younger ones and the *chicas.*"

I winked and he reddened. "*Entendido, mi almirante.*"

"And don't be so formal. Could draw attention. Just relax and enjoy our
little stroll. Another caution: Don't ask *tucos* many questions, and be careful
of hostages you talk with—some may be too close with the *tucos. En boca cer-
rada no entran moscas.*" Flies do not enter a closed mouth.

We walked a few moments in silence until we reached the end of the passageway and started back up the other side toward the landing.

"Seek me out when you have something. We should walk even if we
don't have anything for each other. Why don't we establish a routine of exercising together?"

"*Entendido.*" Alberto looked a little forlorn. His ten-minute strolls around
the circuit would be over. The pounds would melt off him like wax off a
burning candle now that he would be eating Japanese chow and walking

with me. Who knows? Perhaps he would end up eating *papas fritas* with us again.

We reached the staircase and started another circuit. As we entered the passageway, Alberto whispered, "Check out your eleven at fifty meters."

I looked down the other side of the passageway near the barricaded door and saw a truly unusual sight. La Gringa was walking with a young Japanese hostage—either a businessman or junior diplomat. They weren't holding hands or otherwise touching, but they were talking and smiling at each other. Love seemed in bloom. I checked for other *tucos* and saw none.

"Do you think he's . . . ?"

"I don't know, but that would certainly be an essential element of information. See what you can find out. Don't stare."

Alberto dropped his eyes as the lovebirds passed.

"And I need to know the man's name, his occupation, his attitude toward the other *tucos* and us."

Alberto nodded. We reached the barricaded door to the service area. After we turned and took a few steps up the passageway toward the landing, I asked if he knew the names of all the terrorists.

Alberto was silent as he counted on his fingers. "I know eleven for sure: the four *cabecillas*, *las chicas*, and five of the *jóvenes*." He named those he knew, and I checked the names against those I was familiar with. Between us we knew them all. And why shouldn't we? We'd been tight as ticks for a month.

We must have made the circuit more than twenty times—I wasn't counting. We talked very little and not at all about Alberto's duties. The man's round face glistened, and sweat dripped from his chin. His breathing was labored. He'd had enough but I knew he wouldn't quit until he collapsed, and I certainly couldn't have that.

When we reached the staircase, I said, "Okay, *mi comandante*. That will do for today. See you tomorrow." We shook hands. Alberto turned and trudged back to Bravo, chest heaving but head high. He was no longer a powerless hostage; he was now a man on a mission. I had chosen well.

I DECIDED to walk the circuit for another thirty minutes or so. I took off my shirt and tossed it into Charley. It was not yet eleven o'clock, and the second floor was already like an oven.

I did my best thinking while I exercised. As I walked, I reviewed what I knew about each *cumpa*. I chose to call them *cumpas*—short for *compadres*—because that's what they called one another.

I would begin with Cerpa and his lieutenants: the Arab, Tito, and Salvador. Then would come the other male terrorists, and finally the women.

NESTOR CERPA CARTOLINI was a seasoned terrorist with many names. He'd been at the game for twenty years, beginning with the 1978 seizure of the factory on the outskirts of Lima where he had held foremen and managers hostage for more than a year; it was a freelance job with no apparent connection with any known group. He was captured during a rescue that left three policemen and several terrorists dead—including Cerpa's close friend Huertas. Cerpa was released from custody less than a year later.

He joined *Sendero Luminoso*—although he always denied affiliation. He then joined MRTA in 1983 after serving with the Colombian terrorist group M-19. He may have participated in the successful M-19 takeover of the Dominican Republic embassy in Bogotá.

A combat leader from the beginning, Cerpa was responsible for a great number of bank robberies, kidnappings, and assassinations. He planned and directed a prison escape in 1990 that freed forty-six MRTA *cumpas*, including Victor Polay. They escaped through a tunnel under the prison wall dug by the *cumpas*. Most of the escapees were captured within two years, including Polay. By 1995 more than four hundred *emeritistas* were imprisoned.

Cerpa became political as well as military leader when Polay returned to prison. In 1995 he plotted to capture Congress and hold hostages to exchange for *cumpas*, but the plan was thwarted. Cerpa's wife, Nancy, was captured along with Lori Berenson and several other *cumpas*.

Cerpa immediately began planning the attack on the Japanese ambassador's residence to exchange hostages for *cumpas*. He also ordered kidnappings and bank robberies to fund the operations, fleeing to Bolivia to avoid capture during the plotting phases. He sent his two children and mother to live in Nantes, France. A man with well-placed friends in high places in Europe, Cerpa received help from European communists to fund MRTA operations—including the current one.

Cerpa was a vain, arrogant, stubborn, profane, volatile man—all characteristics ill suited for a negotiator. Think of a cornered rat.

. . .

THERE ARE two versions of how Rolly Rojas came to be called the Arab. According to one, the bandanna he wore wrapped around his head with a flap hanging down his neck looked like an Arab's burnoose. The other held that he'd trained with Hezbollah in Lebanon.

Unlike the other *cumpas*, the Arab was light-skinned. Also unlike the others, he put on gentlemanly airs. Among the leaders he was easily the most educated and rational; he was friendly with many hostages after the first week, including myself. He clearly liked to demonstrate how cultured he was, talking frequently of literature and art. He'd studied sociology at the national university, where he also led student demonstrations. He'd paid for schooling by working as conductor on a micro-bus that plied some of the meanest streets in Lima.

Rojas joined MRTA when he graduated. He was sent to train with Hezbollah, then combat-tested as part of the so-called America Battalion—an armed force comprising terrorists from throughout Latin America. He fought in Colombia and Central America.

Upon his return to Peru in 1985, the Arab led MRTA units that carried out kidnappings, bank robberies, assassinations, and attacks on government buildings. He was arrested, tried, and convicted of terrorist activities in 1989.

Less than two years into his eight-year sentence, Rojas escaped from prison with Victor Polay and forty-four other *emeritistas* via the tunnel that MRTA had dug under the prison wall. His great delight now was telling us, in loving detail, how the escape had gone down: how they'd dug, gotten rid of the dirt, shored up the tunnel, and even run electric lights through it. Irony was in the air. Given the great number of errors the prison guards had purportedly made, the escape was probably an inside job.

The Arab offered perhaps our best chance of someone to exploit among the *tucos*, but he was no dummy.

EDUARDO CRUZ was known as "Tito," although the origin of this nickname was a mystery to us other than the obvious: It recalled the late communist dictator of Yugoslavia, who had been a famous guerrilla fighter against the Nazis. Cruz was intelligent, astute, and persuasive. I've never known a greater cynic. Perhaps this was his way of rebelling against having been raised by Jesuits. His soft manner, low voice, and reluctance to look anyone in the face led Ambassador Gumucio to call him *el tuco taimado*—the sly terrorist. He was the revolutionary conscience of the group, the political commissar, the worst ideologue. Perhaps he also owed these traits to his Jesuit upbringing. He told us the priests who raised him taught liberation theology.

Every time Cerpa or the Arab vacillated in the face of government demands and seemed on the point of concession, Tito would gently but firmly remind them of their sworn allegiance to the cause and oath to never surrender. We didn't have the ghost of a chance to turn this zealot. He, too, was a veteran of the America Battalion. With one leg now in a cast as he recovered from his bullet wound, he spent most of his time in the first-floor office.

SALVADOR—he went by the single name only—was a military leader and the best prepared of all the *tucos*. He once told me with a trace of pride he had been a corporal in the marines and very well trained. He had earned, he said, expert badges for his marksmanship with both rifle and pistol. He was another veteran of the America Battalion.

Salvador was in charge of the military exercises and rehearsals that the *tucos* carried out over and over again. He would lead his *cumpas* through a maze of chairs and tables in the living and dining rooms carrying and dry-firing his AKM at imaginary targets.

A violent man, he clearly enjoyed beating or otherwise humiliating hostages—especially Ambassador Gumucio, whom he would hit so hard at times that the blows drove Jorge to his knees. Salvador would be a very hard nut to crack during a rescue and a menace to any escape attempt. He would shoot to kill and was fully prepared to die himself.

CONE—aka the Palestinian—was in his late twenties or early thirties. I assumed he received his nickname from service in the Middle East, but this was never confirmed. A crazed narcissist who was continually looking at himself in mirrors, Cone loved to practice marksmanship at imaginary targets, often while talking to himself out loud. During the first week he was the most brutal of all the *tucos* who terrorized us.

But little by little we were able to gain his confidence, and his attitude softened to the point that some of us thought we might be able to turn him. Like many others, however, Cone had a double personality. When there was no tension, some of the *tucos* were friendly, others indifferent. When stress developed, though, they all seemed to awaken from a nearly hypnotic state to once more become their brutal, violent selves.

If the time came, Cone was charged with hunting down Tudela like a rabbit and shooting him.

TWENTY-TWO—in his midtwenties, tall, and well muscled—was obviously a weight lifter and obviously on the precipice of insanity. During our first week he would enter Charley daily and dry-fire his AKM at us. He delighted in describing with lingering detail how he'd killed policemen in the jungle, severing their heads with a machete, and how they'd continued running a few steps with blood spurting from their gaping necks. He'd gutted them, he continued, and cut out their hearts to make *anticuchos*—and he wanted to do the same with us. He had been the *tuco* who'd slammed me against the broken window in Charley as a human shield after the booby trap detonated.

Toward the end, Twenty-two bleached his hair with peroxide then denied he'd done it. He also donned dark glasses he never removed. A fucking madman.

MARCOS—aka *el Edecan*, the aide de camp—was still in his teens. We gave him the nickname because he seemed forever at Cerpa's beck and call. He followed the leader everywhere, including to the bathroom. Cerpa was fond of the boy.

Then there were *Los Cuatro Charapas*—the Four Jungle Turtles. It was difficult to distinguish one from the other: Rolando, Lucas (Gato Seco or Dry Cat), the Mexican, and Alex. All were in their late teens or early twenties, squat and dark with slow-moving eyes. They spoke a mixture of Indian dialect, Spanish, and Portuguese—a patois of the Amazon. Their speech, appearance, and manner earned them the nickname Jungle Turtles.

Their fighting abilities were doubtful. In the beginning they'd all borne the unmistakable look of terror in their eyes. One carried an RPG-7 with his finger hooked to the trigger, an invitation to accidental discharge. Another had mistakenly detonated a *caza bobo*. All had secured the spoons of their grenades with riggers' tape. All were likely to panic at first sign of a commando assault, perhaps growing too frightened to pull the trigger or toss a grenade. They had rabbit in them. They could flee even before combat.

The two female *tucos* were Luz Melendez Cueva (aka Berta or Melisa) and Giovanna Vilas Placencia (*La Gringa*). Better prepared militarily than Los Charapas, both were ready to kill on command. *La Gringa* was sixteen with a slim, teenager's body and striking face. From the beginning of the crisis she was Dry Cat's lover. Every night you could hear them going at it. *La Gringa* was completely without shame: She'd shriek, shout, and moan as her adolescent hormones raged. The two would fuck whenever and wherever the urge was upon them, even in a passageway. *La Gringa*'s noisy enthusiasm made sleep problematic. Lately, however, they had moved their show to the first floor: *La Gringa* probably didn't want her new boyfriend in Foxtrot to be jealous. With her sex drive she could have satisfied both Dry Cat and the Japanese.

Berta was in her early twenties, with a more voluptuous body than *La Gringa*, but she was considerably more reserved—even shy. She was Tito's lover and spent most of her time on first floor running errands for him. Despite knowing that both women would kill on command, I liked them. They had become so friendly with us hostages that Cerpa kept them mainly on the first floor.

SUCH WERE our adversaries. As I pondered what I knew of each, I began to sweat like Alberto—my trousers looked as if I'd pissed myself. By now I was one of only three walkers left exercising. Lunch was approaching. Time to quit.

I entered Charley and grabbed up a slim bar of soap and folded towel from my rolled-up Red Cross mattress. The mattress was thin but a huge improvement over sleeping on the hard floor. I walked through the door between Charley and Delta. Ambassador Aoki and Chancellor Tudela were seated at a card table playing mah-jongg. Twenty-two sat on the chest barricading the door to the patio. He wore a tight, olive-drab T-shirt that showed off his muscled arms. You could tell the *tucos* who lifted: They all wore tight, olive-drab T-shirts. Twenty-two moved his lips as he read to himself from an Asterix comic book. I was surprised he was literate.

I entered Echo. I was in luck: I had the bathroom to myself. Three buckets of cold water for washing sat in the bathtub. I dipped one half of my towel into a bucket and held it against my face. The cold, wet fabric on my hot skin made me forget my surroundings for an instant. I dipped the towel into the bucket again and wiped it across my chest. Water trickled down across my shrinking belly.

The best part of my day concluded, I unrolled my mattress and tried to sleep for an hour. Although I was exhausted from the workout, thoughts poured through my brain and kept me awake. How could I get my intel to the commandos, who by now were surely well into planning a rescue?

I knew SIN must be attempting to bug the residence, and the most obvious way to do that would be to conceal miniature mikes in objects the Red Cross brought into our prison: crucifixes, chalices, religious paintings, Bibles, other books, changes of clothing, food and drink containers, games, water bottles to fill the buckets, cleaning supplies, mattresses, and pillows. If I could only find a hidden mike and establish a link, I could tell whoever heard me to send a text message over Colonel Fernandez's pager. I needed to speak to the colonel and let him know what was going on.

Now I was wide awake. I went into the passageway, paused, and looked left across the landing toward Alpha. Berta was leaning against the wall next to the open door. She had her AKM cradled in her arms; grenades dangled from her web belt. She had taped the spoons with green riggers' tape. Her orders were to kill everyone in Alpha with grenades and gunfire if commandos attacked. Too hot to wear, her body armor lay next to her on the floor.

I smiled and greeted Berta with a cheery "*Buenas días, señorita*" as I entered Alpha. She smiled and nodded. Berta was much more agreeable and friendly toward me than *La Gringa*, though the teenager's attitude was softening. Would Berta hesitate to kill? I wouldn't count on it. She handled the AKM with practiced ease, and I sensed she had used it before.

Alpha was awash in the snoring of sleeping men as if celebrating the siesta. I saw Colonel Fernandez seated in the open closet where I'd once slept after Diez Canseco left us. That now seemed a very long time ago now. The colonel was reading a book of short stories by Gabriel García Márquez. When he saw me, he closed the book and moved over so that I could join him. I sat with my back against the wall and drew up my knees.

"I know those stories, Roberto. Which one are you reading?"

" 'Chronicle of a Death Foretold.' A good story but an unfortunate title."
I laughed briefly, then lowered my head and talked into my knees.

"Does your pager still work, *compañero*?"

"*Sí, señor.*"

"Received any messages?"

"Not for more than three weeks. The messages stopped coming when I couldn't respond after the *tucos* confiscated the cell phones."

I explained what I intended to do and he was completely on board.

I confirmed the pager number and told him to keep the device close at all times. I reminded Fernandez to make sure it was on vibrator.

"You can be sure. I've got it tucked beneath my balls but, sadly, no vibrations for a long time." He chuckled. Fernandez was a lucky man to have a vibrating pager snug under his nut sack.

"Perhaps that will change." I told him Heredia was at work collecting intel, and I needed him to do the same. He brightened.

"Good," he said. "We've been in this shit hole too long. What's the plan?"

"I'm developing one now. Actually, we'll need two: one if we have to escape on our own and another if there is a rescue attempt. I need a few more *compañeros* I can truly count on for help."

"How many?"

"Not many. Obviously this has to be very, very close-hold. If the *tucos* suspect anything, we'll be in deep shit. We have to be sure of those we choose, and we have to be sure they'll keep their mouths shut. *Secreto de dos, secreto de Dios; secreto de tres, de todos es.*" Secret of two is secret of God; secret of three is secret of all.

We went room by room, name by name, until we had narrowed our list to four: Chancellor Francisco Tudela, air force general Orlando Denegri, Peruvian ambassador (without portfolio) Jorge Valdez, and Bolivian ambassador Jorge Gumucio. We chose these men because we had seen their courage in the face of terrorist threats and beatings. All were astute and would contribute greatly to our planning.

Chancellor Tudela was the senior hostage. He was quiet and prudent. I'd seen him stand up to the *tucos* even though such an attitude brought pain and death threats. On one occasion the *tucos* tied him to a chair and shoved a pistol barrel in his mouth with such force, it bloodied his lip and chipped his teeth.

Although he knew he would be the first to die during an attack, Tudela remained calm, even serene. This perplexed the *tucos*, with whom he continued to talk despite the beatings.

Tudela was also our main contact with the Red Cross and Monsignor Cipriani. He knew more about what was happening outside our prison than any other hostage. That knowledge would be crucial for our planning.

General Denegri was a morale builder. He was joyful, diligent, and effective. He would be my right arm. I needed an active-duty senior officer who could give orders to other, more junior officers: As a retired admiral, I did not have his authority.

Jorge Valdez, a senior diplomat in Peru's Ministry of Foreign Affairs, worked for Tudela. He had a brilliant mind and had demonstrated remarkable courage when the terrorists were about to release him as part of their Christmas present: He'd urged Cerpa to release other Peruvian diplomats instead, pointing out that they were junior to him. Cerpa recognized his greater value as a hostage and freed the others. Valdez may well have signed his own death warrant. The man was fearless.

The fourth *compañero* we chose was the Bolivian ambassador, Jorge Gumucio. Since his country had refused to free the four *emeritistas* it held, he had been a marked man. The terrorists repeatedly beat and harassed him. He remained stoic in the face of these assaults and even cursed the *tucos* to their faces, which of course only led to more beatings.

Jorge Gumucio reminded me of a Bolivian hero during the 1879 War of the Pacific, Eduardo Abaroa. This ruinous war had pitted Peru and Bolivia against Chile. Abaroa—a citizen-soldier of Bolivia during the battle of Calama—refused to surrender to the *chilenos* even though he was outnumbered a hundred to one. When the *chileno* commander demanded Abaroa surrender, he yelled: "*¿Rendirme yo? ¡Que se rinda su abuela . . . carajo!*" Me surrender? Shit! Let your grandma surrender. Yes, Jorge Gumucio had more than a little Abaroa in him. I knew he would be at my side until the end.

We did not include any of the Japanese, because we were unsure we could trust them. Except for Ambassador Aoki, most were friendly with the *tucos* and avoided us. And I was even uncertain about Aoki. The Red Army Faction hijacked Japanese commercial jets in 1970, 1973, and 1977. The government each time gave in to terrorist demands that it free imprisoned comrades and pay multimillion-dollar ransoms. Not surprisingly, the Japanese government now urged Fujimori to negotiate with MRTA to release the hostages rather than choose a military solution, although we did not know this at the time.

In seeking out a microphone I decided to start with a large, silver-plated crucifix that hung on the wall across from the staircase. I told Fernandez I had a message to deliver. The only *tucos* in sight were *La Gringa* and Twenty-two. *La Gringa* was standing in the passageway near the open door to Foxtrot. She was talking to someone in the room whom I couldn't see.

Twenty-two was seated on the second step of the staircase. He was absorbed in his comic book, his back toward the crucifix.

I stood so close to the crucifix that my forehead almost touched the pierced feet of the Savior. I clasped my hands, bowed my head, and mumbled my prayer: "This is Admiral Giampietri. Call 958-4654." I repeated the prayer, crossed myself, and went to Charley. Twenty-two was still reading his comic book and La Gringa had disappeared into Foxtrot. Would Fernandez get a message?

I HAD TROUBLE sleeping that night. So many plans, so many contingencies, so many unknowns. I mumbled my message into various parts of the mattress throughout the night. I was wide awake at sunrise. I got up, folded my bedding, and rolled up my mattress. As I was preparing for the bathroom a thunderous roar of martial music left my ears ringing. The music was so loud, I couldn't recognize the tune. Something with a lot of drums and brass.

The music blared from four huge speakers SIN had positioned on the street in front of the residence. *Son-of-a-bitch,* I thought. *Didn't those* cojudos *learn anything from Waco?* All this noise would do nothing but make the *tucos* edgier—and more likely to rake us with AKMs.

From this point on, the music would continue throughout our captivity from dawn until dusk and sometimes beyond. Siestas were out of the question—at least for light sleepers like me. I never got used to this maddening noise. I decided my first act of freedom would be to piss on those speakers.

10
Chavín de Huántar: The Tunnels

PRESIDENT FUJIMORI gazed down upon the scale model of the ambassador's residence "like God-Almighty brooding on History." But the president was looking into the future, not the past, and he liked what he saw.

Fujimori was alone in the command center except for a bodyguard, the duty officer, and an SF sergeant posted at the entry door. He'd given his staff a well-earned evening off.

The model sat on a fiberglass table that occupied nearly a third of the room, and over the last few weeks the model had been expanded to now show neighboring houses, all numbered or identified by name. In exquisite scale, even the cratered side wall was detailed to show where the terrorists had detonated their breaching charge.

A recent addition was a clear acetate sheet which covered the board the model rested upon. Fujimori focused on three colored lines drawn on the acetate. The lines ran from houses one, two, and four. A solid red line running from House One intersected the wall and stopped the scale equivalent of ten meters from the annex stairs. A dashed red line covered the remaining distance to the stairs. The lines indicated tunnels; the solid segment showed the present progress of the tunnel, and the dashed segment the distance to completion.

Fujimori was not sure when the intriguing idea first came to him. Perhaps it was during one of the many times he thought about Ambassador Aoki. The previous year he and the ambassador had taken a trip up the coast to visit the extraordinary ruins of an ancient culture that had flourished in the Andean highlands two thousand years before the Incas. The ruins were less famous than Machu Picchu, but Fujimori preferred them for the architectural and engineering feats they revealed. He was particularly impressed with a labyrinth of mysterious subterranean corridors linking ceremonial chambers. The corridors and chambers had been cut from stone. Excavating and shoring up the tunnels he had in mind now would be much easier tasks than those the ancient engineers of Chavín de Huántar faced. In these ancient tunnels, Fujimori saw the key to getting his commandos within striking distance, before the terrorists would have time to react. The element of surprise was crucial for success.

There were more lines. Solid green went from House Two, intersected the back wall, and stopped twenty meters from Foxtrot.

A long, solid blue line indicated the main tunnel. It began in a small greenhouse located between Houses Four and Five.

This tunnel had three branches: "Black," "Orange," and "Blue Two." When completed, Blue Two would terminate a meter from the terrorist command center in the first-floor office. Commandos would emerge from the tunnel and breach the office wall with a cratering charge.

As the longest tunnel, the combined length of Blue One and Two would be 197 meters.

Of all the tunnels, the most important would be "orange," the explosives tunnel. This tunnel would run underneath the residence. A marine demolitions expert would place a C-4 charge beneath the three rooms where terrorists would most likely congregate: the ballroom, dining room, and kitchen. The final positioning of the explosives would be confirmed only when there was accurate, timely information about terrorist locations. How to get such information remained a problem, although SIN culled some info from terrorist conversations the mikes picked up. But critical gaps remained. The planners desperately needed someone inside the residence.

When completed, all tunnels would be 1.5 meters high and 2 meters wide. Electric lights would be strung the length of the tunnels. The tunnels would be carpeted, cooled with large electric fans and shored up at intervals with timber.

Fujimori's aide, Montesinos, had ordered sixty miners brought from the mining town of Oruro to dig the tunnels. The miners would work three shifts of eight hours until they completed their task.

Digging had begun New Year's Day and, three weeks later, the dashed lines on the acetate revealed—much work remained. The engineers estimated the tunnels would be ready on or about 15 March. They calculated the amount of dirt to be carted off at nine hundred tons, every bit of it to be taken away at night in police patrol cars and pickup trucks so as not to arouse suspicion.

Now that the tunnels approached the residence, Montesinos implemented his plan to cover the noise. SIN placed four massive speakers on Thomas Edison Street aimed toward the residence. The speakers blared music nonstop for twelve hours, or longer.

Another development pleased the president: Workers had begun construction on an exact, full-size replica of the residence behind the same high, tree-lined walls of Las Palmas Air Force Base that shielded SIN headquarters and the SF compound. Accurate, right down to the tunnels, the workers would complete the replica by mid-March at about the same time the miners completed the tunnels.

Fujimori was particularly pleased with the replica because he had made an important contribution to the project. On New Year's Day he had called on Mrs. Aoki in a drawing room of the Japanese embassy. He brought her a basket of fruit and a package of rice cakes his daughter had prepared. He wished her a happy New Year and told her vaguely that both Peru and Japan were doing everything humanly possible to obtain the release of her husband and the other hostages.

Then he asked her a question that was the true reason for his visit: He wanted to know what kind of material covered the skylight at the residence. She told him regular frosted glass of ordinary thickness.

"Would you like to know more about the construction materials for the house?"

"That would be very helpful, señora."

Mrs. Aoki excused herself for about five minutes and returned with a bundle of blueprints in her arms. Fujimori unrolled one on a coffee table. He studied it closely and saw indeed it was part of an architect's building plan for the residence. The name of a venerable Lima architectural firm was printed in the lower left corner. A Japanese name appeared as one of the firm partners. He did not ask Mrs. Aoki where she had gotten the blueprints, and she did not volunteer the information.

He gave the plans to Montesinos, who checked them against information he had been collecting and told Fujimori they could begin building the replica within the week. The planners had decided on a rescue force of 140 officers drawn mainly from army special forces, Montesinos continued, along with a contingent of fifteen marines who would be responsible for sniper and demolition operations. The force was already being assembled in the Special Forces Division compound at Las Palmas.

LIEUTENANT COLONEL JUAN VALER settled in his chair for yet another dry day of instruction at the army's Command and General Staff College at a military base in Chorillos, a Lima suburb near the ocean. Only twenty weeks of the grind to go after the holiday break. He was an operator, not a staff officer, but he needed the schooling for promotion to colonel.

Itching for action, Valer had just completed two years with the presidential security force. His primary mission had been to protect the president's adolescent son, Kenji. The mission required vigilance, hours of target practice, and quick-reaction drills. Thankfully, neither the target practice nor the drills went beyond exercises. Kenji was a precocious teenager; Valer was very fond of him.

The assignment to the Command and General Staff College was highly competitive. Few special forces officers were selected to attend. The assignment put him on the fast track to a general's star.

But the hostage crisis in Lima now made sitting in a class studying World War II tank tactics seem a complete waste of time. He and other SF officers attending the school simply could not believe what had happened. Where had the security been? How could a ragtag gang of terrorists from the jungle take down the ambassador's residence and seize so many important people? The president himself had very nearly attended and could well have ended up a hostage like his brother.

Most of the officers believed a rescue attempt should take place without delay. They had seen the terrorists on TV, noted their weapons, and knew they had booby-trapped the residence. The rescue force needed to act before the *tucos* hardened their position further. One officer pointed to the quick action of Israeli commandos at Entebbe.

Valer thought the officers were underestimating the *tucos* and not paying enough attention to the dangers of such a Rambo mission. A rushed operation would leave scores of hostages dead and wounded, and SF soldiers would also pay a heavy price. As for Entebbe, the Israelis had the Ugandan army and air force to consider, as well as the likely transfer of the hostages to more secure locations.

The situation in Lima was quite different. Provided the *tucos* did not start executing hostages, time would be on the government's side. Paying a ransom and releasing MRTA prisoners was of course out of the question, but if enough time passed and the *tucos* were convinced they would get nothing from the government, perhaps a deal could be struck to give them free passage out of the country.

Time would also aid a rescue attempt. It would have to be meticulously planned, based on timely and accurate intel, and rehearsed over and over again. Then rehearsed some more.

Valer heard rumors that two plans had already been discussed and discarded as too dangerous. Good decision. Go fever could be fatal.

But as the days passed with both sides refusing to yield, it became likely that a rescue might be the only solution. Valer was relieved when he heard the number of hostages was down to seventy-two.

Valer's train of thought was interrupted by scraping chairs and conversations as students arrived for another sedentary day. Silence settled over the men while they studied notes and awaited the instructor. The classroom door opened and the senior student boomed, "*Firmes, ya!*" The students snapped to attention, expecting to see their instructor stride to the podium at the front of the room. Instead a lean, bronzed colonel wearing special forces and airborne insignia told them to take their seats.

Valer immediately recognized the colonel: He'd been Valer's commanding officer in the Upper Huallaga Valley during the continuing campaign against terrorists and *narcotraficantes*. Something was up. Valer's heart quickened.

The colonel asked all students to leave except SF officers. The students filed into the hallway and closed the door. Three officers remained with Valer. The colonel spoke quietly as he cautioned them that what they were about to hear carried the highest security classification. What they learned here stayed here.

"We are," the colonel continued, "forming a task force of officers at this moment to rescue the hostages. Planning for the rescue has already begun; the task force assembles tonight in the division compound. The force will include marine officers from the Special Combat Unit.

"I know how important the Staff College is for your careers, and if you do not complete it now you will fall behind your fellow officers for promotion. I do not expect you to volunteer for a mission that may never be executed. But I give you the opportunity."

Valer could hardly believe his good luck. He got to his feet, came to attention, and said, "*Listo, mi coronel.*" I'm ready, Colonel.

One other officer stood with Valer. The other two remained seated. The colonel told them to join their classmates in the hallway; he told Valer and the second volunteer to come forward and take seats in front of the podium.

"Well done," he told them. "You've put duty above career. But I will tell you this: If the mission goes down, you two will be at the front of the line for promotions with or without the Staff College."

The colonel told them to report to the SF adjutant, who would give them a preliminary load-out list. He would also tell them where and when the task force would muster that night.

"Come prepared to stay for weeks or even months. We isolate from the beginning. Say your good-byes now. You won't have another opportunity."

Valer and the other officer got to their feet, saluted, and headed for the door.

"Chizito," the colonel said, "I want you to stay for a moment."

Juan's hair—curly with a reddish tint—had earned him the nickname. He had known the colonel for a long time. The colonel was a man who led from the front, a man who set the example, a man who was close to those he led.

"*Sí, mi coronel.*"

"I was sure you'd volunteer. Colonel Williams, who now commands the First SF Brigade, has chosen you with my recommendation to be the main man on the ground—the senior officer going in with the task force."

Juan was stunned and excited at the same time. And a little frightened when he thought of the enormous responsibility. He looked at the colonel and nodded. He asked if the colonel would lead the task force.

"No, Colonel Williams will command the TF. He's assigned me to oversee the training. Colonel Williams is going to have his hands full with the Joint Staff and the president's staff. But he won't be a stranger to us during training. He'll be on site at least once a day . . . or night.

"We have one more job." The colonel took a folded piece of paper from his pocket, unfolded it, and laid it flat on the podium. Valer saw a short list of names. He knew them all. He had put them through the SF basic course when he had been an instructor at the training center. He had fought the *tucos* with a few. He noticed all were majors.

"We need one more assault unit commander," the colonel said. "Choose whom you want."

Juan scanned the short list and immediately pointed to the first name.

"El Frijol?"

"Yes, sir. The Bean."

"How do you know him?"

"I put him through training. Terrific student. Could handle everything we threw at him. Never complained. Couldn't have weighed more than 150 pounds. Short and slender but very strong. Extraordinary stamina."

"Do you know how he came to be called the Bean?"

Juan thought he knew but said he didn't. The colonel obviously wanted to tell the story.

"On the day he graduated from the military academy, his class was standing in formation waiting to be called for their diplomas. They were wearing dress whites. One of the generals seated in the reviewing stand said to the general next to him, 'Look at all those brown faces. Those cadets look just like a big plate of *frijoles.*' "

Juan smiled. That was the story he'd heard. Any cadet from that class at one time or another had been called Frijol. But the name stuck with the major.

"Ever see him operate?"

"A few times. I visited him while he was training and leading *rondas* in Ayacucho—near Huanta. He has a great service reputation."

"Yes, he does."

"I once saw him address several hundred campesinos from his *rondas* in the municipal plaza. He was something to behold. He was firing up his men to go after the *tucos*. The Bean looked just like a campesino . . . or a *tuco*. Wore a woolen poncho, sandals, and a *chullo*. Had taken the *chullo* off and every once in a while would swing it above his head. The crowd responded with booming *gritos*. His men loved him. Would have followed him down the barrel of a gun."

"You've chosen well. El Frijol will be there tonight."

The colonel shook Juan's hand, and they exchanged *abrazos*. Then the colonel was gone. Juan gathered his books and papers, stuffed them in his backpack, and made his way through the crowded hallway toward the building exit. He felt a hundred eyes on him. He took his beret from the backpack, put it on, and walked into the morning sunlight. A condor soaring on a mountain updraft could not have felt freer.

I CALLED the first meeting of the *compañeros* for 2000 in Charley on the second day of thundering music. This was one time I wouldn't have minded if they extended the noise throughout our meeting. No such luck. The speakers fell silent as we began our meeting.

Darkness had descended. Candle power provided the only light in the residence. As we assembled in a corner of Charley, three guttering candles cast long shadows through the room. Visibility was low. We did not expect *tucos* until our *toque de queda*—lights-out or curfew—at 2200. We'd closed the door to the passageway.

I greeted Chancellor Tudela, ambassadors Valdez and Gumucio, General Denegri, Colonel Fernandez, Colonel Marco Miyashiro, and Commander Alberto Heredia. Only the first five men knew of the pager and my attempts to locate a hidden mike. I told them we would meet every night at the same time in Charley. Four of us—Tudela, Valdez, Gumucio, and myself—slept in Charley. I told the others to come at staggered intervals and stay in Delta until the meeting started.

I said we would begin by providing the information each of us had collected during the day. Then we would consider plans, offer new ones, consider contingencies, and closely analyze every concept.

I suggested we start by examining potential avenues of escape. I reviewed what we knew of the windows: All were glass in wooden frames; all were covered with metal screens similar to those of chicken coops; and a few had grating beyond the screens. The *tucos* had originally kept the windows closed and curtains drawn, but after two weeks had allowed us to open the drapes and windows to counter the oppressive heat. Grates on the windows remained locked.

"Does anyone know where the keys are for the locks?" I asked. "I've never seen them unlocked."

Chancellor Tudela spoke up. "Ambassador Aoki told me a single key opens all locks, but he did not know where the key was—though he's fairly certain it's in a drawer on the second floor."

Our first task, then, was to find the key. I had Heredia and Colonel

Miyashiro carefully open every drawer, collect all keys they found, and test them in the locks.

One odd development was that the *tucos* seemed to have done us a favor by removing Mrs. Aoki's trunk and opening the door at the end of the passageway. I asked if anyone knew why. I was sure they had booby-trapped the back stairs to the lawn long ago.

"I think they go back there mostly to take a shit," Heredia offered. "There's a head in the servants' quarters with a Red Cross portable john."

"How do you know that, Alberto?"

"Because I've used it. I once saw Tito buttoning his fly as he returned from the annex. I had to take a dump and asked him if I could use the head. Told him all the others on the second floor were occupied and I was about to shit my pants. Must have found him in a good mood because he said to use the head but not go anywhere else in the annex. I expected him to be waiting for me when I returned but he was gone."

I told Heredia to continue to use the servants' bathroom and establish a routine. We didn't know anything about the annex. If the terrorist got comfortable with Heredia going back there, he could do a recon. We'd designate the servants' quarters and bathroom "India."

Another potential escape route was through the door in Delta leading to the patio. Ambassador Gumucio told us that the men living in Delta had opened the unlocked door, only to find yet another armored door behind it. That door was also unlocked. Fearing it to be booby-trapped, they opened it slowly. No traps.

We now had the beginnings of an escape plan. Inner doors connected Delta and Charley, Charley and Bravo. Bravo and Alpha shared a bathroom. At a given signal, hostages in those four rooms would go through the inner doors, gather in Delta, and go through the door to the patio. We would have to guide hostages in Foxtrot and Hotel up the passageway to Delta through Charley, but once through the patio doors, it was a short run to the breached back wall and safety.

Our only problem was the Japanese businessmen on the first floor. How would we get them past the *tucos* and up the stairs? We considered several ideas and rejected them all as too risky and time consuming. We needed more information before we could develop a strategy to include the first-floor Japanese.

General Denegri brought up a point that had greatly troubled me.

"How," he asked, "will we know who to trust and not trust with information of an escape?"

He answered his own question: "We must be careful with the Japanese. Few of them speak Spanish, and few mingle with us except Ambassador Aoki. I've also seen many Japanese being very chummy with the *tucos*." We decided to tell them nothing, although I knew and trusted several.

"What about Aoki?" Tudela asked. "After all, we're in his house."

"That's right," I said. "But '*Su casa no es nuestra casa. Es casa de los tucos.*' I say we notify him, but we need to feel him out first on his attitude toward an escape." I told Ambassador Valdez I would contact him within the next few days and we would go together to speak with Aoki.

We decided that we really couldn't afford to trust anyone in the Red Cross, either. Any plans to escape would be anathema to an organization that always favored negotiation and a peaceful solution.

The last lighted candle was about to burn out. *Toque de queda* was upon us. The murmur of softly snoring men was already filling Charley and Delta. We agreed to meet the next evening an hour earlier—1900 instead of 2000. Perhaps the SIN DJs would still be at it and the noise would mask our conversation. *No hay mal que por bien no venga.*

11

Only God Can Make a Tree

As February drew near, a Battle of the Bands became a daily routine. The *tucos* countered the noise SIN was making with their own songs of revolution sung at full volume through battery-powered megaphones. To make matters worse, SIN agents and *tucos* vied with each other for the honor of being first to greet the new day. Some mornings, the battle began at 0400.

At least the *tucos* withdrew from the battle after about thirty minutes each morning. However, the SIN speakers continued to assault us for another twelve to eighteen hours.

After the *tucos* finished their songs, they would gather in the foyer and shout various slogans: "Seventy-one days since the takeover of the ambassador of Japan's residence; here, nobody surrenders. *¡Carajo! ¡Patria o muerte, venceremos!*" Following their morale-boosting slogans, our jailers would practice quick-reaction drills: what they would do if commandos attacked. One group of *tucos* would take up defensive positions on the first and second floors to repel or at least delay the attackers, while others would seek out their assigned hostage targets and kill them—then kill the rest of us. Once that mission was accomplished, they would join their comrades to defend the residence. No drill existed for withdrawal. The fanatics intended to fight until the end and then destroy the residence with explosives.

The high-value targets in Charley were Chancellor Tudela, Ambassador Aoki, and President Fujimori's brother, Pedro. One of the two communist radio stations in Lima had revealed Pedro's identity less than a week after the takedown. These stations—*Cora* and *Libertad*—were the link between the *tucos* and what was happening beyond the residence walls. The government allowed no newspapers or magazines into the residence—part of its strategy of isolating the terrorists. To circumvent this an announcer at the stations would read headlines and top stories about the crisis each day as if he were carrying out a civic duty to inform the public. During one such informative reading, an announcer revealed that Pedro was a hostage being kept with other Japanese. The unmasking was followed by beatings and other humiliations. Pedro became my roommate. I made it a point to stay as far away from him as possible.

The terrorists ended their drills at about 0530 and let the hostages use the bathrooms. Before I went to the head I would exercise by running up and down the spiral staircase thirty times to raise my temperature. The exercise also allowed me a limited view of what was going on downstairs. The *tucos* still did not allow second-story hostages to visit the first floor.

We were always cool, even cold at night. A cold bath at dawn was an unpleasant experience. Our caloric intake had been greatly reduced by now; we were losing weight as if we were at a fat farm. I'd lost perhaps thirty pounds.

Other hostages had their own exercise routine. Several would form a line from the landing down the passageway and do light exercises or jog up and down the halls. A few who did not jog lifted weights made of two-liter bottles filled with water. You could not leave your room during this time or you would run into weight lifters or be trampled by joggers.

A Red Cross water truck arrived daily to fill five large tanks located in the foyer. Hoses transported the water from truck to tanks. Hostages then carried large bottles of water to the second floor for the bathrooms and drinking. For a cold bath we could fill the tubs with water from the bottles, but for day-to-day hygiene we used commercial Wet Ones family members sent. We all had our own personal cleaning supplies, but some cretins stole unguarded toothpaste and toilet paper.

There are some habits you don't abandon simply because of difficult circumstances, so I shaved daily. If I ever gained my freedom the world would not see the unshaven face of a defeated man.

For the first few weeks we had only the clothes we'd worn to the birthday party. Underwear was rotting away from skin; socks emitted such a foul odor they were often thrown in the trash that was piling up everywhere.

Then the Red Cross at last collected the trash and brought us fresh clothes from our families. We received up to ten articles of clean clothing each week. The Red Cross also brought medicines from our families if we were ill. Ambassador Gumucio received various pills for his type-2 diabetes, although as he lost weight he needed the pills less and less. *No hay mal que por bien no venga.*

Marcella sent me antibiotics for my bronchitis and also for a worsening case of colonitis. Because of the colonitis, I was using the shitter fifteen to twenty times a day. Some of my smart-ass fellow hostages accused me of trying to escape little by little through the commode.

Although the portable toilets eased our filthy circumstances, they brought their own problems. Four portable toilets were placed side by side in the largest bathroom. The toilets had no doors: everyone had to drop his trousers and defecate in plain view of others. Not a problem for those of us who had been sailors and athletes. However, this lack of privacy upset many. But with each passing day, privacy while taking a shit ceased to be an issue. People appreciated the privacy of the bathroom and often talked and even conspired to the straining rhythm of those on the toilets.

Ironically, the toilets replaced one smelly problem with another. The toilets lessened the pestilent stench of defecation, but replaced it with an equally strong, disagreeable odor of chemicals. This odor penetrated the clothing of hostages who used the toilets; it was easy to identify—and avoid—these men. I solved the problem by visiting the shitter naked.

After we finished our cleaning and personal hygiene duties, we ate a frugal breakfast in our rooms of bread and marmalade washed down by tepid coffee. The Red Cross doctor would not let us eat butter because he feared it would raise our cholesterol. I joined Alberto Heredia in his astonishment at the doctor's lack of perspective.

After breakfast each hostage would roll up his bedding with his mattress to clear the floors for cleaning. The floors were carpeted and because we ate, walked, and slept on them we knew they must be saturated with microbes that could infect our skin. Hostages in some rooms observed the very sanitary Japanese practice of removing their shoes before they entered.

Some rooms were better organized than others, such as Bravo under the leadership of former minister Dante Cordova. Dante prepared a cleaning bill for the hostages that rotated chores weekly. I don't know if Dante's name was on the bill or not. Bravo was the only room where hostages ate their meals on a white linen tablecloth. A police officer found in the tablecloth during a rare visit to the kitchen. The diners spread the tablecloth on top of Inca Kola crates. Cordova did not permit the meal to start until everyone was "at table."

Dante Cordova in addition to being a very orderly person was also very funny. He was a practical joker and each of us at one time or another had been the butt of his humor.

There came a time when several of us decided get some payback. When the former minister took his siesta, he always slept belly up with his mouth open and hands crossed on his chest. We found him in this position one afternoon and drew the curtains to darken the room. Then we placed lighted candles around his mattress, assumed attitudes of prayer, and nudged him awake. He was startled to see he was like a corpse at a *velorio*—a ceremonial viewing of the dead by candle flame. A little gallows humor to lighten our macabre situation.

Other rooms were not as orderly as Bravo, but we were organized to some extent. Cleaning tasks were assigned just as in Bravo. We took turns sweeping the rooms and cleaning the bathrooms. Vice Minister Rodolfo Matsuda scrubbed the bathroom tiles meticulously to kill fungi. Those chosen to sweep and scrub in Charley and Delta were Juan Mendoza, vice minister of energy and mines, and Pedro Fujimori.

Vice ministers of the presidency and agriculture, Felipe Ramirez and Rodolfo Matsuda, taught themselves to cut hair. Cerpa allowed them to use rounded scissors children cut paper with, but would not let them keep the scissors. In the beginning, we looked like sheared sheep after our haircuts. But as time passed the men became true artists of the scissors.

As THE WEEKS PASSED, the *tucos* lessened our restrictions. Those of us in Charley could now roam the second floor. I seized upon two outside jobs: taking buckets of waste from the four portable toilets in the bathroom between Alpha and Bravo downstairs for pickup; and collecting used candles throughout the residence to replace with new. These two chores allowed me to go below and observe first-floor activities.

Colonel Romulo Zevallos, a very resourceful officer, made candle lanterns from used water bottles and pieces of carton. We hung the lanterns outside the rooms that lined the passageway. The lanterns provided enough light for us to stroll and talk at night. Broken glass windows along the passageway provided fresh air. After lights-out, we left only one candle burning in each bathroom. We very much feared fire. The carpets were made of synthetic fiber that would ignite in seconds.

Colonel Zevallos constructed a rattrap that actually worked, though unfortunately he lacked enough materials for the mass production needed. We asked Cerpa to have the residence fumigated to prevent bubonic plague, but he told us to go to hell. He did not want outsiders other than the Red Cross entering the residence for any reason, and the Red Cross wasn't in the extermination business.

LUNCHTIME ARRIVED followed by the tedious afternoon. Our duties finished, we had little to do but listen to the horrid music that mixed Pavarotti with salsa and *tecnocumbia*. Sometimes we tried to stave off boredom with games. The Japanese managed to fill whole afternoons—and most mornings—with round after round of mah-jongg or Go. And they weren't playing for matchsticks. One of them told me he was up ten thousand dollars. Others played various games but without much enthusiasm: gin rummy, bridge, checkers, chess, dominoes, ludo, and reversi or Othello.

Colonel Garrido passed his time working a huge jigsaw puzzle of at least three thousand pieces. It took up a great deal of space and hostages walking through the room sometimes kicked the puzzle apart—accidentally, I hoped—and the poor man would have to start over again. Sisyphus in our midst.

I never cared much for puzzles or games of chance because I found it difficult to concentrate, but I did occasionally play dominoes with the Arab. Our bet was that if I won three games in a row, he would set me free. I often won, and he always reneged.

READING WAS a popular pastime. We amassed boxes of books from families, the government, and foreign embassies. We had a wide choice: novels both dense and long; short novels; a sports magazine, *El Gráfico;* and comic books telling the tales of Asterix and Rin Tin Tin. Asterix enthralled the young *tucos,* although they did not know much about the story and its setting. The Mexican asked me somewhat shyly if I could explain. I told him Asterix was a Gallic tribe during the Roman conquest that resisted the invaders and often made them look like fools. When this word got out, the *tucos* enjoyed the comic books even more. Rin Tin Tin had less appeal.

We put the books in a bookcase on the landing. Most readers chose the shorter ones; perhaps they thought such a selection would somehow hasten the end of our captivity.

A religious painting—*El Señor de Los Milagros*—had recently been hung above the bookcase. The painting came from the family of a hostage. Some would pray before the painting at various times throughout the day and early evening. I joined the faithful although my prayer was unique: I mumbled my message in the hope that a mike was hidden in the frame.

I also continued to pray before the crucifix on the landing—in fact, I said a prayer for all the objects that came in from the outside, but thus far no response from God or SIN.

All hostages welcomed prayer regardless of their religion. Perhaps in the depths of their souls they believed in a superior being, or perhaps they found an inner peace through the meditative act of prayer.

I came to know people very well during the long weeks of our confinement. I knew Supreme Court justice Carlos Giusti was dedicated to enhancing the moral fiber of the judiciary, but I did not know the extent of his commitment. The valiant and charismatic Giusti, father of three daughters, continued in his labors to rewrite judicial documents and rules throughout captivity. A number of bilingual hostages taught language classes.

General Carlos Domínguez taught French, and one of his students was Cerpa. Cerpa spoke very good French because of the time he had spent in France. Sometimes Domínguez would ask Cerpa how to say a certain word or phrase in the language. All went well until the general asked how one says *terrorista* in French.

Cerpa leaped to his feet and replied in an imperious tone: "I am not *terrorista;* I am *guerillero!*" Then he dropped the class.

Tito, on the other hand, persevered in learning Japanese. Congressman Samuel Matsuda was his teacher, and the *tuco* was an apt pupil. Toward the end Ambassador Aoki said Tito could converse with him in the language.

The Spanish classes Eduardo Pando taught the Japanese were tremendously popular. Eduardo had to enlist the aid of Father Wicht as an adjunct to meet the need. Wicht taught the most advanced students. He used the Vargas Llosa novel *Who Killed Palomino Molero?* which contained a fair amount of profanity. One student asked what the difference was between the swear words *cojudo* and *huevón*. The padre replied that both meant about the same—asshole or ass wipe—except for the degree of insult: *Cojudo* was the nastier.

THEN THERE WERE LETTERS. Thank the Lord for letters. Seldom do we truly realize how important it is to maintain contact with the ones we love. Letters compensated in part for being separated from them. Tragically for Japanese hostages—few of whom knew any Spanish—Cerpa made all of us write in Spanish so that he and his goons could read them. More than one Japanese inmate shyly approached me and asked in English how to say "I love you."

Some, including Carlos Giusti and Dante Cordova, wrote far more than letters. Giusti had his thoughts of legal reform to memorialize, and Cordova filled notebook after notebook with chronicles of daily events. He had used eleven notebooks by the end, but none seems to have survived—or if it did, it fell into hands that wanted to keep the information from the public. I also wrote a letter of protest to the government. This document, which I never sent, also disappeared during the rescue.

Those of us who did not participate in games spent afternoons gazing at the limited world beyond our windows. We could see the broad, parched grounds of the residence bordered by high white walls that separated us from what we once knew.

We began to notice a peculiar narrow strip of green that stretched through yellowed, sun-dried grass. It ran from the back wall to about thirty meters short of the residence. It looked as if someone had been feeding the grass with a watering can. We had no idea why the green path existed, because the sprinkler system had failed long ago.

One day we witnessed a startling, pathetic sight. A *perro callejero*—dog of the street—managed to enter the grounds and was trotting toward a meal from the buffet. Just as he was about to enter the tent he stepped on a mine planted by the *tucos*. The poor animal disintegrated before he had time to yelp.

A magnificent laurel tree just outside our windows offered more pleasing activity. Many of us spent hours watching birds that nested or roosted among the leafy branches of the tree, which must have been more than two hundred years old. Its spreading shade cooled our room when the sun was high, and provided us with privacy from the telescopic lenses of the media.

We watched doves so fat with food from the buffet tent, they could hardly reach the lower tree limbs and sometimes toppled to the ground after they landed.

Then throughout one night we heard a rhythmic *toc, toc, toc* beyond our windows. At dawn we saw that the *tucos* had chopped down the tree. It had been blocking the view of the banners with revolutionary slogans that they'd hung from the roof.

We had lost our shade and our privacy. We now had to dress and undress while cowering in corners, or titillating images of our nakedness would appear on TV and in newspapers. The show that nature put on for us, that touched us so deeply, was no more. Only God can make a tree. But any cretin with an ax can destroy one.

AT 1630 SOME of the hostages would gather in Charley and listen to Ambassador Gumucio's radio when he had fresh batteries, which was seldom. The program they listened to was presented by announcer Zenaida Solis. Zenaida was the only person in the media who consistently gave us daily news of our families and events that touched us all. This hour was filled with sadness because Zenaida would play messages from our loved ones. The messages were often accompanied by tears that affected us all. For this reason, I asked my wife not to participate. She complied, but my poor mother could not. The radio often carried her trembling voice. My frail mother was very old and suffered from cancer. Tears leaked from my eyes and coursed down my face when I heard her speak.

We normally ate dinner at 1830 and afterward often listened to opera and classical music on Gumucio's radio in Delta. We set rules for the audience: No one talked or smoked during the music hour.

Dante Cordova, Orlando Denegri, and Pepe Garrido could play the guitar and would sometimes lead us in song. We often celebrated birthdays in this manner. Singing traditional Peruvian songs helped us forget—at least for the moment—our depressing circumstances. We would often sing with such enthusiasm that reporters could hear us from outside the walls. One day the following headline appeared in a local paper: HOSTAGES PARTY IN THE EMBASSY! How disconnected the media was from our reality.

12

"La Cucaracha" with a Salsa Beat

PRESIDENT FUJIMORI was sitting on a couch in his office, resisting the urge to stretch out for a few moments of sleep. He had just returned from an all-afternoon conference with the latest delegation from Japan. He wasn't sure how many conferences of this sort he'd had during the crisis, either on the phone or in person. The longer the crisis persisted, the more concerned the Japanese became that he would choose a military solution without informing them.

Fujimori repeatedly assured the Japanese he would not attack the residence unless the lives of the hostages were in imminent danger. Always careful not to say precisely what he meant by "imminent danger," he dissembled when Prime Minister Hashimoto or Chancellor Ikeda pressed the matter.

On a happier note, preparations for the rescue were advancing largely without incident. They had suffered a minor setback when the main tunnel, "Blue One," collapsed just before the residence wall, and some miners were hospitalized.

The shorter tunnels, Red, Green, and Yellow were now within days of completion; "Blue Two" was only twenty or so yards from its terminus, and near the steps to the second-floor patio. The explosives tunnel under the residence would not be dug until SIN knew for certain where the terrorists and hostages were located. At present the microphones were the only sources of such intelligence, and what they revealed was fragmentary at best. Montesinos and his staff were exploring ways to slip an agent into the residence, but all such plans thus far had been discarded as too dangerous.

As the main tunnellers approached the residence, Montesinos had ordered more diversionary tactics to supplement the blaring music being pumped in from Thomas Edison Street. Some were a bit reckless. Police armored personnel carriers sped up and down the street, with policemen standing unprotected through the hatches shouting insults and making obscene gestures toward the residence. All went well until a terrorist began firing his AKM from an upper window at the APCs. Luckily no one was injured.

SIN had hit upon a clever, simple means of ensuring that the miners kept the tunnels on the correct azimuth should compasses fail underground. A SIN agent with binoculars stationed himself on the roof of a factory that manufactured Unique-brand perfume. Another agent in the tunnel at the farthest point of excavation jabbed a long metal rod through the tunnel roof every five meters or so. The rod protruded a meter above the lawn. This allowed the man on the roof to locate the position of the tunnel. He then radioed the information back to the forward command center.

The agent also noticed something of concern. Narrow fingers of green grass were growing above the tunnels as they progressed. The miners were keeping the clay-based soil wet as they worked to keep dust down and strengthen the walls and roof. This watering had the unfortunate effect of promoting a verdant strip of grass that followed precisely the course of the tunnels. Planners considered sending a commando over the wall to spray Roundup herbicide on the grass, but the danger of land mines planted by the *tucos* made this too risky.

To keep the *tucos* inside the residence and make it more difficult for them to observe these activities, SIN agents from the Andes used slingshots to bombard the terrorists with small stones every time they set foot outside. Andean campesinos grew up knowing how to use these slingshots to herd animals—cows, sheep, llamas, alpacas. *Senderista* fighters used slingshots as improvised mortars to lob lighted sticks of dynamite at police stations.

At first Cerpa complained to Monsignor Cipriani and Ambassador Vincent, but of course they could do nothing. Finally Cerpa decided the stones were a minor provocation and simply told his followers to stay inside.

Although rescue preparations were ahead of schedule, they still had weeks to go. Fujimori was uneasy about the growing pressure from Japan for a negotiated settlement. He needed to appease Hashimoto to buy more time and lull the terrorists into thinking the crisis could have a peaceful outcome. He decided to open formal negotiations with Cerpa at some locale outside the residence under the protection of the Red Cross. This would give the appearance of movement toward the negotiated settlement the Japanese were urging. Fujimori would also embark later on a diplomatic junket to buy even more time. Meanwhile, the commandos were honing their combat skills at Las Palmas.

The rescue force would be divided into three assault units, three support units, and two security units. The assault and support units would be further broken down into four-man elements—the minimum number needed to clear a room. The entire force numbered 140 commandos.

When a marine officer in the explosives tunnel, Commander Carlos Tello, detonated the charges, the three assault units followed by the three support units would flood the residence. El Frijol would lead the first of two assault units out of the tunnels and into the residence. The third assault unit and the support units would blow the front door to the residence with a greased sheet of Flex-X breaching explosive and drive through to the foyer. Three elements of each unit would secure the ground floor. The remaining elements would haul ass up the staircase and kill every *tuco* they encountered. The support elements would follow with fire extinguishers and litters to carry out the wounded.

Colonel Valer emphasized that the mission's goal was to rescue hostages as quickly as possible. There would be no time to take prisoners, which would only give the terrorists the opportunity to kill hostages and detonate their explosives. Every fallen enemy would get two rounds to the head. Years of fighting taught these soldiers that to leave a fallen terrorist alive was to risk a bullet in the back.

Sixteen marine snipers provided security. They were to station themselves on the roofs of the Unique building and a high-rise apartment complex on the other side of the residence. The remaining security elements would cover windows and doors of the residence on the ground.

Since the task force's formation in early January, its men had been putting hundreds of rounds through their weapons each day. Indeed, the commandos had already used up the ammunition allocation for the entire army. The commandos would carry an assortment of weapons: Belgian

P90s, German MP5s, Israeli Galils and Uzis. To clear rooms quickly point men carried 12-gauge Mossberg shotguns loaded with double-aught buck. Valer's chosen weapon was the P90 submachine gun, known to those in the trade as the "room broom."

Up until the rescue, the commandos engaged in seemingly unending physical exercise and quick-action drills. But Valer was saving the live-fire maneuvers until he was satisfied the commandos were completely comfortable with their weapons. For several commandos this would be their first experience in the "kill house," a hostage rescue training building, and Valer would start them out slowly to lessen the danger of blue-on-blue casualties during these live-fire exercises.

The commandos had studied the model of the residence until they knew the layout by memory. In the model, blue figures representing hostages and red representing terrorists were arranged in their last known positions, but with stale intelligence they could not expect that this in any way reflected reality.

On sand tables, the task force plotted their avenues of approach and withdrawal in the compound. But the most valuable rehearsals awaited them after the builders would complete the full-size replica of the ambassador's residence in March. These rehearsals awaited completion of the replica in mid-March.

UNEXPECTED DRAMA at the residence broke the tedium of our usual routine. In the early afternoon the customary din of music was enhanced by the piercing screams of police sirens and the rumble of APCs in front of the residence. We rushed to the open front windows of Alpha and Bravo. We saw APCs speeding up and down Thomas Edison street. Policemen were standing in the open hatches yelling profanities and making obscene gestures.

At that moment Salvador rushed into Alpha with an AKM. He ordered us to the floor, shouldered his weapon, and fired a long burst through an open window. I prayed he did not hit anybody.

The cacophony of police sirens, music, and the revving of APC engines continued to torment us. In February, a helicopter contributed to the agony, beating its way low overhead throughout the day until dark.

The *compañeros* met that night in Charley, as usual. The radio in Delta masked our conversation with the rousing "1812 Overture": clashing cymbals, beating drums, ringing bells, and thundering cannons. Great music.

We reviewed what we had learned so far of our situation. Alberto Heredia and Marco Miyashiro had sorted through some thirty keys and found not one but three that opened every screen and security grille. I assigned Alberto as keeper of these all-important keys.

I asked Alberto if he had learned anything about *tuco* morale and the relationship of La Gringa with some of the Japanese men.

He said he'd heard the Mexican and Gato Seco pissing and moaning about how much they missed their villages near Iquitos—especially their women and booze. The Mexican complained that Cerpa had promised they would be on their way home within two weeks—three tops. They'd been here more than six weeks.

I thought this discontent we might be able to exploit. "Try to gain their confidence," I told Heredia, "but be careful. What about La Gringa and her hostage boyfriend? Do you know his name?"

"Sorry, sir. No one who speaks Spanish seems to know. He may speak Spanish . . . I've seen him talking with La Gringa. Maybe I can ask him what his name is."

"No, don't do that. We'll just call him Sushi."

"Okay. Well, Sushi and La Gringa see each other every day—usually in Foxtrot with the rest of the Japanese. They've got a card table in there, and Sushi is teaching the *tuca* how to play mah-jongg. I suspect something's probably going on beneath the table."

"Is Gato Seco jealous?"

"Not that I could notice. I heard him talking about his girl in the jungle."

Alberto was regularly visiting the bathroom in the servants' quarters. Even the other hostages were using it now. The *tucos* didn't seem to mind. We assumed they had all the escape routes mined.

It was now or never to scope out the annex. I assigned this task to Alberto and Marco.

Then I told the group my own attempts to get a message out had been unsuccessful. I'd been mumbling into every fucking thing I could think of—crucifixes, paintings, rosary beads, chalices, books, thermoses, blankets, mattresses. I'd been absolutely certain SIN had bugged the place. Now I wasn't so sure.

Alberto suggested that they may have been hearing me but for some reason couldn't or didn't want to send a page. Perhaps they feared others were on the frequency.

Party tent at the Japanese ambassador's residence in Lima shortly before the terrorist attack on 17 December 1996 (*El Sol*)

Peruvian foreign minister Francisco Tudela (*c.*) with Father Julio Wicht (*l.*) and Brazilian ambassador to Peru Carlos Luis Coutinho shortly before the terrorist attack on the Japanese ambassador's residence during a celebration of the emperor's birthday (*El Sol*)

MRTA terrorists in a jungle training camp (Reuters)

Terrorist second-in-command Roly Rojas (a.k.a. "The Arab") in the Japanese ambassador's residence (*El Sol*)

Terrorists at a photo opportunity they arranged for journalists after their capture of the Japanese ambassador's residence in Lima. Nestor Cerpa (*c.*) led the assault. (*El Sol*)

Terrorists escort Peruvian foreign minister Francisco Tudela (*c.*) to a press conference in the Japanese ambassador's residence during the first hours after the assault. (Reuters)

The Japanese ambassador's residence during the 126-day siege. Note the TV camera crews on the rooftop in the foreground. (*El Comercio*)

Banners and MRTA flag that the terrorists displayed from a window in the Japanese ambassador's residence throughout the siege (Reuters)

Members of the Peruvian Security Force stationed outside the Japanese ambassador's residence during the first night of the terrorist occupation (Reuters)

A member of the Peruvian Security Force (*c.*) escorts Canadian ambassador Anthony Vincent (*l.*) and Monsignor Juan Luis Cipriani to a meeting with MRTA terrorists. (Reuters)

Peruvian police keep reporters behind a barricade one block from the Japanese ambassador's residence throughout the siege. (*El Comercio*)

Peruvian president Alberto Fujimori and Japanese foreign minister Yukjhiko Ideda walk through the ancient tunnel complex at Chavín de Huántar northeast of Lima after the rescue. The Chavín de Huántar complex inspired Fujimori's plan to assault the terrorists through tunnels and gave the operation its name. (Reuters)

The ambassador's residence under attack by commandos during the hostage rescue. The party tent in the foreground remained up during the four-month siege, complete with a rotting buffet that provided a feast for birds, dogs, cats, squirrels, and rats. (*El Comercio*)

A smoke plume rises after commandos breach the roof with explosives. The second-floor patio that was the hostage escape route is in the right foreground. (*El Comercio*)

Commandos fire through the breached roof into the terrorist armory during Operation Chavín de Huántar. (Reuters)

Flames erupt through the roof after the commandos detonate a breaching charge during the hostage rescue. The second-floor patio in the foreground was a hostage escape route. (*El Comercio*)

A commando directs Peruvian foreign minister Francisco Tudela to safety outside the Japanese ambassador's residence. The blood on Tudela's shirt is Colonel Valer's; Valer died shielding Tudela from terrorist gunfire and grenades. (Reuters)

Commandos assist hostages down the stairs from the patio during the rescue. (Reuters)

Commandos carry a wounded comrade on a litter from the Japanese ambassador's residence during the hostage rescue operation. (*El Sol*)

Commandos carry a fatally wounded officer from the second floor patio after he was shot by a terrorist. (Reuters)

Commandos haul down the terrorist flag atop Japanese ambassador's residence and replace it with the Peruvian flag after the successful hostage rescue operation that ended a four-month siege on 22 April 1997. (Reuters)

Monsignor Juan Luis Cipriani, Archbishop of Ayacucho, weeps at a press conference following the rescue operation that cost two commandos their lives, wounded seventeen others, and killed all fourteen terrorists. One of the seventy-two hostages died of a heart attack after the rescue. (*El Comercio*)

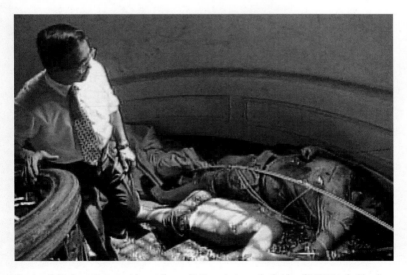

On April 23, Peruvian president Alberto Fujimori views the body of MRTA rebel leader Nestor Cerpa and that of another unidentified guerrilla on a staircase in the Japanese ambassador's residence. (*Reuters*)

Bulldozers demolish the Japanese ambassador's residence in Lima several weeks after the hostage rescue operation. (Reuters)

Commandos pose with flags and arms captured at the Japanese ambassador's residence. (Reuters)

Chancellor Tudela had a stroke of brilliance. "Why don't we use the speakers they've been blasting us with. We'll choose a song unlike any we've heard so far and tell whoever may be listening to play it."

Tudela had a tune in mind: "*La Cucaracha.*"

I ENDED the meeting early. I wanted to start my quixotic quest again. I now had high hopes.

I began my prayers on the landing first before the crucifix, then the painting of *El Señor de Los Milagros*: "This is Admiral Giampietri. Play '*La Cucaracha*' if you hear me. Admiral Giampietri. Play '*La Cucaracha*' if you hear me."

I walked down the candlelit but empty passageway until I came to a new item that had arrived yesterday: a crucifix of the *Cristo Moreno*. I said my prayer and returned to the landing.

Had I forgotten something? Of course, the bookcase!

I selected one book after another and pretended to read the titles in the weak candlelight. I looked around continually. *Tucos* often mounted two-man patrols on the second floor at this time. I saw nothing except a hostage in his underwear walking down the passageway.

I went into rooms and carefully spoke into as many items as I could without raising suspicion: packs of cards, board games, pencils, tablets. Lights-out was drawing near, and most of the occupants were asleep.

I returned to Charley as someone was pinching out the candle flames in the lamps along the passageway. I fell asleep immediately, serene in the hope my prayers would be answered.

·

I ROLLED OUT of bed as the Battle of the Bands began. I looked at my watch in the weak light of the approaching dawn: 0500. Right on schedule, but it was a John Philip Sousa march that hammered my ears from the speakers. I groaned: No "*La Cucaracha.*" Then the terrorists joined the fray shouting their anthem, "Los Molinos." I resigned myself to another futile day of prayers. I pulled on my trousers and prepared for my morning run up and down the staircase after the *tucos* finished their noise in the foyer.

Then they fell silent. John Philip Sousa stopped. I approached the landing to begin my exercises and the sweetest sound I'd ever heard broke the silence: "*La Cucaracha*" *with a salsa beat.* I nearly broke into a Mexican Hat Dance on the spot, but contained myself and started running the stairs. I must have finished in record time. I saw Francisco Tudela leaning against the wall. He smiled and flashed me a discreet thumbs-up.

The lively tune filled the residence for another magnificent five minutes. The other *compañeros* sought me out and expressed their joy with smiles, a quick pat on the back, winks. At that moment the only thing that could make me feel better than the music was freedom itself.

The *tucos,* viewing the music as a sign of disrespect, proceeded to take their anger out on us. They ordered us into our rooms and began the same tired drills they had put us through during the first weeks of our captivity. And we went without breakfast. A small price to pay.

Of course now the problem was I couldn't be sure which item or items I'd spoken into had the hidden mikes. With nothing more than a gut feeling, I went back to the common areas, to the portrait of El Señor de Los Milagros, the silver-plated crucifix, the crucifix of the *Cristo Moreno,* and books in the bookcase.

My first prayers were for the listeners to call Fernandez's pager. Then I took a break to avoid raising suspicion. I continued this pattern interspersed with my duties of hauling honeypots from the shitters to the front door and replacing burned-out candles. After lunch I changed my prayer: I began giving brief, essential elements of information: where the hostages were located, where the terrorists were located, and their daily schedules. No page.

That night I discussed the problem of locating the mikes with the *compañeros.* Someone—I couldn't tell who in the darkness—told us of a conversation he'd had with General Domínguez about a note the general's wife had sent him that read: "Put your trust in El Señor de Los Milagros." The general said he had done as his wife ordered: He prayed daily before the painting. The prayers calmed and filled him with hope.

"Do you suppose . . . ," I began.

Tudela finished the thought: ". . . the painting is bugged and the general took his wife's counsel too literally."

We ended the meeting, and I made straight for the painting.

Two days passed and despite numerous prayers the pager remained mute. I became frantic. On the morning of the third day, as I walked the circuit with Alberto, Colonel Fernandez and General Denegri caught up to us from behind and in a breathless whisper Denegri told me, "A message has arrived for you on the pager." Both men were beaming like children in a candy store.

We finished another circuit and went to Charley. Alberto stood guard at the open door. We were permitted to close doors at night but not during the day. Fernandez showed me the brief message: YOUR WIFE WILL SOON SEND YOU A GUITAR. No doubt with a microphone, I thought. I told Fernandez to delete it, and we established a procedure for him to tell me of future messages.

Fernandez would write the message on a scrap of paper. The pager had a capacity for only twenty words. He would give the message to a *compañero*, who in turn would deliver it to me in Charley. I would wait for a moment when the bathroom in Echo was vacant, enter, and quickly read the message. Then I would swallow the paper it was written on. I must have swallowed at least a hundred messages during the captivity, which no doubt contributed to my persistent stomach disorder.

A week later, on February 15, the Red Cross brought not one but four guitars in handsome cases. There was no mistaking the guitar meant for me. A message supposedly from my wife had been written on a note that accompanied the guitar: PARA QUE RECUERDES MIS NOCHES SIN TI, TE AMO! MARCELLA. So that you will remember my nights without you. I love you! Marcella.

I know my wife and she did not compose this *cursi* message. Yes, it was in her handwriting, but she would not express herself in this way—especially for so many eyes to read. Certainly SIN or navy intelligence had dictated the words to her.

That night in consultation with the *compañeros* I decided to keep the guitar in Charley and make the room my communications center. During the day when the door to the passageway was open, one of the *compañeros* would serve as lookout.

We also realized we needed *ayudantes*—helpers—to maximize intelligence collection. We agreed we could trust most military and police officers and several civilians to collect information without question. But we would not tell any *ayudante* about the contacts we had made with the outside.

Among the civilians we recruited were Dante Cordova, Eduardo Pando ("Dr. McCoy"), Pedro Fujimori, Pedro Aritomi, Father Wicht, and Jorge San Ramon. We divided the military, police, and civilian *ayudantes* among us. Each *compañero* would bring me the intelligence his helpers gathered and I would retransmit it to the outside.

According to a pager message my call sign was "Mariner." In addition, code words were assigned to the terrorists: Cerpa, Tito, Salvador, and the Arab were "Big Pigs." Cerpa and Tito were further identified with names from Orwell's *Animal Farm:* Napoleon and Squealer. The other male terrorists were Piggies, while the two females were Piglets. I provided the letters I had assigned our rooms on the second floor, Alfa, Bravo, Charlie, etc. The other areas of the residence would now be known as: "parlor" (dining room–ballroom combination); "office" (terrorist command center); "pork chop" (kitchen); "tree house" (rear service area); "Hell" (first floor); "Purgatory" (spiral staircase); "Pearly Gates" (landing); "Heaven" (second floor beyond the landing).

The commandos who would rescue us were "Angels," and we, the hostages, were "Bishops."

Each night the *compañeros* would summarize by category the intel helpers had provided. I would then transmit that intel to the listeners. The listeners would acknowledge through the pager. They also asked for information we had not provided. I often spoke into the guitar more than twenty times daily.

The first few messages I sent established intel categories, layout of the residence, location of hostages, and hostage morale. Among the categories I focused on were terrorist positions and routine. I continually transmitted intel to be certain it was timely. Army general Arturo Lopez Pardo Figueroa provided very valuable information on *tuco* munitions and armament. Police commander Gerardo Haro joined his shipmate Commander Alberto Heredia in keeping tabs on *tuco* morale and movement.

Our comm plan worked perfectly; messages streamed from and into the residence. Then it happened. The heavy use of the pager killed the batteries, and we had no replacements. We were back to transmitting in the blind without knowing whether the mike batteries had also failed.

We attacked the problem at the next meeting of the *compañeros.* We ruled out getting the right kind of batteries from the Red Cross. The only batteries we received—and very seldom—were for transistor radios. What we needed were special batteries for pagers or cell phones. We could not even request the correct batteries: The *tucos* would inevitably learn of the request and want to know why we needed such devices. They would search us, our rooms, and meager possessions. Certainly my guitar would be carefully examined. And we would all be strip-searched. No more hiding place for the pager.

Albert Heredia provided some intriguing information. He'd overheard Salvador asking Twenty-two if he knew where the black plastic bag with the cell phones was. Twenty-two said he'd placed it with the rest of the trash for pickup. After giving the moron an ass chewing, Salvador ordered him to find the bag immediately. Not a hard task with the helpful Red Cross. A Red Cross worker told Twenty-two he knew where the bag was and would retrieve it. The worker went to a pile of garbage bags stacked near the front gate, found the prize, and gave it to Twenty-two, who in turn delivered it to Salvador.

I asked Alberto if he knew where the bag was now.

"Yes, sir. In the service area next to the door to the passageway."

"Terrific. I want you and Commander Haro to load up on batteries from those cell phones. Don't take all of them, and don't take any cell phones. Put our dead batteries back into a cell phone. One of you stand guard while the other gets the batteries."

Alberto and Gerardo returned the next night with six batteries. We were back in business, and business was good as March approached.

13

El Frontón: A Peruvian Alcatraz

THROUGHOUT MY CAPTIVITY I dreaded the prospect that Cerpa would single me out for special treatment because of my role in putting down a bloody prison uprising in 1986. But he never mentioned the incident—probably because the prisoners were members of *Senero Luminoso* and not MRTA.

The aging prison of El Frontón was situated on a rock pile called San Lorenzo Island at the mouth of the bay. El Frontón housed the worst criminals and was site of the country's executions until Peru outlawed capital punishment. Newspapers used to publish two standard photos that announced each death of prisoners not already incarcerated at El Frontón: The first showed the condemned man boarding an open boat with guards for the short trip to San Lorenzo; the second showed the boat returning with a wooden coffin.

As the war with *Sendero* intensified during the early 1980s, El Frontón filled with the most dangerous and vicious terrorists we captured. Prison officials put them in a large, oblong cellblock called "the Blue Pavilion."

The terrorists soon controlled the cellblock. They bribed poorly paid guards or frightened them so much the guards left the *senderistas* alone to manage their affairs.

The terrorists established a rigid hierarchy that oversaw everything from meals to indoctrination to punishment. They hung banners from walls that celebrated the "three swords of communism": Lenin, Mao, and Abimael Guzman—"El Presidente Gonzalo."

The Blue Pavilion had two stories and was surrounded by a low wall that was half concrete and half fence. An exercise yard was between the perimeter wall and the cellblock. *Senderistas* often staged parades and rallies in the exercise yard to honor the revolution and its heroes.

The Pavilion was situated at one end of the island forty meters from a small beach cluttered with rocks and boulders. The beach was some five meters below the level of the Blue Pavilion.

As time passed, the terrorists turned the Blue Pavilion into a minifortress. They constructed a maze of concrete inner walls as defensive positions, and dug a huge basement to store explosives, weapons, food, and water. They dug tunnels for shelter from government attacks to retake the Blue Pavilion. One of the tunnels opened onto the beach. *Senderista* "prisoners" coordinated with comrades on the mainland, who sent fishing boats at night to ferry armed groups ashore for sabotage and assassinations in Lima. What better operations center than a prison? Who would think to look for active saboteurs and assassins in a prison?

As June 1986 approached, *senderista* inmates at Lima's main prison, Lurigancho, bought or coerced autonomy over their cellblock as comrades had at El Frontón. *Senderistas* at a third prison in Callao, Santa Barbara, followed suit.

The situation became intolerable and the government, now headed by President Alan García, moved to disrupt the terrorists and take back the cellblocks.

The strategy was to disperse the terrorists to other prisons and periodically transfer them to prevent organization and resistance. The cornerstone of the removal program was a new prison in Lima, Canto Grande. When the Republican Guard began the transfer, *senderistas* at the three prisons mutinied. Their defense was well planned: they had fortified the cellblocks and had an assortment of weapons from lances, knives, slingshots, and Molotov cocktails to rifles, pistols, grenades, and explosives.

President García moved swiftly to put down the uprising. He was motivated in part because he was about to host a prestigious International Socialist convention. Delegates from nations around the world were already arriving. More than five hundred foreign journalists were arriving with them. Among the delegates were twenty-two presidents and seventy leaders of political parties. SL's timing was exquisite and intentional.

García ordered the Republican Guard to retake the prisons. The military would support the Guard if necessary.

1400, JUNE 18. I reported for duty with twenty-one FOEs at the San Lorenzo pier. I presented myself to the Republican Guard general on the island.

The situation on the island was chaotic. For starters, we knew nothing of value about the enemy. We did not know how many inmates were common criminals, how many *senderistas* occupied the Blue Pavilion, how they were armed, how many hostages they held, or what fortifications they had built. We knew nothing of the cellar and tunnels they'd dug.

And we had no time to learn this essential information through such efforts as a recon, consultations with prison officials, review of prison records, or interrogation of former inmates. We were, in a word, *fregados*—fucked. Too bad. The Republican Guard, with our support, had to continue the mission.

We did, however, discover some one hundred *senderistas* were in the Blue Pavilion armed at least with rifles, pistols, and grenades. They'd captured three prison guards and were torturing them. The favored instrument of torture was a white-hot poker the *senderistas* applied to tender parts of the body. A *senderista* had forced a pencil up the penis of one hostage.

The Republican Guard contingent numbered a hundred men—about the same number as the *senderistas*. A ratio of one-to-one was not good for an attacking force, but the Guard had its orders.

The general told me to take my FOEs to the far end of the island, where a small beach was situated behind and below the back wall of the Pavilion.

My men and I maneuvered through rocks and boulders to the beach without drawing fire. I couldn't believe it. Perhaps this would be an easy day. No such luck.

I went forward with a FOE to check out the target before we emplaced our charges of C-4 explosives on the Pavilion wall. The FOE and I crawled up the shallow slope to view the back wall of the Pavilion. I knew when we reached our observation post we would be exposed and dangerously close to the building. A few small boulders provided some cover and concealment, but not much.

When we were within about twenty-five meters of the target, the FOE raised his head to check out the wall and the Pavilion erupted in gunfire. Well-aimed rounds from a guard tower struck boulders near our head and showered us with rock fragments. We tumbled back down the slope to the relative safety of the beach. We joined other FOEs who had taken cover among boulders and rocks.

Massive gunfire came from the second floor and guard towers of the Pavilion. We did our best to return fire but could not keep our heads up long enough to take aimed shots. We hugged the sloping beach and held MP5s above our heads for wild bursts. Doing anything was better than doing nothing—even if it was wrong.

The *senderistas* stopped their fusillade. An uneasy silence engulfed us. Then we heard shots snap around us again as the tiny lethal missiles broke the sound barrier. The man next to me, Petty Officer David Palacios, took a fatal round to the head. I heard David gasp as he fell, "*Dios mío. They've killed me.*"

Men of my security team threw me to the ground. I instinctively thrust out my hand as I slammed into the rocks. A razor sharp stone opened a nasty gash. Blood rushed from the wound; I wrapped the wound tightly in a bandanna.

Where the fuck did those rounds come from? I wondered. We would later learn *senderistas* had fired from a hidden tunnel entrance behind boulders on our left flank. We'd thought a sniper in a guard tower had targeted us. We took no more rounds. The terrorists had vanished.

We regrouped and prepared to move out. Gut-wrenching screams from the Blue Pavilion stopped us in our tracks. A hostage moaned a pitiful mantra for the terrorists to kill him: "*Máteme, máteme. Dios mío, máteme.*"

We couldn't wait to get out of that hellish place. One by one we maneuvered back through rough, rocky terrain to the pier. As I suspected, the *senderistas* held their fire. Ammo resupply for them would not be easy.

At the pier the Guard general decided only a night assault could succeed, but he doubted his men were adequately equipped and trained to do more than shoot at the terrorists in the Blue Pavilion from a nearby hill. The Guard had no mortars, RPGs, or night-vision devices. The general requested that the Joint Command reinforce his troops.

2300, JUNE 18. We arrived back at the beach. Under cover of darkness, two of my men with wire cutters opened a hole in the perimeter fence. The demolition element slipped through the opening and scurried like sand crabs to the Pavilion wall. They loaded C-4 on the wall and capped in.

Two FOEs spooled out the firing wire from the blasting cap to a galvanometer and hellbox behind a boulder on the beach. One FOE checked the circuit with the galvanometer: the needle jerked. He attached the bare end of one firing wire strand to the positive post on the hellbox and the bare end of the other to the negative post. He inserted the handle of the hellbox and yelled, "Fire in the hole!" He twisted the handle; the charge went high-order. We had crouched below the slight beach berm and covered our ears. We still felt the heat and concussive wave of the blast. Sand stung our eyes and debris fell around us.

The explosives did their work well—too well. A large section of the wall collapsed, but part of the second-story floor swung down as if on hinges and closed the hard-won opening. We gained one benefit: FOEs rescued a prisoner who fell from the second story when the floor collapsed. The man had refused to join the mutiny, and *senderistas* were torturing him when our charges detonated. The FOEs brought him to the CP. A black knife handle jutted from between his shoulder blades. One of my corpsmen removed the knife, cleaned and closed the wound.

The grateful man told us all he could about the situation in the Blue Pavilion. He said the *senderistas* had tortured and executed several prisoners—both terrorists and common criminals—who refused to join the mutiny. He did not know precisely the number of defenders in the Pavilion other than "many, many." He confirmed what we'd learned about the variety of *senderista* weapons. He told us he'd seen several wooden boxes marked "dynamite."

I could see the man was in pain and ended the questioning. I told the corpsmen to give him pills to ease the pain but nothing strong enough to knock him out. No morphine. He had to help us help him when we withdrew. We couldn't carry the man on a litter up through all those boulders and rocks.

When we returned to the pier I learned that the Joint Command had ordered a force to the island that would go through any breach at any time: Peruvian marines.

0300, JUNE 19. A detachment of marines arrived at the pier under command of their second ranking officer. The navy had been unable to locate the commander, navy captain (colonel) Juan Vega Llona, but were looking for him.

0600, JUNE 19. I returned with my men to the Blue Pavilion, but this time established the CP on the military crest of a low hill overlooking the entrance to the prison. I sent seven men forward under covering fire to throw smoke and fragmentation grenades through windows near the door. Another FOE with a rocket launcher would fire a missile at the door immediately after the grenades exploded.

I watched through binoculars from the hill. As smoke swirled from detonating grenades, I saw the FOE launch his missile. A second later my man fell, struck by a well-aimed round from a sniper in a guard tower.

Two FOE grenadiers were at the stricken man's side in seconds. They dragged him beyond the perimeter fence and carried him up the hill. The sniper round nearly severed his spine. He survived, but to this day his left side is completely paralyzed.

The FOE grenades had detonated on target inside the building but with absolutely no effect. The terrorists had hidden in the secret cellar. The missile the wounded FOE had fired slammed into the armored door but did no more than blacken the metal.

I sent a demolition element back to the Pavilion. We covered their advance with automatic weapons fire. They placed their C-4 on the wall and door, capped in, and fired mechanically with a thirty-second delay. The C-4 did its job. The explosions obliterated the armored door and opened a hole in the wall you could drive a jeep through. The second floor did not collapse.

The demolition element returned to the CP without drawing fire and we withdrew to the pier, where I learned Captain Vega Llona had arrived to assume command of the marines.

0900, JUNE 19. I retired from the battle. I remained on the pier and listened to grim radio traffic while combat raged at the Blue Pavilion. The marines fought their way through the breached wall and drove the prisoners from the first floor. As the prisoners retreated to the second floor, they fired point-blank at the charging marines. Petty Officer (gunnery sergeant) Edilbert Jiménez fell mortally wounded. Lieutenant Commander (major) Luis Enrique de la Jara rushed to his man's side and a *senderista* gut-shot him.

Enrique surely would have died if Captain Vega Llona had not braved *senderista* fire to carry the wounded man out of harm's way.

The terrorists fought hard to defend the second floor. Three marines died and twenty-one were wounded during the attack.

1300, JUNE 19. I was ordered to depart San Lorenzo and have my wound tended while the battle at the Blue Pavilion continued. I arrived shortly afterward at the Callao Navy Base. When I left the island, the Blue Pavilion still stood. The marines opened and fought their way through additional breaches. They engaged the terrorists in close quarter battle that often included hand-to-hand combat.

1500, JUNE 19. I saw thirty-five *senderistas* who had surrendered to the marines arrive at the naval base. Despite their losses, the *senderistas* in the Blue Pavilion continued their fierce resistance. They killed those they caught trying to surrender.

In yet another attempt to defeat the hard-core terrorists, the marines detonated a charge to open an additional avenue of attack. The explosion breached the wall but caused a sympathetic detonation of dynamite that the terrorists had positioned nearby to throw at the marines. The sympathetic detonation collapsed walls and floors. The cellar and tunnels collapsed as well, killing several of the resisting terrorists.

In an ingenious attempt to snatch victory from the jaws of defeat, Abimael Guzman began the next phase of his operation: A *senderista* prisoner proclaimed to the media that the navy had destroyed the Blue Pavilion to kill people inside who had quit resisting and were trying to surrender.

An investigation revealed the support columns for the cellblock were forced outward, indicating that a powerful blast from inside the building had struck and bent them.

On the second day after we had defeated the mutineers, lawyers filed a petition charging that navy officers had murdered *senderista* prisoners. Few lawyers could have prepared this complicated lawsuit so quickly after the battle. Nor was there any need for such swift legal action. But the result was a media frenzy that Guzman counted on to convince the public that the navy had indeed violated the prisoners' human rights. Guilty until proven innocent.

The trial court dismissed the lawsuit, and the lawyers appealed and appealed yet again until finally the case reached the Peruvian Supreme Court. The Supreme Court soundly rejected the claim just as the lower courts had. To pursue a lawsuit from the trial court through appellate courts to the Supreme Court was a very costly process. But Guzman believed—correctly as it turned out—the propaganda value would be well worth the cost.

Not long after the recapture of the Blue Pavilion, Abimael Guzman proclaimed: "The valiant prisoners of war at the cost of their own lives achieved a great moral, political, and military victory for the party and the revolution. Their sacrifice enabled a great leap forward in the struggle for a new order in Peru."

As civil courts were deciding whether government forces had committed crimes at El Frontón, navy investigators, prosecutors, and judges were also considering whether navy personnel were guilty of wrongdoing at the prison. Peru follows a centuries-old practice that originated in Spain called the *fuero militar* to judge members of the armed forces accused of crimes committed in the line of duty.

A military system of justice beginning with trial and continuing through appeal determines if the accused is guilty or innocent. Countries worldwide follow this practice, including Great Britain and the United States. The military judges its own subject to civilian oversight.

Peruvian navy courts investigated the alleged crimes *senderistas* claimed navy officers committed during the battle of the Blue Pavilion. No court found compelling evidence of any crime.

By 1988, civilian and military courts had exonerated those of us who fought at El Frontón. That should have been the end of the matter—but it was not. The *senderistas* and their sympathizers turned up the heat, and the pot boiled again.

In 1981 Peru had agreed to accept the limited jurisdiction of the Inter-American Court of Human Rights, which is a tribunal of the Organization of American States. Several countries refused to sign the agreement—including the United States. These nations were absolutely unwilling to surrender sovereignty over their citizens to a foreign court.

Within six weeks of the battle at El Frontón a petition was filed with the Inter-American Court on behalf of three *senderista* prisoners who perished in the fighting. This petition triggered *nine years* of investigations and court proceedings.

I testified before dozens if not hundreds of international and national investigative and judicial bodies. I couldn't begin to tell you the exact number or the names of these organizations. The witch-hunt was continuing when the hostage crisis began.

But Captain Vega Llona and I had more to worry about than biased international commissions and misinformed courts. Within months of El Frontón, SIN learned that SL had placed us on a death list and were already making plans to murder us.

The government sent us out of the country. I went to the United States as a naval attaché in Washington, DC for two years, while Captain Vega Llona was assigned to the Peruvian embassy in La Paz, Bolivia. Within a year, terrorists on a motor scooter had gunned him down near the embassy.

SL plotted to kill me as well. Agents from the DEA and FBI notified me that SL had hired a Colombian drug cartel to carry out the assassination. The US government gave me a permit to carry a weapon, and DC police patrolled my neighborhood the entire time I was in the United States.

I could have remained outside Peru as long as necessary, but I refused to let terrorists keep me from my homeland. I returned in 1989 and was promoted to admiral. I continued to fight in our War on Terror for another four years. When I retired I was the second-ranking admiral in the navy.

After I left active duty, the government appointed me president of the Peruvian Institute of Oceanography. I continued to manage my successful deep-sea diving and salvage company. I was blessed with a loving family: my mother, wife, two sons, and two daughters. Grandchildren were on the horizon. I still had bodyguards, but the terrorists had made no attempt on my life. I was beginning to think I'd weathered the storm and was steaming full speed ahead with following seas.

Then I received the little white envelope a week before Christmas 1996.

14

People's Tribunal

MARCH ARRIVED. The weather cooled. The gray sea mist we called *La Garua* drifted in as fall approached. More than two months in captivity and counting.

A new development raised our spirits and improved morale: The government had agreed to resume "conversations" with MRTA monitored by a trio of "guarantors."

These talks took place outside the compound in a nearby house on Thomas Edison Street. The Red Cross chose the house, picked up the terrorist negotiators, and delivered them in an armored sedan. The Red Cross also installed a phone in the house with a direct line to the terrorist command center, and videotaped each meeting. The meetings were under the protection of the Red Cross to ensure that the government would not ambush the terrorists. A Red Cross flag fluttered above the house where the talks took place.

The three guarantors were Ambassador Anthony Vincent of Canada, Archbishop Cipriani who represented the Holy See, and Michel Minnig of the Red Cross. Minister Palermo represented the government, as he had during the earlier talks. Because President Fujimori did not personally attend the meetings, neither did Cerpa. He sent the Arab as his representative. The Japanese insisted they have an observer and sent their country's ambassador to Mexico, Teruseke Terada.

The first meeting lasted four hours and addressed procedural matters. As he would after each meeting, Archbishop Cipriani briefed the swelling gaggle of journalists and spoke into any number of microphones for radio and TV. He said both sides had established procedures for future meetings and had begun work on an agenda. The second meeting would be the following day and "address matters of substance." What Cipriani did not tell the media was that a total of ten meetings had been scheduled.

The substantive matter discussed the following day was the hostage–prisoner exchange. In fact, all meetings in one way or another focused on this issue and improved jail conditions for incarcerated *guerilleros*. The guarantors did not participate unless talks stalled between the parties. The Arab could contact Cerpa over the landline whenever he wished. The government promised not to tap the line.

At the third meeting two empty chairs were at the conference table should Cerpa and Fujimori decide to attend. One chair remained empty throughout the talks.

The Arab presented MRTA demands: The government must free all prisoners and transport them to the central jungle. The *guerilleros* would free all but fifteen hostages. The *guerilleros* and hostages would join the freed prisoners for the trip to the jungle. Upon safe arrival, MRTA would hold the hostages for twenty days and then free them. End of crisis.

Palermo responded with the government's position: It would release no prisoners. The government would, however, guarantee safe passage for the terrorists to a third country if they released the hostages, laid down their weapons, and removed or rendered safe all explosives.

Cerpa through the Arab rejected the proposal and urged the government to present another with more reasonable terms.

On February 21 Cerpa attended the fourth meeting instead of the Arab. A SIN agent, Rafael Bartet, represented the government in place of Palermo. Montesinos chose Bartet because the agent had successfully persuaded jailed SL leader Abimael Guzman to sign a peace accord that called for his followers to lay down their arms. MRTA knew the substitute representative's name but not his precise government affiliation. After the meeting, Archbishop Cipriani assured the media that progress had been made.

Palermo returned for the fifth meeting and brought an assistant, José Payet. Cerpa also brought an assistant, the Arab. Cerpa offered to exchange all hostages for fifty-five prisoners—a number considerably lower than the original 440.

The guarantors believed this was a reasonable number and recommended the government accept the deal. Fujimori responded at a news conference: He would liberate no prisoners. The next day Cerpa said he would not accept less than the original 440 prisoners in exchange for the hostages. Back to square one.

As the talks stalled, we redoubled efforts to gather and transmit intelligence to our SIN listeners. We were especially alert for conversations among the *tucos* about negotiating strategy but we heard nothing.

We also drove on with our own plans for escape if the talks failed and a rescue was not forthcoming soon. Talks had been going on since shortly after Christmas, and now nerves were fraying. I became more and more impatient with the listeners and asked time after time when we would be rescued. They never answered. I finally began swearing at them, calling them *conchatumadres* (motherfuckers), *cojudos* (assholes), and other choice words. The more they remained silent, the more I cursed them, until finally I gave up.

The *compañeros* had devised a more modest plan than the mass escape, which surely would have resulted in many dead and wounded hostages. Now that we had the keys for the windows, we decided to escape by that route. But the drop from the second-floor window to the lawn was four meters—far enough to break bones in the elderly and others in poor condition who did not know how to hit and roll to cushion their fall.

So Alberto proposed an alternative: The room with a connecting bath in the service area had a balcony that was only about three meters from the ground. The terrorists had wired the door to the balcony shut, but the wire would not be difficult to remove. The balcony was only a few meters from the breached wall from which the terrorists had breached to enter the compound.

The room—India—had the added advantage that *tucos* seldom visited there, although a few of us thought La Gringa and Sushi had midnight trysts in the service area among the *caza bobos*. We would have to be alert for that threat, although the *enamorados* would likely be so absorbed in making the beast with two backs, they would be oblivious to all else.

The plan called for us to seize control of the second floor and hold it for fifteen minutes with weapons we took from the *tucos* guarding us. We would be able to defend our position for more than fifteen minutes if we could somehow gain access to the armory in Golf, which was unlikely.

While the security group kept the *tucos* at bay, the rest of the hostages would assemble in India, with its balcony. We'd then tie ten mattresses together with line and lower them from the balcony to the ground. Two of us would leap to the ground with one end of a blanket stretched between us. The other end would be secured to the balcony. We would tie our end of the blanket to the mattresses and fashion a slide from the balcony that elderly hostages could use. Once on the ground, they would flee through the breached wall. Everyone else including the security group would jump and follow through the breach.

We had two serious problems: first, we would have to disarm the *tucos* on the second floor; second, we would have to somehow bring the Japanese on the first floor up to the second. We calculated we could handle no more than two armed *tucos*. We also reluctantly concluded that the Japanese on the first floor might not be able to join us. An outside force would have to rescue them.

I told the listeners of our plan and requested that commandos storm the residence through the front door when they heard shooting inside. I also asked that snipers be positioned on the roof of the Unique building to protect us as we jumped to the ground from the balcony. The listeners remained silent despite my increasingly desperate messages.

A CRITICAL QUESTION we had to answer was when to tell the other hostages of our escape plans and what they were to do. These hostages included all the Japanese except Pedro Fujimori, who was an *ayudante*. We decided to wait until the very last minute. We feared someone might panic and give the game away if we spoke too soon.

We all agreed we could trust Ambassador Aoki and decided to let him know of the plan now. But we also agreed he should not know about our contact with the outside.

The next morning during the exercise period Jorge Valdez and I approached the ambassador while he was walking the circuit and asked if we might speak privately with him in Charley.

When we explained the escape plan he seemed startled and remained quiet for a moment. I saw his face redden beneath his cap of gunmetal-gray hair. He became so angry his voice trembled when he spoke. He accused me of being a narrow-minded, stupid militarist and that such a scheme would end up killing us all. He waved a finger in my face as he spoke. I'd never seen the man in such a state.

I met his hostility with my own. The only difference was that my insults were laced with *lisuras*—profanities. Jorge joined in. Faced with this onslaught, the ambassador left the room.

I looked at Jorge. "Do you think the *conchatumadre* will tell anyone?"

Jorge did not think so because life would become unbearable for all the hostages. The *tucos* would assume everyone was planning to escape.

Jorge was right. Two days passed and the terrorists did not act any different. In fact, Aoki came to me the day after our confrontation and apologized. I accepted, and we exchanged curt bows. But the ambassador told me he did not want to know of any further escape plans. Not a chance. Shortly after our conversation I noticed a diplomatic officer who worked for Aoki began sticking to me like glue.

Although no one snitched on me to the *tucos*, someone did tell Michel Minnig I was planning an escape. He became my third cross to bear. The day after Chancellor Tudela told Forty-four the facts of life, Minnig personally brought me my lunch in Charley. He sat beside me as I ate and said in an imploring tone, "Admiral, I beg you not to proceed with your escape. I am confident a breakthrough in our talks is at hand. A hostile act on your part will not only destroy any chance for a negotiated settlement but also put your fellow hostages in grave danger."

He looked at me with spaniel eyes and I replied, "Don't worry. I would do nothing detrimental to my fellow hostages." *Jesus,* I thought, *the enemy within. As if we don't have enough fucking problems.*

My repeated use of the guitar took its inevitable toll on the microphone batteries. A pager message notified me transmissions were weak and barely audible. The message advised that my wife would send a Bible.

The Bible arrived in a few days. I went to Charley, opened the Good Book, and spoke into it. The listeners replied immediately. I was Lima-Charley: loud and clear. They reminded me I could whisper very softly and they would still pick up my transmission. The Bible gave me mobile comm—I could wander the second floor, and even the first at times, pretending I was devoutly reading scripture. Talk about real-time intel.

The government and MRTA met for a seventh time on February 27. Afterward, the Arab told me, "In the meetings we talk, tell jokes, and make friends but no progress at all."

Cerpa complained about Fujimori to a group of hostages: "In this country the only one who makes decisions is Fujimori and he never attends the negotiations. Because he is never present, I will stop attending." We were once more between a rock and a hard place. We fought despair.

An eighth meeting on March 3, also led to nothing.

But hope flickered to life the first week in March when Fujimori flew to Cuba for consultations with Fidel Castro. Fidel received the president warmly but said he would not mediate an end to the crisis. However, he did agree to provide asylum for the terrorists and allow them to remain in the country for a year. His only condition: that Peru acknowledge Cuba had no connection with MRTA. Castro also wanted the guarantors—Canada, the Red Cross, and the Vatican—to join Peru in the petition for asylum.

While Fujimori was in Cuba an incident occurred that put me in grave danger. The two communist radio stations, *Cora* and *Libertad,* had served throughout our captivity as the voice of MRTA. Announcers for these stations even went so far as to call hostages "oligarchs who deserved execution." They also spoke of Cerpa with something approaching reverence, congratulating him on his boldness and ranking him among the greatest fighters for the masses. The stations also continually described what police were doing in the neighborhood and where they were positioned.

I don't recall the exact day, but early one morning General Denegri found me in my room and gave me very bad news: Jorge Gumucio had just heard Manuel Romero of *Cora* tell his audience what a shame it was that newspapers had identified me as a high-ranking officer who had directed operations against MRTA. Several freedom fighters died in these operations. He went on to report I had been in charge. My neck was in the noose. I feared a People's Tribunal was at hand.

These were secret mock trials Cerpa held for the worst enemies of the people. Rumor had it that the accused would be hauled before Cerpa, Salvador, Tito, and the Arab in the first-floor office. The accused would sit on the floor before the tribunal with his arms tied at the elbows behind his back. Twenty-two would slip a sawed-off broom handle between the accused's back and the rope and twist to make a Spanish windlass. The sadist often twisted the rope so tightly, it would nearly dislocate a shoulder. The only reason the *tucos* did not do any real damage was that they knew the Red Cross doctor examined us every week.

Following the inevitable guilty verdict for crimes against the people, Cerpa would pronounce sentence: death. Twenty-two would then jab the barrel of a revolver into the neck of the accused and pull the trigger. Until now, the hammer had fallen on an empty chamber.

I did not wait long to learn my fate. Cerpa, Salvador, and Twenty-two appeared in the doorway. Salvador and Twenty-two each grabbed an arm at the elbow and frog-marched me from the room. We followed Cerpa down the staircase and into the office. The two terrorists screamed *lisuras* and threats into my ears while they wrenched my arms. I clenched my teeth against the pain.

I was ready for the command to sit on the floor but Cerpa ordered me to stand. He sat behind a large mahogany desk. His lieutenants flanked him. Cerpa got right to the point: He told me in an accusatory tone I was to be judged as an enemy of the people. He began the interrogation.

"Are you Admiral Giampietri?"

"Yes."

"Have you been chief of naval operations?"

"Yes."

Cerpa leaned forward and glared at me.

"That proves you are an enemy of the people, an enemy of the revolution! You have ordered the execution of our comrades."

Thanks to General Denegri I'd anticipated the accusation and prepared a reply. "No, you've been misinformed. The chief of naval operations is in charge of ships, airplanes, and submarines. Nothing more. We have never used ships, airplanes, or submarines against MRTA."

The interrogation continued. Cerpa tried to catch me in a contradiction. He said I'd ordered the execution of a "Comrade Quispe." This, he continued, was the son of a close friend who had been with him during the siege of the textile factory in 1978. Marines under my command, Cerpa claimed, had killed Quispe in the department of Ucayali.

I told Cerpa that a thirty-eight-year-old commander had been in charge of the Ucayali operation. I asked the terrorist what year the son of his old friend had died.

"It was 1989."

"Well, I couldn't have been involved because at that time I was assigned as naval attaché to the Peruvian embassy in Washington, DC."

The answer seemed to confuse the terrorist. He told me to sit down and walked from the room.

Salvador, Tito, and Twenty-two scowled at me. The Arab asked if I had visited Disneyland or Disney World while I was in the United States.

Cerpa returned with General Denegri in tow. "The general says he knows you. Claims he worked with you." Cerpa asked Denegri what kind of work that had been.

"I was an air force observer on the admiral's flagship during a joint exercise. He was chief of naval operations at the time." Denegri spoke with such finality that—luckily for me—Cerpa appeared impressed.

"All right, Admiral. You may go." He had decided I was a harmless old retired admiral.

As I walked up the staircase with Denegri, I realized this was the first time Cerpa had called me by my rank. Incredibly, after the tribunal the *tucos* paid less attention to me and several—including La Gringa—even became friendly. This new attitude facilitated my work. *No hay mal que por bien no venga.*

15

Chavín de Huántar: The Tunnels Revealed

THE MEDIA MONSTER feasted on and threatened us every day. My close call at the kangaroo tribunal was just the latest example of how great the threat could be.

Within minutes of the terrorist takedown—by now more than three months back—local TV stations had cameras on scene and rolling. Within hours of the takedown a horde of TV, radio, and print journalists from around the world had joined their Peruvian colleagues. Fox, CNN, ABC, CBS, NBC, *The New York Times*, the *Los Angeles Times*, *The Washington Post*, *The Miami Herald*, *Time*, *Newsweek*, *U.S. News & World Report*, and even *Rolling Stone* were among the many TV networks, newspapers, and magazines that settled in for what they hoped would be a long, profitable stay. NHK and the BBC headed the foreign TV contingent on station and ready.

As the crisis deepened, several hundred journalists, photographers, and TV cameramen gathered daily behind barriers police had erected a block from the residence. The scene was surreal and became known among Peruvians as "the MRTA Road Show."

A permanent gaggle of journalists teetered on stepladders and perched in trees as they aimed telescopic lenses toward what experts grimly called the "crisis point." Police with riot shields lounged between the journalists and the crisis point.

Religious and other fanatics walked in front of the barricade toting any number of figurines, paintings, and crucifixes. Prayer and rosary beads dripped from the barricade. A common sight said much about Peru's woes since the sixteenth century. Two elegantly attired women would square off daily with Quechua shamans who were decked out in colorful ceremonial dress to exorcise demons. The women would scream at the Indians and brandish bejeweled crucifixes as if to ward off vampires.

Well-heeled media conglomerates paid top dollar to rent homes with a view, however slight, of the residence. A room or rooftop with a good view could fetch as much as one thousand dollars a day—this in a country where more than three-quarters of the population earned less than fifty-eight dollars a month.

Local TV channels shared in the bonanza: They rented equipment to the foreign networks for what the market would bear. *Frecuencia Latina,* a leading Peruvian TV station, loaned its satellite facilities to US and Mexican companies at a rate of two thousand dollars a minute. A smaller Peruvian station, RTP, struck a deal with NHK to obtain state-of-the-art TV equipment without cost after the Japanese departed.

The media monster was ever-vigilant for the revealing photo, sensational rumor, or exclusive story—the more macabre, the better. The insatiable beast put the hostages at risk daily.

But the gravest danger occurred in late February: Local and then foreign media announced that the government was digging tunnels under the residence wall. Enterprising reporters had noticed pickup trucks going to and from houses behind the residence most nights. One night reporters followed the trucks to the gates of Las Palmas Air Force Base. The truck beds had tarps stretched over them, but loose dirt leaked from beneath the tarps throughout the trip. One magazine wrote that an "unnamed source in a position to know" said commandos would use tunnels to attack the *guerilleros.*

The hostages and terrorists learned of the tunnels from transistor radios tuned to *Cora* and *Libertad.* The terrorists immediately began listening for tunneling and checking for other signs. They pulled back the rug in the office and saw a long crack in the concrete floor. And they heard what they believed were digging sounds in the first-floor bathrooms.

Cerpa ordered Dante Cordova and Francisco Tudela to come down and listen. "Our comrades," Cerpa began, "have been hearing noises we have reason to believe come from the digging of tunnels. Listen for yourselves."

Cordova dropped to his knees and put his ear to the floor. "I can't hear anything."

Cerpa grew angry. "But you can clearly hear noises!" he yelled. "A tunnel is being dug and you cannot tell me differently!"

Cordova again pressed his ear to the floor. "Yes, now I do hear very faint noises. Must be rats."

"Yes," Tudela said. "Rats."

The terrorists were confused. They wanted to believe rats were making the noise but feared miners were at work.

Cerpa called a meeting of his lieutenants to consider the problem. After several hours the terrorists decided they had to prepare for the worst. They changed the guard and patrol assignments to focus on the first floor. The younger terrorists were stationed in the office and bathrooms. If commandos opened holes in the floor, the *tucos* would rake them with 7.62mm rounds from their AKMs and toss grenades into the tunnels.

Cerpa ordered the barricaded windows and doors of the first floor reinforced with furniture. He assigned Salvador to oversee the first-floor defense. Salvador redoubled the military drills through the ballroom and dining room.

Cerpa had one or two terrorists sleep in every room with hostages. He and his aide slept with us for the first week; after that the two women took over. The women were tougher on us than Cerpa. They would not enter our rooms until around midnight and made as much noise as possible. They shined flashlights in our eyes to ensure everyone was present and awake.

The women did provide unintended comic relief when they shared the portable toilets with us. While one *tuca* was taking a dump the other stood guard at the stall without a door. Several hostages suddenly felt the urge to relieve themselves. After viewing the spectacle, hostages whispered obscene comments about the entertaining position of the girls astride the shitter.

The change in the terrorist routine hampered but did not stop our plans for a rescue or escape. Because the women entered Charley late, we continued our nightly meetings. We took the added precaution of speaking in English should a terrorist barge past our lookout and enter the room without warning.

Tension, always in the air, became almost unbearable. I immediately notified the listeners of the changed enemy situation but transmitted fewer messages because of heightened *tuco* security.

Not long after Cerpa started reinforcing avenues of approach to the residence, he, the aide, and two *charapas* entered Charley and took the armored door from the closet. Then they removed the armored door to the passageway. I had a sick feeling someone had informed Cerpa of our conspiracy. Cerpa ordered his men to use the doors as barriers on the first floor.

The tension affected *tucos* as well as hostages. They became unhappy and quarreled among themselves. The younger *tucos* railed against their leaders in loud voices for having lied to them about a quick return to the jungle. Cerpa punished more than one of his underlings and made all shave their heads except his aide, Twenty-two, and the women.

The punished *tucos* became careless in their duties. More than one fell asleep on watch. This would help if we decided to escape at night. On the other hand, their carelessness became a danger for us: We feared a hostage might grow more desperate than we already were and initiate his own escape by seizing an AKM from a sleeping *tuco*. If this happened, so much for our escape plans. To guard against a Peter Rabbit among us, we would gently and surreptitiously nudge sleeping guards to awaken them.

ON MARCH 3 Cerpa allowed the ninth meeting to take place even though he was now convinced the government had tunneled beneath the residence walls. He attended with the Arab and continued the numbers game with Minister Palermo. The guarantors said they would consider the issue and hopefully reach a compromise number. During the meeting, terrorists hung a banner from the roof that read: PEOPLE OF PERU! REMEMBER FUJIMORI DOES NOT SPEAK OR RULE FOR YOU!

The next day Cerpa suspended the talks. He stunned the guarantors and delighted the media when he accused the government of digging tunnels to attack the residence.

Fujimori immediately called a press conference. "I'm not going to confirm or deny," he announced, "if we are digging one or several tunnels or none at all. Nor will I confirm or deny we have air assault teams prepared to seize the residence after the terrorists have been incapacitated with paralyzing gas. I will say nothing about our plans to end the crisis. The international community surely will understand our position."

On the following Sunday, March 9, Monsignor Cipriani celebrated Mass in the residence. He remained afterward and talked with us for more than two hours. As he was leaving, he gave us encouraging news the talks would start anew the following day.

Cerpa, the Arab, and the guarantors showed up for the meeting, but not

Minister Palermo. Fujimori later issued a statement that read: "The MRTA unilaterally suspended the dialogue at a point when real progress was being made with the excuse Peru was not acting in good faith. The time is not yet ripe for conversations to resume. Both sides need a period of reflection."

This may have been a good strategy for the president to show Cerpa who was boss, but it was terrible for us. We had been captives for eighty-three days with no end in sight.

ONE OF FUJIMORI'S worst fears—and he had many—was realized when the terrorists discovered the tunnels. Up until this point he had been successful with his smoke screen of negotiations and trips abroad to cover military preparations for an assault.

During February, Fujimori had traveled to Canada, the United States, Cuba, and the Dominican Republic. In Montreal he had a "summit conference" with the prime minister of Japan, Ryutaro Hashimoto. Afterward he and the prime minister issued a joint declaration, which stated among other things that meetings would commence between Peru and the MRTA in search of a peaceful solution to the crisis. Fujimori was careful to ensure that the following language appeared in the declaration: "The preservation of mental and physical health for the hostages is an indispensable condition for successful conversations." Fujimori saw this condition as justification for an armed assault at any time. The hostages were constantly in danger of being killed. This certainly was already affecting their mental and physical health. The Japanese did not object to the loophole language.

Fujimori met with President Clinton in Washington, DC. Clinton buoyed Fujimori's spirits when he endorsed Peru's handling of the crisis—especially its firm resolve not to release prisoners. Fujimori nevertheless told Clinton he would use every reasonable means to achieve a nonviolent end to the crisis.

Fujimori also appeared before the Organization of American States in Washington. The secretary general of the OAS, César Guevara, endorsed how the Peruvian government was handling the situation. Fujimori later made an announcement that claimed MRTA had abandoned its demand for a prisoner release in the face of Peru's firm opposition. Fujimori emphasized that his patience would guarantee a peaceful outcome.

The next day the MRTA mouthpiece in Europe, Isaac Velazco, told the

French media the *guerilleros* had not abandoned their imprisoned comrades. He said: "President Fujimori makes much of his Oriental patience. We say we have patiently resisted colonialism and neocolonialism for more than five hundred years. We are prepared to patiently resist much longer, as the present facts demonstrate. We are the children of Túpac Amaru." When Fujimori learned of the MRTA response, he reminded himself that the Spaniards had drawn and quartered the rebel Inca leader in the public plaza of Cuzco.

Fujimori had planned on flying to Cuba from Washington but thought better of it. He did not want to alienate Fidel by appearing to be a stooge of the gringos. Fujimori instead traveled to the Dominican Republic, where he spoke with President Leonel Fernandez at the airport. The Dominican Republic had provided safe haven for terrorists in the past, and Fernandez agreed to consider that possibility for MRTA.

Fujimori returned to Peru with the backing of several important nations. He was confident he could continue the strategy of appearing to seek a negotiated settlement while preparing for a military solution.

Now this—the discovery of the tunnels. He determined to meet the threat head-on: He put the commandos on high alert to launch an assault at any time even if it meant the tunnels might not be complete. Fujimori would not restart direct talks with the terrorist to avoid appearing weak, but he would communicate indirectly with them through the guarantors. That ploy should stave off complaints from abroad.

The Japanese vice chancellor, Masahiki Koumura, would arrive in a few days on March 18; Fujimori hoped renewed contact with the terrorists— however indirect—would placate the Japanese. What was that expression about mushrooms in the dark?

LIEUTENANT COLONEL VALER joined the colonel as he did every morning after breakfast with the men. The colonel gave him the bad news about the tunnels. He told Valer the men were now on high alert and should be ready to board helicopters at a moment's notice in full combat gear. They would use the contingency plan if ordered to assault the residence early. Two Russian-made tanks would be on station at the residence. One tank would smash through the front gate and door, while the other would lead APCs with commandos on board around the residence to assault through the dining room and back doors. Commandos would fast-rope onto the roof from a helicopter and blow the door to the second floor. The plan had too many variables and would take too much time, but the commandos had no alternative if ordered to attack early.

The colonel asked Valer as he did each day how training was going and what he had scheduled for the day.

"Training is on schedule and we're at full strength. I had intended for the commandos to do more live-firing on the ranges, but with your permission I would like them to start going through the kill house now."

"Permission granted. We're working around the clock to get the replica finished ASAP. The engineers and architect tell me they can finish in a week."

"My men will be ready to use the replica by then. We'll start with dry runs and then move quickly to live fire, including demo. We need to calculate the correct size of the charges: enough to kill and disable the *tucos* but not bring down the residence and harm the hostages." Valer wanted to confirm another important detail yet again about the replica. "I would like to make certain, Colonel, that the walls are being built with bullet traps."

The colonel smiled and gave his usual answer: "Yes, Chizito, the walls are still being built with bullet traps. You'll no doubt want to inspect them. See you tomorrow morning."

VALER CALLED the SF school and told the training officer, who knew nothing of the mission, he would need the instructors he had picked for the kill house today rather than next week. The officer grumbled about how that would screw up his training schedule but Valer cut him off: "Just make sure those men report to me within the hour. They know to come prepared for a long stay."

Valer had chosen the best instructors available—all enlisted men—to train the commandos for the kill house. He sat in a briefing room with the sixteen men of El Frijol's assault unit and listened to an instructor explain the procedure. Different instructors would do the same later with the other two assault units.

The instructor began: "I know you officers will pay attention because if you don't, you or your buddy will end tits-up in the kill house. And you wouldn't be the first.

"Today I will explain how you go through the door and clear a room of tangos or *tucos,* take your pick.

"I know that for many of you this will be a review, but you can never get enough experience in the kill house. You first form a combat train of four men to go through the door. Never approach the door head-on: The doorway is the 'Fatal Funnel.'

"What," the instructor asked, "is the doorway?"

"The Fatal Funnel," the commandos shouted.

"And don't forget or you'll end up dead. Every enemy weapon will be trained on the doorway ready to fire when the door opens or perhaps even before. Of course you will have to enter the Fatal Funnel to reach the room, but your time in the funnel should be as short as possible. A second or less." The instructor chalked stick figures and diagrams on a green board while he talked.

"As you approach the door outside the funnel, you get nuts-to-butts and keep the muzzles of your weapons pointed up. You bring the weapon to bear as soon as you enter the room, careful not to sweep your buddy.

"The door will either be closed or open. If you can handle a closed door you'll have no problem with one that's open. How do we handle the usual closed door? The man with the shotgun leads the way and blasts the doorknob—or where the doorknob should be. He then gives the door a mule kick and stands aside to let the train through the doorway.

"If the door doesn't open, the quickie-saw man cranks his machine, cuts vertically down the door from top to bottom, and gives the door a mule kick. The quickie saw cuts metal. If the door still doesn't open—and you'd better pray it does—the sledgehammer man goes to work. All the while the clock is ticking.

"Regardless of how you open the door, you follow the same procedure to enter and clear a room. The shotgun man throws a crash—a flashbang grenade—into the room and steps aside. The next man enters and goes right or left down the wall to the corner. He sweeps the room with his weapon through a forty-five-degree arc from the corner toward the center. The second man through the door repeats the same movement but goes the opposite way from the first. The third man follows the first, stops about halfway down the wall, and sweeps through a forty-five-degree arc from the center of the room toward the corner. The fourth man—who usually carries the shotgun—repeats this movement down the opposite wall toward the second man in the corner. He stops about halfway down the wall and sweeps through a forty-five-degree arc from the center toward the corner."

The green board was filling with chalked combat trains, other stick figures, doors, and squares to represent rooms.

"I'm sure you understand that when anyone sees a tango at any time, from any place in the room, he fires two head shots. The cardinal rule you must always remember when bringing your weapon to bear on a tango is this: *You never sweep your buddy!* If your barrel is swinging toward your buddy, you must raise it immediately. What is the cardinal rule you must always remember when you are bringing your weapon to bear?"

"Never sweep your buddy!"

"What do you do if you are about to sweep your buddy?"

"Raise your weapon!"

The instructor saw a few commandos scribbling furiously in their small green notebooks. He smiled. "Gentlemen, no need for notes. Keep your attention on me. We'll walk you through these procedures many, many times in the kill house before we begin live fire.

"Back to our original positions along the wall on either side of the Fatal Funnel. If anyone sees anything—tango, furniture, another door, anything that could be a danger—that commando yells 'Moving' and identifies the danger." The green board continued to fill with chalk markings.

"Of course if the danger is a tango, the commando doesn't yell anything—he cranks off head shots. Don't fire center mass—the tango may be wearing a bullet bouncer.

"Suppose the potential danger is a couch along the far wall. The first commando who sees the couch yells, 'Moving! Couch!'

"Does the commando then move on the couch? He does not. He waits for another commando—any commando—to yell, 'Move!' At that point the commando closes with the danger and renders it safe.

"Once you have cleared the room you are ready for the next. If you see a door in the cleared room, you stack your combat train beside the new door and start the procedure again.

"You mark a cleared room with either a red or green chem lite: green if no one is in the room, red if nonthreatening persons are in the room. A dead tango is nonthreatening."

Laughter.

"Okay. This has been a quick-and-dirty explanation of how you go through the door and clear a room. Save your questions for the kill house. That's where the real learning begins. We'll put you through many, many dry runs with BFAs on your weapons before you load live rounds. Yes, sir?"

Valer had risen to get the instructor's attention. "Outstanding presentation, instructor, as usual. How many times have you been through a kill house?"

"I've lost count, sir. Well over a thousand."

"Who trained you?"

"The US Army Delta Force and the Israelis. We combine the best of both approaches. We believe Delta is a little too careful and the Israelis a little too loose. We like the way Israelis set up a kill house; a lot less expensive than Delta. Delta has all sorts of electronic stuff like pop-ups. We use stationary stand-ups like the Israelis and reuse targets after we tape over the bullet holes."

Valer smiled and again commended the instructor for a job well done. The instructor left the room, and Valer addressed the commandos: "I have nothing to add except we will not be using crashes and with any luck at least a few doors will be open. But don't count on it. See you at the kill house."

WE GOT AN UNEXPECTED and sorely needed morale boost on March 17: Peruvians by the thousands paraded through Lima in a show of solidarity with the hostages. Priests rang church bells, drivers honked horns, and firemen cranked sirens. An emotional time. Tears welled in the eyes of many hostages.

We also received the good news that talks had started again with the guarantors acting as mediators. And the *tucos* unintentionally did their part to make the *compañeros* happy: They moved the Japanese businessmen from the music room on the first floor to India in the annex. All hostages were now on the second floor. I notified the listeners.

Cerpa did something else that attracted my attention: He organized a game of *fulbito* or mini-soccer among his followers every afternoon. They would usually begin the match around 1500. Two teams of four each would play on the floor that ran from the ballroom through open double doors into the dining room. The Red Cross provided a soccer ball, jerseys, shorts, and even sneakers. Cerpa and his lieutenants always played—sometimes together, sometimes on different teams. All but two of the *tucos* who did not play watched the matches. The *tucos* who did not play or watch stood not-very-attentive guard duty on the second floor.

Cerpa began *fulbito* to distract his followers and improve morale. He worried that the *guerilleros* were gaining too much weight and losing their physical edge. The *fulbito* started on April 1—April Fools' Day. I notified the listeners.

16

Chavín de Huántar: Dress Rehearsal

PRESIDENT FUJIMORI was in the command center at SIN headquarters when I transmitted the extraordinarily good news that Cerpa had moved the Japanese businessmen to the second floor and scheduled daily *fulbito* games. This news allowed final preparations for the rescue.

The tunnel complex was ready except for the demolition branch that stopped just short of the residence. Miners were waiting until the engineers told them what rooms to dig under to complete the tunnel. Fujimori and his staff could now have charges placed under the ballroom, dining room, and kitchen without fear the detonation would harm the Japanese. And—incredibly—charges under these rooms would kill or incapacitate most if not all terrorists except the two on the second floor. Fujimori could hardly believe his luck. All that remained before he ordered the commandos into the tunnels was a timed dress rehearsal through the replica.

Fujimori was now less concerned about the sham peace process, although he would continue it until after the rehearsal. The exchanges with the terrorists through the guarantors were serving their purpose. He had calmed the Japanese delegation with assurances he was committed to a peaceful resolution of the crisis. He always added the loophole: "provided the mental and physical health of the hostages is not endangered."

The Japanese vice chancellor urged Fujimori to be more flexible on the prisoner exchange issue and consider releasing Cerpa's wife. Fujimori was noncommittal but said the matter of Cerpa's wife "was difficult." The vice chancellor also asked the president to "increase the pace of negotiations." Fujimori readily complied.

Between March 20 and 25 the guarantors met four times with the terrorists and other times with a government representative and even Fujimori himself. The guarantors believed a deal was possible when on the twenty-fourth they showed Cerpa a list of 271 prisoners and asked him to choose ten names, five of whom the government would select for exchange. Cerpa chose eleven. When the guarantors showed Fujimori the list, he did not reject the proposal out of hand but said it "required study." The guarantors saw light at the end of the tunnel, but it proved to be a train when Cerpa incredibly demanded all 271 prisoners on the list be exchanged.

A phone call Fujimori received from Prime Minister Hashimoto motivated the president's direct contact with the guarantors. Hashimoto had pressured Fujimori to reconsider a prisoner–hostage swap and threatened to cut economic aid to Peru if he ordered an attack that harmed Japanese hostages. The president once more assured Hashimoto that he would do all in his power to settle matters without an attack. He added that if armed intervention became necessary to save the hostages, the military commander would take every precaution to ensure no hostage was harmed—especially the Japanese.

After Fujimori received word from the Mariner that the terrorists routinely played *fulbito* at 1500, he decided it was time to do something about rogue Red Cross administrator Jean Pierre Schaerer. Montesinos had advised Fujimoto that this Swiss national was practically—and perhaps literally—in bed with the terrorists. SIN had picked up damning conversations of Schaerer passing information to Cerpa and the other leaders. Montesinos added that agents believed Schaerer was also passing information to Cerpa over the secure phone in the Red Cross conference room across from the residence. Montesinos's men were reluctant to tap the line because the government had formally agreed to allow private conversations. But the agents learned that every night Schaerer had duty in the conference room, the phone in the residence office rang around 0200 and Cerpa answered. The mikes picked up only parts of Cerpa's conversation but confirmed he was talking with Schaerer. Time for Schaerer to go.

AMBASSADOR GUMUCIO'S RADIO brought the good news talks had resumed between *tucos* and government—albeit through the guarantors. At least we had dialogue again. And when we learned that President Fujimori had met personally with the guarantors, we became cautiously optimistic that a peaceful end to our torment might be at hand.

As a military professional I recognized my duty to escape despite the danger. But as a husband, father, and son I prayed several times daily we would walk through the front door free men without a shot fired.

More good news from the radio. The government had declared the Swiss-Argentine *cojudo*, Jean Pierre Schaerer, persona non grata. Within an hour of that declaration, SIN agents shoved his ass aboard a flight back to Switzerland.

Our cautious optimism eroded and then gave way to pessimism when the renewed meetings led nowhere. The terrorist leaders were also affected. Divisions among the leaders appeared. Cerpa's priority was the release of his wife. He now didn't seem to care much about the other prisoners. The Arab didn't seem to care about any prisoner exchange. He wanted money, so that he could purchase a grocery store in a third country and lead a profitable, quiet life. But Salvador and Tito stood firm: They insisted on a full prisoner–hostage swap. I reported this development to the listeners.

We feared for our lives if the talks did not succeed. We believed that the terrorists—especially Salvador and Tito—were prepared to selectively mutilate and execute hostages to force an exchange.

The guarantors presented yet another proposal from Cerpa at the final scheduled meeting on March 26. One group of MRTA *guerilleros* and hostages in the residence would travel to Cuba, and a second group to the Dominican Republic. A commission on human rights would decide the question of amnesty or commutation of sentence for the imprisoned comrades. Congress would elect members to the commission, which would be independent of the government. The decision of the commission would be final. The guarantors would supervise improvement of prison conditions. The final point would be the most difficult for Fujimori: A few prisoners would be released to travel with the *guerilleros* to Cuba and the Dominican Republic. Cerpa's wife, Nancy, would be among them.

Cipriani took heart when Fujimori did not immediately reject the proposal. The archbishop believed this could be a sign that the president was studying the proposal and might accept it or accept with minor changes. Cipriani decided he would travel to Ayacucho for Holy Week. He told the press before he left that he was optimistic the parties could agree on a peaceful solution.

Cipriani returned on the twenty-ninth and met with the hostages. Then he met with Canadian ambassador Vincent and Japanese ambassador Terada. After this meeting he delivered the following speech to the media: "I meditated on the crisis while I was in Ayacucho. As you must know, the same God who created man and gave his only begotten son to be crucified for our sins meant this as a signal for the world to become civilized. Resolute journalism blind to humanity speaks of vacillation, weakness. We confront a human not a political problem. Respect due all human beings demands everyone involved either directly or indirectly with negotiations be treated with this respect. We of course condemn violence: This is not the way to solve problems. He who commits a crime must be punished but without having his dignity destroyed. Therefore, with Easter approaching to celebrate the resurrection, we must talk of forgiveness and mercy . . . I feel too often when a glimmer of hope appears, there are those who act to destroy it. I ask you as journalists to respect our work, not denigrate it. Please do not speculate. Speculation can destroy progress." Cipriani used the word *forgiveness* six times during his speech.

We heard the archbishop over the radio. More than one hostage wept. Hope touched all and pessimism dissipated. But not for long. The next day, Easter Sunday, Fujimori reiterated his position through the media that under no circumstances would he release prisoners.

Cerpa heard yet again Fujimori's vow never to free prisoners, including his wife. Cerpa told Cipriani and the hostages: "Because the government continues to refuse our proposal for a prisoner exchange, a solution is far from being achieved. Our main point is a prisoner exchange. Until Fujimori agrees, there will be no peaceful end to all this." Back to the starting line.

Cipriani met with Fujimori a few days after the president's speech and said he and the other guarantors "didn't have much gas left in the tank." Fujimori replied that he, too, was nearly out of gas. The hostages had been running on empty for a long time.

THE COMMANDOS finished the kill house training without incident and had been rehearsing the assault plan through the tunnels and replica for more than a week. Valer told the colonel the men were ready to begin going through the replica with live rounds rather than blanks.

The colonel gave the order to proceed and advised Valer of the new situation within the residence: All the Japanese were now on the second floor, and the terrorists played a game of *fulbito* on the first floor every day at about 1500. Only two terrorists guarded the hostages during the game. The colonel believed a dress rehearsal could be ordered anytime.

"We could use another ten days, sir."

"I'll tell Colonel Williams, who will discuss it with the general. We certainly do not want to go until all is ready—unless we have an emergency."

For the next ten days Valer drove the commandos hard. They took short breaks while engineers and demo men calculated the correct amount of C-4 to detonate under the ballroom, dining room, and kitchen. They placed cows and dogs in these rooms and cranked off various amounts of C-4 starting with one kilo. That amount only terrified the animals, who bolted from the residence with manifestly weakened sphincters.

Two- and three-kilo shots maimed and killed a few cows but left the dogs unharmed and yelping. Four kilos yielded the desired effect: The shots killed all the cows but only stunned and slightly wounded the dogs; more importantly, the exploding C-4 did not bring down the replica. Valer told the colonel the commandos were ready for the dress rehearsal. The date was April 13.

The commandos did not have to wait long. President Fujimori and Vladimir Montesinos arrived in the compound on the morning of April 15. The chief of the Joint Staff, army general Nicolás de Bari Hermosa, was with them. The general ordered the commandos to conduct a dress rehearsal. Thirty minutes later, before *La Garua* swallowed the smoke from the explosions, the president told the commandos they were superb and would soon fight for the glory of Peru.

"Watch," he told them, "for certain moves on the political scene that will mislead the terrorist into thinking we have lost our resolve and will not attack anytime soon. You are at this moment within days of entering the tunnels."

17

The Tightening Screw

As we moved deeper into April, *La Garua* thickened and temperatures dropped. Captors and captives alike felt the cold even more because of our limited caloric intake and plunging weight. Days passed without sunshine. When the sun did come out, we pressed ourselves against windows for any hint of warmth. Sunshine and warmth were balm for the spirit as well as the body. Now we lacked both.

The *tucos* also suffered from the increasing cold. Most were from the jungle and unused to the damp, penetrating chill of a coastal winter. They asked the Red Cross to bring warm clothing for them. The government would not allow it. Cerpa retaliated by keeping clean clothing from us.

Depression afflicted everyone in the residence. Some hostages began sleeping seventeen hours a day. Others exercised to the point of utter exhaustion and beyond. Many spent entire days listening to the radio.

Minnig concluded we needed psychotherapy. He approached us and suggested we meet with psychiatrists to unburden ourselves. Many of us laughed in his face. What an absurd notion.

Ambassador Aoki wanted us to at least take antidepressants. He became particularly concerned for our mental health when he entered a room and saw a hostage with his head tilted to one side and jumping up and down. Aoki thought the man was going over the edge. He did not know the hostage had just taken eardrops and was merely trying to get the drops to settle.

Cerpa slipped into a dark mood. He spent most of his time in bed. When he was not sleeping, he stared at the ceiling and listened to the radio. One day he shouted to no one in particular: "The media does not talk about us anymore! Perhaps we should make our hostages mow the lawn. What a sight for the world to see: pieces of ministers and military officers flying through the air when the mines explode. Perhaps the media would once again start paying attention to us!" If anyone needed a shrink, it was the *tuco* leader.

Contact with the listeners raised my spirits sometimes, but I became disconsolate if they did not respond to messages. When I was not collecting and transmitting information, I tried to calm myself by reading. I was unsuccessful. I kept reading the same page over and over while I dwelled on the awful things that might soon happen. I lost my capacity to understand English—a language I had spoken and read for twenty years.

I delivered the following message through the microphone in the Bible: "Dark moods affect all. Optimism gone. Situation dangerous. Angels must come soon." I often placed the Bible near Cerpa and the other leaders while they raged against Fujimori, so that the listeners could hear for themselves how volatile matters had become. The listeners remained mute. My frustration grew.

A curious attitude developed among several hostages toward our captors: anger and a dangerous willingness to express it. I recognized this attitude as part of a process many terminally ill people go through: surprise, depression, anger, and finally resignation. The will to live weakened. Many hostages began to wish for the torment to end—even if it meant death.

Hostages began to confront *tucos* with no apparent concern for serious, even fatal consequences. As a reaction to government intransigence, the *tucos* had begun chanting vulgar, insulting remarks through megaphones every morning in the foyer. During one chant they repeatedly shouted, "Guard dogs of the oligarchs are cowardly motherfuckers who eat Fujimori's shit!" One of the hostages, an air force officer, made a loud, rude noise. Salvador and Tito rushed to the officer's room and warned that if he made the noise again they would be forced to take "harsh measures."

An army officer in the room confronted the *tucos* and yelled that the noise was nothing more than a loud fart—something one cannot control. "Meanwhile," the officer said, "you shout insults at us for no reason at all." The two men scowled and left the room. This officer was either exceptionally brave or simply didn't give a damn how the *tucos* with AKMs in their hands and knives on their belts would react.

But the most dangerous moment—and moment of greatest bravery—occurred one morning when the *tucos* insulted Bolivia. "Bolivia" they shouted, "is a nation of shit-eating faggots!" They had insulted Ambassador Gumucio's country in this manner several times in the past, because the Bolivian government infuriated the *tucos* when it refused to release four imprisoned *cumpas*. Gumucio had endured the insults in silence. But not this time.

The ambassador approached a *charapa* standing guard on the landing. He told the youngster in a very loud voice to go below and tell his comrades "they are a bunch of *huevonazos*"—big assholes—"who dare insult my country because they have weapons."

The startled *charapa* stared at Gumicio and then hurried downstairs to deliver the message. In the meantime, I could see Gumucio was enraged and tried to calm him. I trembled at the thought of what the terrorists would do to the man. I walked away and whispered into the Bible: "Something very dangerous about to happen. Stay alert."

I closed the Bible as Cerpa, Salvador, and Twenty-two rushed up the stairs and grabbed Gumucio. They said they would take him below for a "serious talk."

"I have nothing to talk about with you *hijos de puta*."

Twenty-two and Cerpa grabbed Gumucio by his arms. The ambassador resisted. Hostages who had gathered on the landing started toward the terrorists. Salvador raised his weapon and the hostages hesitated. Cerpa and Twenty-two hustled Gumucio down the stairs.

In the foyer Cerpa yelled that Gumucio would face a People's Tribunal. Gumucio yelled back, "Take your People's Tribunal and shove it up your terrorist ass."

I ran to Golf, where the Arab was cleaning his AKM. "A fight has started," I told him. "You'll stop it if you don't want to see someone killed and police storm the building." I quickly explained the situation to the Arab, who was the brightest, most even-tempered *tuco*. We rushed from the room and saw that many hostages had gathered on the landing and were shouting. The Arab pushed through the crowd and hurried down the stairs. He had a frightened look on his face.

An incredible act of solidarity took place among the hostages. We began to sing the Peruvian national anthem, "*Somos Libres*"—We Are Free. We stamped our feet hard on the landing. Salvador and Twenty-two ran up the stairs and threatened us with their AKMs. We ignored them, continuing to stamp our feet and sing our anthem. The *tucos* stared at us with their mouths open.

When we finished "*Somos Libres*" we gave three loud *gritos*: "¡Viva Perú! ¡Viva Bolivia! ¡Viva Japón!"

In the face of such solidarity, Cerpa relented. He brought Gumucio to the second floor. As the two men reached the landing, Cerpa asked Gumucio: "Are you truly so brave, Ambassador?"

"When it concerns my country, yes, I am. You would see how truly brave I could be if you didn't have an AKM in your hands."

Cerpa flushed but said nothing. He realized he could no longer intimidate the ambassador and left without a word.

The courage of Gumucio and other hostages confused and worried the terrorists. As we lost our fear of death, we also abandoned our vacillating and obedient attitude. Cerpa and the other leaders met in the office to discuss this alarming development. Afterward the Arab spoke to our leaders in Charley. He urged us to speak with Cerpa or other senior *guerilleros* if we had complaints. He said open lines of communication were essential if we were to maintain tolerable cohabitation. What was the Arab saying? That we were all in this together?

Although the hostages welcomed this conciliatory attitude, the terrorists angered us with their stupid unwillingness to accept what the government had offered—safe passage. We believed Japan had sweetened this offer with assurances that country would give the terrorists a multimillion-dollar payoff once they released the hostages in Cuba or the Dominican Republic. Big payoffs, after all, were the way the Japanese government typically settled hostage crises.

Minister Tudela and Ambassador Aoki pleaded with Cerpa to accept the offer of safe passage. Tudela emphasized again that he knew Fujimori would never release MRTA prisoners—at least none of the leaders. Aoki hinted broadly that his country would pay a hefty sum of money in exchange for the hostages. Both men emphasized the significant achievements of MRTA: They had forced the government to negotiate; the government promised to improve prison conditions; they had informed the world of their grievances and demonstrated their power.

Cerpa wavered. He called his senior staff together and put the matter to a vote. He was in favor of taking the money and running to Cuba. Salvador and Tito were determined to accept nothing less than a prisoner swap and voted against Cerpa. The Arab yearned for a financial settlement but feared Salvador and Tito would lead an uprising and perhaps kill Cerpa if he compromised on the issue of prisoner release. The Arab reluctantly threw in with the two zealots. The microphones picked up the argument and terrorist vote.

Through Minnig, Cerpa increased pressure on the hostages to write Fujimori demanding compromise and the release of prisoners. The Red Cross disgusted many of us when this supposedly neutral organization sided with the terrorists. We wrote no letters.

On April 14 Monsignor Cipriani made one more attempt to sway Fujimori. Cipriani had at least tentatively convinced the terrorists to prepare a final list of twenty-one prisoners to be released as part of a settlement. Through Herculean efforts over four long months the prelate had persuaded the terrorists to reduce their original demand for 440 prisoners to a fraction of that number. Among those on the list were Cerpa's wife, Nancy, Victor Polay, Lori Berenson, six Chileans, two teenagers, and a man of seventy.

Fujimori agreed to free only the teenagers and old man. Cipriani pleaded with the president to free Cerpa's wife as well. Fujimori answered with finality: "We will liberate no MRTA leader."

Cipriani announced to the media his health had worsened under the strain of the negotiations; his doctors had ordered bed rest, and he would not be able to resume his efforts for two or three days. He said he feared for those within the residence and their families. He pointedly did not limit his concern to the fate of the hostages.

When the *compañeros* learned of the latest failure, we met and evaluated the situation. We agreed it was dire and we could not count on the government, although I had finally forced a reply from the listeners that implied a rescue was at hand. A few days earlier I had sent an angry, frantic message. I said if we did not hear from them within the next hour we would proceed with a plan to break out on our own. An almost immediate response appeared on the pager: YOU MUST CONTROL THE BISHOPS. THEY MUST DO NOTHING TO THREATEN D DAY. I knew then a rescue was near. But when? I asked the listeners; they did not reply.

The *compañeros* decided we could not wait long for a rescue. We agreed to escape through India on April 25. Clandestine rehearsals began the next day.

We heard some good news, however slight, over the radio on April 17. Our families, friends, and other Peruvians of goodwill marched that day by the thousands through Lima to mark the fourth month of our captivity. The crowd massed in the Plaza de Armas before the presidential palace. People prayed, sang, and filled the air with balloons and white doves. Fujimori met privately with wives of hostages. Nothing happened.

FUJIMORI DREADED his meetings with the wives of hostages. He would much rather deceive the media and Japanese government than these poor women. He was relieved he would fire the interior minister that afternoon as prelude to the rescue. The wives would at least not have to suffer the hell of uncertainty much longer.

The next day brought unexpectedly good news for Fujimori: Cerpa announced he would no longer allow doctor visits to check on the medical condition of hostages, many of whom had potentially fatal ailments that required weekly examinations and sometimes injections. Fujimori called the Japanese prime minister and told him what the terrorists had done. He added that their action had placed the health of the hostages at great risk. The prime minister responded in a weary voice that he understood.

After speaking with Hashimoto, Fujimori called Montesinos on the secure phone and told him to order the commandos into the houses behind the residence. That night police cruisers began delivering the commandos to the houses four men at a time. This was not the first time they had been in the houses; throughout their training the commandos had secretly visited dozens of times in small groups. They had pre-positioned such items as ladders, stretchers, fire extinguishers, radios, and explosives. Now the commandos would enter the houses for the last time and await orders to occupy the tunnels.

THE MASS DEMONSTRATION at the Plaza de Armas buoyed our spirits somewhat. Then Cerpa halted the doctor visits that had been part of our weekly routine since the takedown four months ago.

Cerpa must have believed he could force Fujimori to be more cooperative in return for renewed medical visits. I doubted it. Cerpa's provocative act would do nothing more than heighten the danger of an armed attack. We intensified rehearsals for a breakout.

On Sunday, April 21, the pager vibrated at 0900. Fernandez did not bother to write the message down for delivery but came directly to me in Charley. Heredia and Denegri were with him. Tudela and Gumucio joined the two men and formed a screen for privacy as I read the message. The listeners confirmed our standing codes: FIRST FLOOR HELL; SECOND FLOOR HEAVEN; SPIRAL STAIRCASE PURGATORY; LANDING PEARLY GATES; HOSTAGES BISHOPS; COMMANDOS ANGELS. The message nearly maxed out the pager's twenty-word capacity. A minute or so later the pager vibrated again with a message that continued the codes: FOUR LEADERS BIG PIGS (CERPA NAPOLEON, TITO SQUEALER); OTHER MALES PIGGIES; FEMALES PIGLETS. The messaged ended with instructions for me to read back the codes. I opened the Bible and complied.

The pager vibrated once more. WHEN FUN BEGINS HELL, SEND "PIGS IN PARLOR!" WHEN ONE OR TWO PIGGIES/PIGLETS HEAVEN, SEND "MARY IS SICK!" I read back the codes.

The screen went blank, then: ANGELS 3 MIN. AFTER THUNDER. ALL BISHOPS ON FLOOR. I acknowledged and asked if this would be a drill.

The listeners did not reply immediately. After five minutes or so they sent: DRILL. GO THROUGH SEQUENCE, OPEN DOORS AS LAST ACT. I had told them about only two doors: the first door and armored door to the patio. *Rehearsal my ass*, I thought. Throughout the day and even after lights-out, I sent more than eighty messages. The listeners answered only a fraction.

I slept little that night. Finally we were on alert, on standby. Only the *compañeros* and a few trusted *ayudantes* knew what the next day was to bring. I wrote a short will and shoved the paper in my pocket.

18

"The Pigs Are in the Parlor!"
"Mary Is Sick!"

APRIL 22. Our 126th day in captivity began like most. Our jailers assembled downstairs in the foyer, where the Arab led PT. Two of his henchmen remained on guard at the top of the stairs. We started our daily round of cleaning chores under their watchful eyes.

As I mopped the hallway I could hear the Arab counting cadence: "One, two, three, one! One, two, three, two!" Four-count jumping jacks. When the count reached a paltry fifteen, the terrorists stopped and began to run in place. They chanted the usual slogans as they ran: "One month is nothing! Two months are nothing! Three months are nothing!" Then: "¡Qué se mueran los enemigos del pueblo! ¡Qué todos se mueran! ¡Aquí nadie se rinde, carajo!" Let the enemies of the people die! Let them all die! No one here will surrender, goddammit!

The enemies of the people paid no attention. We were well beyond the point of intimidation. I stifled a yawn and continued to mop.

Soon the mindless chanting stopped. Cerpa, trailed by the Arab, Salvador, and Twenty-two, climbed the stairs to confront and harangue. Cerpa ordered us into our rooms. The terrorists followed me and stopped in the doorway for a head count. All present. They would do the same in the other rooms. As was their custom, the terrorists sang their tiresome anthem, "Los Molinos." The song was a tribute to fallen comrades in the Andean town of the same name, where we had cut down seventy and captured many more. *We* should have been singing of Los Molinos—our finest hour so far against the criminals. I prayed an even finer hour was close at hand.

For the past several days Cerpa had followed the singing with a menacing tactic he had not used for weeks. Two terrorists would leap into the room and level their AKMs at us. Cerpa and the Arab would follow with grenades held high ready to toss. I suspected Cerpa had ratcheted up the harassment as prelude to a demand we plead with President Fujimori to release the imprisoned terrorists, including Cerpa's wife and the American, Lori Berenson. *Que estupidez.* What stupidity. Fujimori was as immovable as the Andes—especially now that he knew the terrorists might well be on the eve of their destruction.

I noted with some alarm that Cerpa had lately taken to planning strategy—such as it was—with the Arab, Salvador, and Tito in a voice barely above a whisper. But he screamed threats to kill us all one by one if the government did not meet his demands. I feared Cerpa had finally realized the residence was bugged and would soon search for hidden mikes. We had little time left.

Finished with their threats, the terrorists allowed us to go to the bathroom and begin our own PT. Most of my companions were listless and went through the exercises halfheartedly. They were depressed—resigned to an awful end. Long gone was the widespread enthusiasm and hope of the first few weeks. One disappointment after another had eroded optimism. Now most of the seventy-two hostages believed our remaining days were few. Many had begun to move like the living dead.

0900. The terrorists called Ambassador Aoki to the first floor. In a surreal ceremony Cerpa congratulated him on his wedding anniversary. "Our most sincere congratulations on your anniversary," Cerpa told him. "It's a shame circumstances do not permit you to celebrate this happy event with your wife. We want you to know how much we respect you and wish you and your wife good health."

Aoki took little comfort. He knew he was third on the list to be killed, after Foreign Minister Tudela and Pedro Fujimori, the president's brother.

A little later a young terrorist appeared in the upstairs hallway and asked Father Wicht to give another talk on economics. At the insistence of the Arab, Wicht had already given four such talks, but of course he agreed to address the subject yet again. He went downstairs and presented his lecture to Cerpa, the Arab, Tito, and several young *tucos.* I walked halfway down the stairs and counted an audience of eight in the ballroom. All had their weapons either cradled in their arms or held at their sides.

Wicht spoke of the communist model that forbids private participation in the means of production and exchange. He pointed out that the model works only in the abstract and used the Soviet Union as proof it could not function in the real world. I heard the Arab and Tito surprisingly agree with the priest—at least on the point that the Soviets had failed to solve the problem of poverty. Some pigs, they seemed to realize, remained more equal than others.

While the terrorists were distracted with talk of economic theory, I took the opportunity to send my first message of the day. I went to my room and rummaged through the bag with my clothes until I located the Bible. I took the Good Book in hand and began my daily pacing around the landing and down the passageway. I mumbled what appeared to be my incessant reading of scripture. No one paid any attention, including the two terrorists lounging on the landing at the top of the stairs and listening to Father Wicht's lecture below. I had simply become an aging reactionary lost in his religion.

As I turned and walked away from the terrorists, I spoke directly into the tiny mike within the book's spine. Using code, I told the listeners: "The sea stinks today. Fishing will be good. Four big Pigs plus five Piggies, one Piglet in Hell. All armed. Two Piggies and one Piglet in Heaven, one Piggie in Purgatory. Two wearing T-shirts: CRISTAL and ALIANZA. One wears national soccer team jersey. Long sleeves."

I closed the Bible and entered Delta from Charley. I sat in a chair near the barricaded door to the upstairs patio and waited for the pager Fernandez had given me to vibrate with a return message. The message soon arrived but the tiny screen told me only to stop moving around. Weak signal breaking up. More bad fucking news.

I put the Bible on the ledge of a shuttered and chained window next to me. Now the problem was I'd have to leave my communications link, meander through the residence to collect intel, and return to the Bible. Instead of real-time intel I would be passing on information that might be stale. But I had no choice.

I returned to the landing and again walked toward the stairs, this time swinging my arms as if exercising. All seemed normal. Jorge Gumucio was seated outside Charley listening to music on his transistor radio. He winked at me as I passed.

Colonel Pepe Garrido was at his accustomed place in the room of the Supreme Court justices working on his puzzle of three thousand pieces. Carlos Blanco was at his side, watching in fascination as the colonel went about the interminable task of selecting the right piece. Pepe was seldom correct but remained serene—as if he knew someday he would solve the puzzle. I thought of Colonel Buendía in García Márquez's *Cien Años de Soledad* waiting patiently day after day, week after week, month after month, year after year for a government pension that never arrived.

I turned, walked back past Gumucio, and looked into Charley. Ambassador Aoki and Foreign Minister Tudela were playing cards. Tudela smiled at me as I walked toward the landing. Aoki ignored me.

I approached the terrorists on the landing, then turned away and walked back down the passageway toward the servants' quarters in the annex, passing and glancing into the room where the Japanese businessmen stayed. I saw one of the younger Japanese seated at a card table with the infatuated teenage terrorist, La Gringa. They gazed into each other's eyes and were quite likely playing footsie. A Go board was on the table between them. The man had patiently taught La Gringa the game. They now played almost daily whenever the girl's military duties permitted. Several of us wondered if they were lovers—and, if so, how they managed it.

I noted that La Gringa had carelessly leaned her AKM out of reach against the wall behind her. She'd draped her web belt over the rifle as usual. Grenades with the spoons taped dangled from universal ammo pouches hooked to the belt.

ALL WAS NOT as usual in the tunnels beneath the ground surrounding the residence. The commandos had entered the tunnels two days before, and many of the ninety men in the assault, support, and security teams had suffered a debilitating attack of diarrhea after eating stale field rations. The men had withdrawn in groups of ten back through the tunnel openings in the three houses beyond the rear wall. Medics rehydrated and pumped antibiotics into the commandos through IVs. They also gave them generous doses of Lomotil.

With medicinal plugs in place, the commandos returned to the carpeted and fan-cooled tunnels to once more await the preliminary signal to attack. This signal would come when the red overhead lights in the tunnel pulsed green. At that point the commandos would move forward to the line of departure and wait until they heard two orders through their earphones: "Detonate charges!" followed by "Attack! Attack! Attack!"

The forty-eight commandos in the assault team sweated beneath their bulletproof vests and balaclavas while they once more checked their weapons—an assortment of Belgian P90s, German MP5s, and Israeli Galils and Uzis. Lieutenant Colonel Valer had told his men the lights could turn green anytime within the next three hours. If not, they would fall back to the houses for fresh air and sleep.

The men had long ago written letters to loved ones for delivery should they die in the attack. Nothing more to do but wait and sweat.

1145. The hostages continued their routine as if today would be much like every other day. After I completed my chore with the honey buckets, I joined other hostages in the kitchen who were filling five-gallon water jugs from large vats. The jugs were heavy when filled, and we banged them against furniture as we stumbled toward the stairs.

As I carried water into the bathroom between Alpha and Bravo I felt the pager in my pocket vibrate. Alone in the bathroom, I retrieved the pager and read its message. The listeners were worried. They wanted to know what was happening downstairs. They heard alarming noises.

For the first time I now knew the tunnels ran directly beneath us instead of stopping in the garden as I'd thought. The knowledge thrilled me, but my joy was tempered with a realization that the commandos would almost certainly insert after demolition charges had breached the ground floors. I feared the impact the explosives would have on the load-bearing structures of the residence. If the commandos loaded too heavy, we might all perish beneath collapsing floors, walls, and ceilings. And the terrorists had rigged their own explosives throughout the place, which would surely detonate sympathetically when the commando charges went high-order. Not a happy thought.

I told the listeners the noises they heard came from hostages bumping into furniture with heavy water bottles.

1312. Members of the Red Cross arrived with lunch. They brought a special meal of sushi and tempura for Aoki to celebrate his wedding anniversary. No sake. The other Japanese shared this meal while the rest of us ate ravioli. I had no appetite but forced myself to eat the stuff as I normally would. I almost gagged. I might as well have been eating wet cardboard.

The Red Cross left at 1414 with the remnants of our meals and the nearly empty coffee and tea thermoses with their hidden mikes. The workers—a few of whom from the beginning had sympathized with and even aided the terrorists—remained ignorant of the aid they were providing SIN.

IN THE TUNNELS the commandos lunched on canned meat and canned peaches in syrup. Each man also received a small bag of candy for quick energy. They reviewed yet again the tactics for the rescue.

At 1400 Colonel Williams ordered Valer and his men out of the tunnels and into the houses for a few minutes of fresh air. Then they returned to watch the red lights.

SHORTLY AFTER the Red Cross left, the pager in my pocket beckoned. I was already seated beside the window ledge with the Bible on it. I opened and placed the Bible on my lap. I used it to conceal the pager while I read the message. It was as if a cold hand had suddenly clutched my heart: TODAY WHEN PIGS BEGIN MINI-SOCCER IN HELL, ANGELS FOLLOW THUNDER. COPY?

"Copy," I said into the Bible.

USING CODE INFORM WHEN PLAY STARTS, HOW MANY AND WHO PLAYS, HOW MANY WATCH, HOW MANY IN HEAVEN. COPY?

"Copy."

The pager displayed yet another message: REMEMBER GO, NO GO CRITERIA. NO GO UNLESS AT LEAST 8 PLAY AND NO MORE THAN 2 IN HEAVEN. OUT.

I couldn't have spit if my life depended on it. Military professionals the world over who have faced combat know the terror that uncertainty brings just before the battle starts. We deal with it through almost superhuman concentration on mission details. Heroes are those who attain a kind of serenity at the moment of greatest danger—Hemingway's grace under pressure. I prayed such grace would touch us all. How, I wondered despite myself, would it go down once I uttered the code that would set events in irreversible motion? But I thankfully had details to occupy me.

The number of *compañeros* now stood at ten. In addition, several helpers or *ayudantes* were ready to follow our orders, although they still didn't know precisely what was happening or why we gave the orders.

For days now several other hostages seemed to have known that something was in the air; we'd deflected or otherwise shrugged off their questions.

These men seemed to have fallen prey to the famous Stockholm syndrome and had long been currying favor with our captors. We had little doubt they would run straight to their masters if they thought we were planning an escape.

Still, with so little time remaining and so many suspicions among us, Chancellor Tudela and I decided it was time to risk "loose lips sinking ships." At last we told all *compañeros* that we'd established contact with the intelligence service through hidden mikes. We also revealed that SIN was sending messages on the pager Colonel Fernandez had managed to hide beneath his testicles each time the terrorists searched him.

Then I began my well-rehearsed tasks with Ambassador Gumucio, who was now leaning against the wall of the passageway just outside Charley and Delta. These two rooms were key, because the route to freedom ran through them and out the presently barricaded and bolted doors to the upstairs patio. The commandos would meet us on the patio when they climbed the stairs from the lawn.

I entered the passageway from Charley and greeted Gumucio with a too-hearty, "*¡Buenas tardes, Jorge! ¿Cómo estás?*"

The ambassador's mission was to increase the volume of his radio to cover the noise we would make when we moved the massive chest blocking the first bolted door to the patio, and to warn us if any terrorist approached. He would turn off the radio to signal the rescue would commence in three minutes.

Jorge fixed me with his usual sardonic look and replied, "*Jodido pero contento, compañero. Jodido pero contento. ¿Y tú?*" Fucked up but content. And you?

I put my hand against the wall and leaned close to his ear. "Couldn't be better. All is in place. They'll be coming for us soon. Stay here and wait for my signal."

For once the man was speechless. Just as well. I headed to the end of the landing to pass the word to *compañeros* in Alpha and Bravo. I whispered instructions to them as I located each either on the landing or in the room. Several had just settled in for a siesta. But they were wide awake when I left them.

As I passed the spiral staircase on my return to Charley I saw half a dozen terrorists in the foyer. Several were on their hands and knees using red and black markers to prepare yet another set of banners. They would hang these banners from the second-story windows and the roof as propaganda to feed the insatiable media monster pressing as close with its cameras and satellite dishes as security barriers would allow.

I peered over the curving balustrade and saw that one banner would be displayed on April 28 to commemorate the battle of Los Molinos. What was it with these *cojudos*? Why were they so fascinated with defeat? Perhaps they believed they could turn history on its head by endlessly proclaiming the battle a glorious victory rather than the catastrophe it had been.

The other banner was more traditional: It would celebrate Mother's Day—the second Sunday in May. The terrorists apparently did not believe a quick solution to the crisis was at hand. So much the better for us.

I knew the mini-soccer game in the ballroom would not start until the terrorists finished their posters. I couldn't see the leaders; Cerpa, the Arab, Salvador, and Tito were probably in the first-floor office trying to figure out what to do next. I returned to Delta and the Bible.

1415. The Canadian ambassador, Anthony Vincent, arrived for what appeared to be a negotiating session. But he left the office after a few minutes to address those of us who had assembled in the foyer and on the stairs. Another delay. The *fulbito* would not start until after Vincent left. In halting, tortured Spanish the ambassador tried to lift our spirits, but he could not hide his fear all might end tragically. His mood was somber, and I could see hostages drop their heads as he spoke. He should have kept quiet.

"Archbishop Cipriani," he said, "is sorry he could not come, but he's ill."

We took this as a sign the archbishop simply had nothing left to offer the terrorists in return for our freedom. I grew impatient for Vincent to leave so that the soccer would start and we could bring this awful time to an end. We'd done the math: We calculated at least a third of us would die. We did not care. We wanted it finished.

Ambassador Vincent told us we were in his prayers and in the prayers of millions around the world. Then he mercifully left, and the hostages returned to their rooms.

I lingered at the top of the stairs and soon saw the terrorists assemble for their game. All were dressed in shorts and wore shirts with logos of various Peruvian teams. The players also all wore sneakers.

I'd seen enough. I knew the time had come. I returned to Delta and took the Bible from the window ledge. I opened it and began to speak: "The Pigs are in the parlor . . . I say again, The Pigs are in the parlor. Copy?"

＊ The pager rested within the open Bible next to the hidden mike. The return message was immediate: COPY. PROCEED.

"Eight at the trough. Three big Pigs. Five little Piggies. Napoleon and Squealer among big Pigs. Copy?"

PROCEED.

"One big Pig, one Piglet watch. Alpha Kilo Mikes against wall. Two Piggies in Heaven playing cards with two Japanese on landing. Armed. One Piglet playing game in Foxtrot with one Japanese. Armed. One Piggy in Heaven at Pearly Gates. No weapon within reach. One-zero in Hell, four in Heaven. No go. Will advise. Copy?"

COPY. WE'LL WAIT FOR YOUR WORD ONLY 2 IN HEAVEN.

Two of the terrorists upstairs had to leave to satisfy our go criteria. Jorge Gumucio was now seated in his chair outside the door to Charley and Delta, where he could see me. His radio was on. Several men in Charley were lying on the floor as if sleeping—but none were. Father Wicht, Jorge San Ramon, and Eduardo Pando were playing cards in Delta. These men would help me move the chest away from the bolted door to the patio. Once the chest was out of the way, we would unbolt but not open the door. We would do the same with the second door.

I put the pager in my pocket and left Delta. The two little Piggies continued to play cards with the Japanese businessmen. One Piggy leaned against the balustrade and watched. He yawned as I passed.

I noted with satisfaction that Colonel Miyashiro was in animated conversation with two other hostages at the entrance to Bravo. These young military men had courageously volunteered to take out or at least delay any terrorist who might attempt to enter Charley while I was sending the code to attack. As for Miyashiro, I had absolute faith in him. He was the man who had captured the notorious Abimael Guzman.

I walked down the passageway and confirmed that one of the *compañeros* was at or near the door to all rooms with hostages. When Jorge Gumucio switched off his radio, they would warn every hostage to hit the deck. Everything was in place—except for two terrorists too many upstairs. I stood by Gumucio, listening to the radio and waiting.

I didn't wait long. In one of those exceptional moments that reaffirmed my faith in God, Salvador appeared at the head of the stairs and told the terrorists playing cards and La Gringa that Cerpa wanted to see them. The *tucos* followed Salvador downstairs with their weapons.

Only one Piggy remained. He had moved to a large window near the stairs that overlooked the lawn. He would be an easy target for the snipers I was certain had deployed on the roof or top floor of the Unique perfume factory. The factory towered above the residence directly across from the window where the Piggy stood.

At last all was in place. I entered Delta and told my helpers the time had come to move the chest and unbolt the door. "They'll be coming for us in less than five minutes," I said.

I nodded at Gumucio and he turned up the radio. The sweet melody of a traditional Peruvian waltz, "*La Flor de la Canela*," filled the air.

We put our shoulders to the chest and quickly moved it aside. We had more difficulty with the heavy bolt. It had rusted and at first would not budge. I was pushing so hard, my arms started to tremble. I swore at the unyielding chunk of iron: "*¡Conchatumadre!*"

Finally the bolt began to move. The movement was slow and accompanied by a screeching I was sure the Piggy could hear. But the ever-alert Gumucio had already turned up the volume again to cover the noise. He'd also begun to sing along with the radio.

I left Delta and entered Charley, where I picked up the Bible I'd laid aside to clear the door. Adrenaline quickened my heart.

I spoke into the Bible. My voice was too loud but I didn't care: "Door cleared." I checked my watch. "It's 1714. Sorry—1514. One in Heaven, one-three in Hell. I hear helicopters."

SEND CODE. THUNDER AND ANGELS IN THREE MINUTES.

I looked at Gumucio, who stared back. He'd stopped singing. I jammed my thumb down like Caesar ordering death in the arena. Gumucio switched off the radio. My fellow hostages in Charley stopped what they were doing and lay facedown on the floor, hands clasped behind their heads, elbows pressed against the sides of their faces.

On the landing, Colonel Miyashiro ordered the two Japanese seated at the card table behind the Piggy into Bravo. One man hesitated. Miyashiro grabbed him by the neck and flung him through the doorway.

The landing and passageway emptied. Only the Piggy remained, standing by the window, gazing across the lawn with his rifle and grenades behind him out of reach.

I spoke into the Bible for the last time: "Mary is sick! Mary is sick!"

I closed the book and made the sign of the cross. Less than three minutes remained. I wondered if I'd offered up my last Our Father.

19

Forty-one Seconds from Terror to Freedom

VLADIMIR MONTESINOS was in the SIN command center as always to monitor transmissions between his agents and the Mariner. Today, he prayed, would finally be the day. The longer the commandos remained on alert in the tunnels, the more they would lose their combat edge, which had been honed to such sharpness over the past four months.

When he heard me utter, "Mary is sick! Mary is sick!" Montesinos punched a number on his cell phone. He was disappointed his hand trembled.

The president awaited the call in the Palace of Justice, where he was answering a judge's questions during a hearing on his ex-wife's petition for more spousal support. In keeping with the opsec plan, Fujimori was going about his daily schedule as if all were normal. The bitter divorce had been more entertaining for Peruvians than any *telenovela*. The national media reported, magnified, and otherwise distorted every detail of the entire sorry episode. The terrorists would certainly know of the hearing and be lulled into thinking today would be uneventful: The president would be preoccupied with this personal embarrassment.

Fujimori barely listened to the magistrate's questions; the man often had to repeat himself. Fujimori's cell phone buzzed on the table in front of him and he cut the man off: "One moment, Your Honor. This is an important call."

Fujimori did not even bother to turn away from the judge. He put the phone to his ear and heard Montesinos say: "Mary is sick, *señor presidente*, Mary is sick."

The president thought he detected a tremor in his aide's voice. Fujimori spoke in his usual clipped manner when a crisis was upon him: "Ready for *la cuenta regresiva*?" The countdown?

"*Sí, señor.*"

"All Pigs in the parlor?"

"*Sí, señor.* All but one who is in Heaven."

And about to enter the fires of Hell, Fujimori thought with some satisfaction. "*Macho o hembra?*" Male or female animal?

"*Discúlpame.* Piggy above, both Piglets below."

"*Comienze la cuenta regresiva.*"

"*Sí, señor.*"

Fujimori snapped his cell phone closed and addressed a perplexed judge: "The hearing will have to wait for another day."

Minutes later the president was at the command center after a thrilling ride in his armored Mercedes behind a brace of police motorcycles with sirens in full cry.

"*¡LUZ VERDE!*" The ninety commandos of the assault and support groups in their tunnels alerted like dogs on point when they heard "green light" crackle in their earphones. But they'd heard the same order the day before and nothing followed except word to withdraw.

Today would be different: The overhead lights turned from red to green and the commandos heard the order, "*Abra la boca!*" Today they would not withdraw through the main tunnels up into the houses just behind the walled compound of the residence. Today, within the next two minutes, they would open the mouths of main and branch tunnels and scramble onto the parched lawn to assault the residence.

The men leaned forward and gripped their Belgian P90s, German MP5s, Israeli Galils, and Uzis. Several snapped on the halogen flashlights secured to their gun barrels with riggers' tape. Men with Mossberg 12-gauge shotguns chambered shells of double-aught buck.

Men of the support group in the tunnels yanked lanyards releasing plywood platforms holding less than six inches of topsoil that separated the commandos from fresh air, success or failure, life or death.

Several tunnels failed to open. The topsoil, unwatered for months and baked hard by the hot sun of a Peruvian summer, refused to collapse. Men sweating heavily beneath helmets, balaclavas, and body armor battered the unyielding earth with flat-headed mining tools called *topos* or moles. The men succeeded in punching the *topos* through all but one of the tunnels.

Tree roots were hopelessly entangled across the tunnel mouth that four men of an assault element were trying to climb through. The men retraced their steps, found a clear tunnel opening, and prepared to hoist themselves to daylight. The delay put them a fatal forty seconds behind schedule to storm the second-floor patio.

As the men were opening the tunnel mouths, they heard another order over the net: "*¡Entrando al bravo!*" Forward with courage! The men would climb from the tunnels as soon as they heard explosions.

Commander (major) Carlos Tello of the marines' Special Combat Unit was at his post in the explosives tunnel. He bent over a heavy-duty truck battery and prepared to close the circuit that would detonate four and a half kilos of C-4 each beneath the ballroom, dining room, and kitchen. Tello had calculated the demo and placed the charges.

Cables connected the explosives to the battery. If the charges failed to blow electrically, Tello had double-primed them to fire mechanically.

His earphone filled with the *cuenta regresiva: "¡Cinco, cuatro, tres, dos, uno: Fuego!"*

All charges went high-order. The ground trembled and bucked as if Lima were suffering yet another monster quake. Assault and support groups fought through dust and debris to daylight. Chavín de Huántar was under way.

I HAD TAKEN my position behind the door to the landing from Charley. The first explosion lifted me at least a meter off the deck. I was momentarily stunned but still conscious. Two other explosions slammed the residence. Walls shook and glass shattered. The Bible with the mike flew through the window, its pages fluttering to the ground.

Several smaller explosions joined the thundering noise as booby traps detonated. Smoke and debris swirled so thick I couldn't see my hand in front of my face. Fires flared.

I remained flat on the floor and yelled for other hostages in the room to do the same. I had told all hostages many times that if commandos came, the only way they could identify us was if we remained perfectly still on the floor. Movement of any kind invited death. With such restricted visibility, commandos often threw themselves on prone bodies and checked for weapons to determine if the person beneath them was hostage or *tuco*.

I heard the voice of the terrorist Cone yelling at the door and saw him thrust his AKM into the room. A white rag was tied to the barrel. I knew he had come for his target, Chancellor Tudela. Cone peered through the drifting smoke and saw that Tudela was not on his mattress or the couches next to the wall. He did see the minister of agriculture, Rodolfo Muñante, who screamed for the terrorist not to kill him.

Cone ignored Muñante and continued to search for Tudela. Muñante later claimed Cone had spared him as an act of mercy. Nonsense, I'd thought. The terrorist simply did not want to waste time killing Muñante because his target was Tudela. The chancellor, intelligent man that he was, had stayed away from his accustomed place in Charley: He'd taken a position in Delta near the armored door to the patio we'd left ajar. The explosive shock waves blasted the door from its hinges and blew the second, armored door aside. Still dazed, Tudela found himself looking onto the patio and freedom. He crawled forward.

Colonel Valer and his team at that moment had reached the stairs to the patio. The plan was for him and his men to follow an assault unit up the stairs—but that unit had been delayed when they could not punch through their tunnel. Valer did not hesitate. *"¡Vamos, comandos! ¡Síganme!"* Let's go, commandos! Follow me! The colonel took the steps two at a time with his men close behind.

Valer scrambled up and onto the patio with his Herstal P90 ready for an aimed burst of four. But he was unprepared for the sight that confronted him.

Crawling crab-like toward him less than two meters away was the balding Tudela in a white shirt. And above Tudela floated a grenade tossed by a green-shirted terrorist who was now about to fire a killing burst with his AKM from across the patio.

The 7.62mm rounds ripped into Valer as he launched himself atop Tudela. One round struck the commando in the neck above his body armor; two other rounds tore through his liver. Colonel Valer died within seconds.

One of Cone's bullets hit and broke Tudela's ankle. The grenade that Cone had thrown bounced harmlessly on the patio tile. In the confusion of the moment, the terrorist had pulled the pin but neglected to remove the tape securing the spoon. Commandos would later find four other such unexploded grenades where terrorists had flung them into rooms filled with hostages.

A commando behind Valer lifted him off Tudela. A splash of Valer's arterial blood blossomed like a red flower on the back of Tudela's white shirt. Two other commandos from Valer's unit hosed down Cone with their MP5s, then trampled his body as they ran through the doorway with two other commandos to clear Delta. Almost immediately after the commandos entered Delta a stream of hostages crawled onto the patio led by Eduardo Pando and Pedro Aritomi. Valer's pooling blood soaked Eduardo's pant leg as he crawled through it.

One of the commandos who had sprinted through the doorway to Delta went directly to Charley. His duty was to find me. I heard his voice close to my ear: "Admiral, I'm here to get you. Don't worry. We've killed the only *tuco* in these rooms."

I looked into the man's face, streaked with camouflage grease, and immediately recognized him as a marine officer I'd trained in special operations. I cannot describe the absolute bliss I felt in that moment. I was at last free. My life was no longer in the hands of madmen. I would later calculate the time it took for the marine officer to reach me after the initial explosion beneath the ballroom: forty-one seconds.

The officer asked me to direct him to Bravo. I pointed to the connecting door, which was partially obscured by smoke but still on its hinges. We had unlocked the door before the assault. Three commandos joined the officer, and together they entered Bravo. The commandos encountered no terrorists—only a roomful of eternally grateful men who were no longer hostages.

I made my way carefully past other commandos into Delta and toward the patio. I addressed the commandos and identified myself in a very loud voice. I did not want to become a friendly fire casualty.

I dropped to the patio tile and began to roll toward the stairs on the far side. I didn't want to risk walking or even crawling. Because of my size I would have made a good target for any lurking terrorist.

I worked my way down through commandos coming up the stairs in a combat train. Other hostages were directly behind me. When we reached the lawn, a commando directed us to sit against the wall of the residence. From time to time other men joined us. Some were bleeding and limping, and several were on stretchers. I thought one of the wounded on a stretcher was Carlos Giusti but I couldn't be certain.

I also saw several badly wounded commandos on stretchers and a black zippered bag containing Colonel Valer's body. My joy was replaced with an overwhelming sadness as I saw the carnage. And fighting still raged within the residence. More casualties would surely follow. I feared many hostages would die, just as we'd projected.

WITHIN SECONDS of the C-4 detonations beneath the residence, two other explosions boomed just outside. One breached the common sidewall with the Unique building; the other breached the common back wall with the houses.

The assault and support units from Unique headed across the front lawn to link up with commandos who had battered in the doors to the circular driveway. Other assault units deployed to cover the roof and windows on the first and second floors. Four men in a support element ran to the massive front door between the Doric columns. One man positioned a greased mat of Flex-X to blow the door. Another commando held the mat in place with a long pole while two of his comrades taped the mat to the door. Taping complete, one of the commandos pulled the ring on a fuse lighter, and ten seconds later the exploding Flex-X hurled the armored door down the foyer toward the staircase.

The door struck the *tuca* Berta Melendez and fractured her skull. As commandos ran into the residence several paused before the prone terrorist to give her a double tap.

The charges under the ballroom and dining room had killed six terrorists instantly and stunned others. These men regained their senses, grabbed weapons, and headed up the stairs to execute hostages and detonate their own explosives to bring down the residence. Cerpa was one of the survivors and the first to reach the stairs. Commandos who had entered through the front door mingled with terrorists on their way to the second floor. The smoke from fires and explosions was so thick, the men could not distinguish friend from foe.

Halfway to the landing a commando looked down through rising smoke and saw hairy legs in basketball sneakers beside him. The commando brought his Uzi to bear and squeezed off two rounds center mass. The force of the bullets slammed Cerpa into the balustrade. The commando heard the terrorist's last words: *"Estamos fregados."* We're fucked.

THE ASSAULT and support units that had climbed through the breach in the back wall while their comrades were blowing the front door met trouble immediately. The commander in charge of the assault unit stepped on an antipersonnel mine that somersaulted him into the air when it exploded. Medics reached him in seconds. He was still alive but losing blood fast. A medic located a vein and inserted an IV for a blood expander transfusion. The commando leader survived, but his left leg was so mangled that surgeons later had to amputate above the knee.

Miraculously no other commando stepped on a mine. But doom from another source awaited them as they mounted the stairs to the rear annex: a labyrinth of primed and ready *caza bobos.*

The point man was Lieutenant Raul Jiménez. He tripped the first of several booby traps in a chain. Semtex and shrapnel severed arms and legs, and tore out eyes. Jiménez took a scrap of steel through his throat and was dead before he struck the stairs. The assault on the back of the residence through the annex stalled.

LA GRINGA had just entered the passageway on the second floor and when the shock waves of the first explosions threw her to the floor. She quickly recovered and her training took hold. Thoughts of Go vanished as she thumbed the selector switch on her AKM from safe to automatic. Glass fragments crunched beneath her feet as she stumbled down the passageway toward her target: the Japanese businessmen in Foxtrot.

She stepped over the threshold, raised the AKM to her shoulder, and locked eyes with her *enamorado,* who cringed on the floor in front of her. La Gringa lowered the AKM and stood still as a tombstone. Then she turned and stepped into the passageway, where a commando decapitated her with a blast of double-aught buck from his Mossberg.

AMBASSADOR AOKI did not see La Gringa enter Foxtrot. After the initial explosions another hostage threw one of the thin Red Cross mattresses over him. The ambassador did not know his benefactor but would be forever grateful. Aoki had realized early in his captivity that he would be among the first terrorist targets if Fujimori ordered an assault. The terrorists repeatedly practiced how they would track him down and kill him. The ambassador was relieved he had decided to play mah-jongg with the Japanese business-men. But he knew the terrorists would soon search him out when they dis-covered he was not in Charley.

The thirteen men in Foxtrot remained flat on the floor as they'd been in-structed. They heard terrorists shouting to one another and commandos yelling "¡Lucha, lucha, lucha!" Fight, fight, fight! Who would come through the door? The commando or the tuco?

A few minutes passed. The men could no longer hear either the terrorists or the commandos. They knew that if they stood and moved about they risked being shot, but they began to think no one was coming for them. They were partly correct: Jiménez's team had the mission to secure Foxtrot, but they were busy evacuating their wounded comrades and the body of their leader. The fear of more booby traps also slowed them.

Every Japanese seemed to rise as one. They first checked the passageway and saw it ablaze. No joy there. The only way out would be to jump from the balcony—but its double doors were chained and padlocked.

Eight men pushed the doors hard five times. On the sixth effort the lock on the chains snapped and the doors opened. The Japanese crowded onto the balcony.

Commandos below them yelled, "Jump! Jump!"

The distance was some twelve feet, and the Japanese hesitated. Then they saw flames from the passageway ignite the door to the room and felt the heat as the door caught fire. Three sat on the edge of the balcony wall and launched themselves into space. One leaped far enough to catch the canopy of the party tent and break his fall. The remaining men landed on the lawn. One suffered a broken leg; another, a badly sprained ankle.

The rest of the Japanese quickly followed. Many sprained ankles and knees but no broken bones. Ambassador Aoki managed to grab the tent canopy and make a soft landing. Commandos directed them to join other freed hostages against the residence wall beyond the stairwell to the patio. Medics carried men on stretchers who could not walk.

. . .

COMMANDOS WITH fire extinguishers sprayed foam on flames throughout the residence and slowly brought fires under control. A Waco lesson learned. Other commandos in assault elements went room-to-room looking for *tucos*. They shouted "Clear!" after they checked each room and tossed a red or green chem lite in the doorway. The only *tucos* they found were dead. *Tucos* on the stairs had taken so many double taps, their heads were little more than shredded chunks of bloody meat. Standard military procedure.

Two commandos started down the passageway to clear Golf. They knew Golf was the terrorist armory and they might well take fire. They slowed their approach; their caution was rewarded. As they neared the open door they saw a grenade fly from the room and bounce away from them toward the end of the passageway. A second grenade appeared that bounced toward them. They managed to dive into Foxtrot but not before one commando caught a backside full of shrapnel.

SALVADOR, LIKE CERPA, had survived the initial blasts, but he'd had better luck on the stairs than his leader. Salvador stepped onto the smoke-shrouded landing and took advantage of the confusion to disappear down the passageway. He was headed toward his target in Hotel: the magistrates.

Pepe Garrido had prepared the justices for the commando assault. All but three were now prone on the floor; a few had covered themselves with mattresses. Carlos Giusti, Mario Urello, and Luis Serpa chose to stand in a double closet with a sliding door. Hugo Sevina followed his colleagues and with their help managed to hoist himself onto the overhead shelf. The men closed the door.

Salvador appeared in the doorway with his AKM locked and cocked. Men screamed for him not to shoot. The terrorist hosed down the room anyway, his selector switch on automatic. The 7.62mm rounds snapped above the hostages on the floor but pierced the closet door. A round struck Carlos Giusti in the leg and severed his femoral artery; Mario Urello took rounds in the leg, knee, and buttocks; a round hit Hugo Sevina in the stomach and perforated his intestines.

The sound of a splintering door at the end of the passageway interrupted Salvador's deadly task. The terrorist headed to the MRTA armory in Golf. The armored door had withstood the blasts and protected the ordnance behind it.

Salvador unlocked the door with a steady hand. Before he entered he fired a short burst at a commando coming through the door from the annex. The man fell back.

Once in the armory Salvador had at his disposal a generous quantity of RPG-7 rockets, hand grenades, and ammunition. He knew how to use them all. No spoons on his grenades would be taped.

Salvador dragged a case of grenades to the door, pulled the pin on one, and rolled it to the right down the passageway toward the annex. He looked left and saw two commandos coming slowly at him from the landing. He pulled the pin on another grenade and tossed it. He would continue to lob grenades right and left from the armory as long as he could pull the pins. This terrorist was in charge for the moment. But the moment would soon end.

Two commandos—one SF and one marine—climbed a ladder to the roof and hurried across it until they were directly above the armory. In less than a minute they capped into a two-kilo mat charge of Flex-X and cranked it off with a hellbox.

The detonation caused secondary explosions from grenades, Semtex, and RPG-7 rockets. What remained of Salvador wouldn't fill a jungle boot. The last *tuco* was no more. All the hostages were out of the residence. All the terrorists were dead. The time was 1602.

A commando raced to the front corner of the roof, snatched the MRTA flag from its pole, and flung it to the ground while his mates gave full-throated shouts of victory. A slight, fox-faced commando brown as a bean clenched his fist and pumped his forearm piston-like, bringing to mind a vintage Alex Olmedo celebrating a passing shot. Victory truly seemed complete.

20

Requiem for a Rescue

ALL THE HOSTAGES from Alpha, Bravo, Charley, and Delta survived, but we did not know the fate of those in the other rooms. The commandos gathered us in front of the residence, where President Fujimori awaited. He approached and said: "Admiral, I commend you. I've been listening to you on the radio since you first began transmitting."

"Thank you, Mr. President, you heard the good with the bad. Sometimes I was so desperate I raged against everyone."

"Now we'll talk only of the good," said the president. "We can talk of the bad later."

Those were the final words President Fujimori ever spoke to me concerning my role in the rescue. Several months later he called me at home and asked the name of the officer who'd had the pager. That was it. Never met with or heard from the man again. And if a so-called hot wash-up meeting was ever convened to evaluate and draw lessons learned from the rescue, I wasn't invited.

After exchanging these few words with the president at the residence, I approached the marine officers of the Special Combat Unit who had so valiantly risked their lives to save us. They came to attention and saluted. I embraced and thanked each man for his extraordinary courage and professionalism. I'd trained most of these officers.

Someone had brought President Fujimori a chair that he stood on with megaphone in hand to tell us Operation Chavín de Huántar had been an enormous success: All hostages had been rescued without a fatality. Later we would learn the devastating news Carlos Giusti, the Supreme Court justice, had died of a heart attack in the ambulance on the way to the hospital.

Our joy was tempered further with the terrible news that two commando officers, Lieutenant Colonel Juan Valer and Lieutenant Raul Jiménez, had lost their lives helping save ours. Seventeen other commandos had been wounded, some gravely.

The president continued to speak as flames devoured the ambassador's residence and Senora Aoki's kimono collection with it. When Fujimori finished, commandos and former hostages joined in singing the national anthem.

We boarded buses parked on Thomas Edison Street that would take us to the military hospital. We were bruised and dirty. Many hostages had unkempt beards. We drove through streets lined three and four deep with citizens who cheered wildly when the buses passed. President Fujimori leaned out a window in the first bus and waved a Peruvian flag as a symbol of victory. I was elated but my thoughts were scrambled. I did my best to focus on the present.

After doctors examined me at the military hospital, the first family members I saw were my sons, Luis Felipe and Sergio. The emotion I felt was indescribable. We got in the family car and drove home. When I arrived, many people had assembled to greet and cheer me. I went straight to my wife, Marcella, my daughters, Alesia and Angelina, my blessed mother, my brothers and sisters. Tears flowed as we embraced.

Other friends and neighbors had come to celebrate my return, together with the merely curious. So many people filled the street, it looked like a demonstration.

I entered my home and the first thing I saw was the Christmas tree with lights ablaze and a mound of gifts beneath its branches. The tree had remained in place throughout the terrible four months of my imprisonment. How strange it was to be opening Christmas gifts in April. I did not complain. Joy to the world.

I finally excused myself to take a bath. The many kisses, handshakes, and *abrazos* had left me dizzy with happiness. I luxuriated in the tub of hot water I'd been denied for such a long time. I changed clothes and returned to the party. The phone rang incessantly, even more than when I'd been promoted to admiral.

When the party was finally over, I sat alone with Marcella and we cried as we gave thanks to God. I'd made a contract with Him that He had honored. I hoped I had done and would continue to do the same.

I went to bed and felt a curious pain throughout my body. I was unused to sleeping on a real mattress with real sheets, pillows, and blankets. It was all too much. I could not sleep. A whirlwind blew through my mind flinging thoughts, memories, and emotions every which way. I still could not believe the long nightmare was over. Something deep in my subconscious made me feel as if more awful events were to come.

IN THE MONTHS ahead the media monster that had feasted on me during the crisis continued to pursue with its insatiable appetite. I was continually harassed with demands for interviews and "photo opportunities." Writers who wanted to benefit from my pain offered to write my story—for 50 percent of the book's profit.

I resisted the media for two reasons. First, above all else I wanted to protect my family from the physical and emotional danger public exposure of my role in the rescue would pose. I'd learned from my previous fight against terrorists that publicity fueled absolutely serious death threats. I'd been forced to take my family out of the country for two years because of such threats after my involvement in the battle to put down the *senderista* mutiny at El Frontón prison in 1986. My fellow officer who took part in that combat, Admiral Vega Llona, had already paid the final price at the hands of terrorist assassins.

The second reason I resisted was to avoid the appearance of being in competition for the celebrity others sought so assiduously—the inevitable glory hounds: president of the republic, chairman of the Joint Chiefs of Staff, head of the *Servicio de Inteligencia Nacional,* and even fifteen-year-old Kenji Fujimori. The president proudly and absurdly claimed his son had been a trusted adviser throughout the crisis and had been the one who discovered through his telescope that terrorists were mining the lawn.

My efforts to remain beneath the radar were successful until the day two months after the rescue when the Japanese government invited me to Tokyo for an awards ceremony. I traveled with fourteen other hostages. The commercial attaché of our embassy in Tokyo met us at the airport. Chauffeured limousines drove us to one of the most elegant hotels in the country, located across from the emperor's palace in the heart of the city.

We had a "working breakfast" with our ambassador in Japan, Victor Aritomi, who as usual arrived precisely on time. He outlined the schedule for our visit. We would meet with former Japanese hostages, senior military and police officers, and members of the nation's Center of Civil Defense. We would visit the beautiful and orderly cities of Kyoto and Nari.

After breakfast the ambassador took me aside and said, "Admiral, I'd like you to give an interview on Japan's leading television network, NHK."

"Mr. Ambassador," I replied, "I've refused interviews in Peru for many reasons, but the main reason is I want to shield my family from terrorist reprisals."

He insisted. "This is a very important matter. You would help me a great deal with the Japanese government if you granted an interview. You may of course answer whatever questions you choose."

I reluctantly agreed, and NHK scheduled the interview for that afternoon.

I thought the interview would be in my hotel room but at the appointed time an NHK representative arrived and took me to a TV studio.

The interview was exceptionally uncomfortable and at times felt more like an interrogation. The reporter continually pressured me to reveal details of my role in the rescue. I resisted until at one point—just as if I were in the hands of a police interrogator—the reporter took out a tape recorder and placed it before me.

"Look, Admiral," she said in a *gotcha* tone, "I want you to listen to this tape and see just how much we know about what you did in the residence."

She switched on the tape recorder and I heard my voice transmitting vital information to the listeners shortly before the commando assault. So much for a low profile and responding only to questions I chose to answer.

I was disgusted. Somebody in the government must have given the tape to NHK. Another example of how others were willing to sell out me and my family for their own purposes.

When the interview ended, I asked the reporter if she would wait until I left the country to broadcast it. I knew the Japanese terrorist group Red

Army Faction had close ties with MRTA and might attempt to assassinate me before I returned to Peru. She said she would delay the broadcast and also told me she would give me a classified report the network had on the crisis and rescue.

I visited Japan on two other occasions. She never delivered the report. She told me her superiors had ordered her not to.

After several months, while I continued in my post as president of the Institute of Oceanography, I outlined this book. I had not intended to publish it but to leave the manuscript as a remembrance, a memoir for my grandchildren.

My only contact with the government was through the Ministry of Fisheries. I never received any official notification concerning the rescue or my part in it, not even from the armed forces. I was curious about this lack of communication but lost no sleep over it.

One day during a ceremony at the naval academy unrelated to the rescue, I encountered Vladimir Montesinos. I told him I'd very much like to know how the rescue had been planned and executed. He clapped me on the back and through that Cheshire cat grin of his promised to call and tell me all about it. "Perhaps," he added, "we could talk over lunch and a few beers at the Granja Azul." I never heard from the man.

Just as well. In 2000 a terrific scandal erupted when a Lima TV station aired videos of Montesinos bribing members of opposition parties to join Fujimori's party, which would give the president control of Congress. Millions of dollars changed hands. Montesinos himself had made these and several hundred more secret videos to use as blackmail if recipients of the government's largesse failed to uphold their end of the illicit bargain. The videos, stolen by political enemies of Montesinos, became known as "Vladivideos."

There was much more. Perhaps the most disturbing revelation was that Montesinos had sold arms to the notorious Colombian terrorist organization FARC (Colombian Revolutionary Armed Forces). Montesinos fled to Venezuela, but that country extradited him to Peru. He now shares a supermax prison with Victor Polay and Abimael Guzman. Peruvian SEALs guard the notorious inmates.

Not long after the Vladivideos began to appear on television and Montesinos's flight to Venezuela, President Fujimori took a trip to Japan, his ancestral homeland, where he retained citizenship. Once he arrived in Japan, he faxed his resignation as president to Congress.

A great witch hunt ensued as Fujimori's political enemies attempted to charge, try, and convict anyone associated with the disgraced president. Guilty until proven innocent.

In their zeal to discredit him, Fujimori's enemies turned their attention to what had been the president's crowning achievement in the War on Terror: the hostage rescue. The effort was helped immensely by the former Japanese hostage Hidetaka Ogura.

In 2001—nearly five years after the hostage crisis—Ogura wrote the Peruvian national prosecutor and accused commandos of having executed terrorists who tried to surrender. Fujimori's detractors were elated, and the witch hunt intensified. Never mind that not one other hostage—including all the Japanese—corroborated Ogura's version.

A particularly scurrilous rumor with absolutely no basis in fact began to circulate that Montesinos had secretly infiltrated the commandos with his own assassins. These men, according to the tale, had orders to execute any terrorist who attempted to surrender. And who originated such orders? Alberto Fujimori. Political payback is hell. Fueled by this rumor and other charges of "human rights violations," a hostile government demanded Japan extradite the disgraced ex-president.

MY TURN in the barrel soon arrived on a dismal *Garua*-shrouded day in 2001. One of my bodyguards came to my home and gave me an official-looking document. I could tell from the look on his face that it held bad news. Indeed, it was a subpoena from the Judicial Council directing me to appear as a witness into allegations of "first-degree murder."

I felt like a ship's captain about to founder on treacherous rocks. Owing to my battles in the War on Terror, I was no stranger to subpoenas, but this was the most shocking. The subpoena was not in an envelope. Who knew how many hands the document had passed through, how many eyes had seen its contents. Who among the many readers may have been a terrorist or terrorist sympathizer? A nice gift for those who would assassinate me: the time and place I was to present myself for interrogation.

The politically motivated investigation churned on for fifteen months, and in March 2002 the court ordered the terrorist corpses exhumed for evidence of "extrajudicial executions." Experts—none of whom were from the armed forces of Peru or any other country—conducted minute forensic examinations of the decomposed remains. Among these experts were officials from the Institute of Legal Medicine and the Peruvian Forensic Anthropology Group.

The government at this time was headed by a new president, Alejandro Toledo, who had for a very short time been a fellow hostage. He was among the first male hostages the terrorists released on December 20, only three days after the takedown. He'd departed the residence in company with the leftist politician Javier Diez Canseco. The two men had addressed the media and urged the government to negotiate with the terrorists. They read a petition on behalf of the terrorists.

The experts and media made much of the fact that many bullet holes perforated terrorist skulls. Generals William Zapata and Jaime Patiño, who had heroically directed the overall operation, meticulously explained how commandos must fire into a fallen terrorist's head to make certain the terrorist is dead and will not rise up to shoot a commando in the back. Commandos who do not follow this practice during hostage rescues such as Chavín de Huántar risk paying the ultimate price. For giving this professional opinion, President Toledo's government jailed General Patiño for two weeks; he is still facing charges. No good deed goes unpunished—especially if the deed is lost in the labyrinth of Peruvian politics.

THE GOVERNMENT permitted relatives of the dead terrorists to hold ceremonial reburials complete with laudatory speeches and coffins draped with the Peruvian flag.

The Forensic Anthropology Group issued an ambiguous report—challenged by several independent experts—concluding that the commandos had indeed committed "extrajudicial executions." The prosecutor, Richard Saavedra, seized upon the conclusion to charge former president Fujimori, SIN director Montesinos, chairman of the Joint Chiefs of Staff General de Bari Hermosa, and all commandos who had saved us with having committed first-degree murder. The conditional language of the indictments was peculiar: "If murder would have been committed, the accused would have participated." Alice in fucking Wonderland.

At the request of Prosecutor Saavedra, the judge hearing the case, Cecilia Polack Boluarte, ordered the preventive detention of generals Patiño and Zapata and eleven officers of the army and navy for alleged first-degree murder of the terrorists Eduardo Cruz Sanchez aka Tito, Emma Luz Melendez Cueva aka Berta, and Victor Pecero Pedraza.

Public outcry over these outrageous, so-called judicial actions was enormous and consequences swift. Judge Jorge Barreto replaced Judge Polack and released the jailed officers. The minister of the interior, Fernando Rospigliosi, said detention of these men represented an obstacle in the War on Terror. The defense minister, Aurelio Loret de Mola, also rejected the unjust actions of Saavedra and Polack: "We do not believe [the actions of these officials] were justified. [Chavín de Huántar] was not a secret campaign but an open, successful military operation." The discredited actions of these judicial officials had the further invidious result of revealing the names of the commandos, so that terrorists knew against whom to exact revenge. Terrorists had worked their vengeance on scores of military and police officers throughout the years. Leading examples include navy admirals Jerónimo Cafferata, Carlos Ponce, and Juan Vega Llona. Terrorists murdered General Lopez Albujar in front of his sons. So many military judges who handled cases of terrorism were assassinated, they wore hoods to conceal their identities while on the bench. Such actions, of course, led to a hue and cry from the radicals that the military was violating the civil rights of terrorists.

Five years after the rescue the armed forces were finally permitted to recognize the heroism of the commandos. In an emotional ceremony, the commanding general of the army and chairman of the Joint Chiefs of Staff, Bustamante Reátegui, decorated all the brave officers who had saved us. One of these officers, José William Zapata, gave a powerful speech in which he said: "This recognition and distinction fills us with immeasurable pride and strongly reaffirms the love we have for our Peru and its citizens. We will continue to defend until the death the noble ideals for which our nation stands."

I was honored to receive the Andrés Avelino Order of Combat for my part in the rescue.

You may be sure it did not take the Israeli government five years to recognize the heroic commandos who rescued a hundred hostages at Entebbe in 1976. And how many terrorists survived that rescue? Zero. The idea that Israel should have investigated and jailed its heroes because they killed all the terrorists is laughable.

The same could be said of any suggestion the British government should have investigated and jailed the British commandos who in 1980 rescued nineteen hostages being held by terrorists in Iran's London embassy. One of six terrorists survived that operation. Here's a quote the media attributed to a high British government official: "The rescue would have been an unqualified success but one bloody terrorist survived."

In December 2001 MRTA commemorated the fifth anniversary of the terrorist takedown with the following statement on its international website: "We reaffirm our military promise to continue fighting for the freedom of the people and our imprisoned comrades. We vow to strengthen our military force to achieve equality and justice for all. Only in this way can we ensure the enormous sacrifices of Túpac Amaru and his finest sons down through the centuries have not been in vain."

Although I was rescued on April 22, 1997, I fear I will forever be a hostage. Still, the terrorists cannot change the outcome of that glorious moment ten years ago any more than they can change their disaster at the battle of Los Molinos.

Epilogue

By LATE 1996 I'd begun to believe we'd finally emerged victorious against *Sendero Luminoso* and MRTA after sixteen years of bitter combat. During that dark period twenty-five thousand Peruvians had lost their lives, forty thousand children had been orphaned, and the war had cost the nation twenty-five billion dollars in ruined infrastructure. But all that was behind us: The leadership of both groups now spent their days in new, secure prisons rather than terrorizing Peru. Abimael Guzman and Victor Polay served life sentences for their hideous crimes. Both were fortunate the country no longer had the death penalty. Peruvians were at last free to go about their daily business and enjoy family and friends without fear. Wishful thinking.

The MRTA takedown of the Japanese ambassador's residence and my four months as a hostage shattered the illusion all was well and we had the devil on the run. Reality struck me in the face with a red-and-white bandanna emblazoned with a hammer and sickle. I questioned whether the government could ever eradicate terrorism through military means alone. We'd won many battles but the war smoldered still. We were mired in what has been called an "asymmetrical war"—a war without fronts, a war that has an important political dimension as well as military.

Terrorists could absorb combat losses and forge ahead in the political field, especially when they had sympathizers and even allies among government officials and the media. I determined to confront the enemy in the political arena as I had in the military.

During my time as a hostage, those long nights without power, sleeping on the floor and subsisting on meager rations, I wondered what could have made such zealots of the young men and women who held us. What experiences had made them so willing—perhaps even eager—to die for such a ruinous cause?

The answer is complex, but one thing is certain: Their lives must have been so bleak, so hopeless that anything else would have been better. The younger people who held us had been so marginalized, they knew little or nothing about the world beyond the borders of their villages. Toward the end, when the prospect of free passage to Cuba loomed, several asked hostages questions such as: How long would it take to reach Cuba by bus? When told they would fly to the island, they clamored for information about what it was like to ride an airplane.

Several hostages ridiculed this ignorance; I did not. I was appalled at how my government had failed these people and thousands more like them who lived in the mountains, jungles, and slums of our coastal cities.

After the rescue I resolved to do what I could to remedy such ignorance, such an abysmal lack of education, such resentment toward our government. Clearly the inequality in our society and the unfair treatment it breeds play into terrorists' hands. If we do not overcome this inequality, providing resources and hope to those the terrorists would recruit, violence will be our constant companion.

I decided to enter political life—something that would have been unthinkable for me had I not spent four months as a hostage. The decision was difficult primarily because it would mean I could not cloak myself and my family in the relative safety of obscurity. I would be on a public stage for all to see—including those terrorists who considered me a mortal enemy. Sometimes in my darker moments I wondered if I shouldn't just paint a target on my back.

I kept a fairly low profile in the beginning: I campaigned for local office as a member of a movement called *Vamos Vecino*—Let's Go, Neighbor. The people of Callao elected me to their city council for a two-year term. I think during that time I contributed to building a better Peru, albeit on a small scale. I also learned that Peruvian politics breed enemies.

My experience on the council confirmed something I had always believed: Only a national party with dedicated, disciplined members organized right down to the village level can ever truly change the abysmal conditions that foster terror. The one political party with those qualities was *Alianza Popular Revolucionaria Americana*—APRA. The party originated in the 1920s as a populist, democratic challenge to the wealthiest Peruvians—the so-called forty families who controlled the country through the military.

Although party rhetoric sounded very much like that of the Peruvian Communist Party, APRA was not in the thrall of a foreign ideology. APRA stood for the worker, the peasant, and an emerging middle class. Unlike the Peruvian communists, APRA did not preach class warfare but a uniting of classes to confront those few who governed and were adamantly opposed to any redistribution of wealth. Also unlike the communists, APRA championed democracy.

As the party's popularity and reach grew, government repression escalated. *Apristas* formed militias and fought back. In 1932 Haya de la Torre narrowly lost what many thought was a rigged presidential election. Party members took to the streets by the thousands. Demonstrations were particularly violent in the coastal city of Trujillo north of Lima—Haya de la Torre's birthplace and an APRA stronghold.

Battles between the army and militias raged through the streets of Trujillo. Combat was unrelenting and savage. APRA executed sixty army officers. Retaliation was swift and brutal. Backed by airplanes that bombed the city, the army killed more than a thousand *apristas*. Thus began a feud between the military and the party that endured for more than a generation. The government imprisoned Haya de la Torre and outlawed APRA; the party operated clandestinely for the next fifteen years.

In 1945 APRA regained legal status and supported José Bustamante for the presidency. Bustamante won in a landslide and brought APRA into the government. This began the party's move toward the center as an important player once again in national and local politics. APRA organized, proselytized, and regained its lost status as the most popular party in Peru. It spoke for the unemployed, the urban worker, the campesino, and the entrepreneuial middle class.

There were bumps along the way. Renegade *apristas* who were navy sailors mutinied in 1948 and seized the flagship of the Peruvian fleet. When APRA as a party refused to use violence to gain power, disaffected members deserted and took up arms. The military suppressed their most ambitious revolt in the sierra during the late 1960s. MRTA is the direct descendant of those former *apristas* who chose bullets and bloodshed over the ballot box.

Before he went over to the dark side, Victor Polay had been a protégé of Haya de la Torre and close friend of another rising APRA star, Alan García.

After the people elected García as the first APRA president in 1985—at the height of the war with SL and MRTA—I had the honor to meet him. I came away from that meeting with the cautious but nonetheless genuine feeling this man was truly of the people. And the leader of the strongest, best-organized, and most popular party Peru has ever known. APRA is the main reason militant communism has been the god that failed in Peru.

Still, when I ran for the Callao City Council, I could not bring myself to join APRA. The anti-military nature of the party—however far in the past— gnawed at me. Then in 2003 a choice was thrust upon me that would change my life.

A close friend of Alan García approached me at a funeral and with little prelude told me the former president wanted me to run as his first vice presidential candidate during the 2006 elections. García also wanted me to lead a national front. The idea of a front appealed to me as a way different groups could come together for the good of Peru. Inclusion rather than exclusion should be the policy. The country had always been dangerously fragmented—one region pitted against another, one class against another, one institution against another.

When the 2006 elections were officially called, Alan García invited me to participate in the organizing meeting for the front, and I accepted. Afterward I received a call from Jorge del Castillo—a García confidant and future prime minister of Peru.

Jorge said, "Alan wants you to become an APRA congressman and run as his first vice president during the elections." We scheduled a meeting with the APRA leader.

At that meeting Alan García and I discussed many topics, including the anti-military tradition of APRA. García made it clear that this stance was a thing of the past: Peru could not afford such grudges.

I asked if he would visit and have a frank discussion with members of the General Officers and Admirals Association. He readily agreed. Alan convinced all who were present that he was sincere when he said APRA and the military could make common cause for a better Peru. The alternative was the hammer and sickle.

After García's successful meeting with the association, I decided to ac-

cept his invitation to join the APRA ticket. I admit I was not particularly enthusiastic with the decision at first. I had family and friends I enjoyed spend-
ing time with; I had a successful diving and ship salvage business that more
than paid the bills; I was not anxious to become an even more attractive target for terrorists.

But as the elections drew near and campaigning intensified, I became
convinced I'd made the right decision. I traveled with García throughout the
country and often on my own. I visited poverty-stricken mountain and jungle villages and urban slums. People lived in terrible circumstances: straw
huts, malnutrition, pestilence, no electrical power, no sewage, little or no access to education or health care.

Despite all this, people I met and talked with at length still hoped for a
better future. I was now part of an effort that had a real chance to deliver that
future, or at least work toward it.

THE ELECTORAL PATH to the presidency is difficult and dangerous. You hear
shots fired, explosives detonated; police and bodyguards hover close to you;
small planes ferry you through jungle rains and mountain mists that limit
visibility to less than a hundred feet. And to become president you must run
the gauntlet twice unless you win at least 50 percent of the vote the first time
through. Rarely does a candidate accomplish this feat.

Presidential candidates from twenty parties competed in the first round.
The three favored candidates and their parties were Lourdes Flores (National
Unity), Alan García (APRA), and Ollanta Humala (Union for Peru).

On a political continuum, Flores would be right of center, García left,
and Humala far, far left. Humala, a former army colonel, yearned to be the
Hugo Chávez of Peru, the Evo Morales of Peru. He would nationalize anything that moved and much that didn't. He would repudiate Peru's free-trade
agreement with the United States. He would legalize the cultivation of cocaine for any use. He would establish a commission to replace the old Constitution with one more to his liking. He would champion an axis running
from Cuba, through Venezuela and Peru, to Bolivia.

In January 2006 Hugo Chávez invited Humala to a celebration in
Venezuela honoring the Bolivian president-elect, Evo Morales. During the
celebration Chávez publicly endorsed Humala for president of Peru.

The conservative candidate, Lourdes Flores, favored close ties with the United States and warned Peruvians not "to go down into the abyss with Humala."

Humala told an Argentine newspaper that if Flores were elected, she would be overthrown within a year. Humala knew something about military coups. In 2000 he attempted to overthrow Fujimori and was imprisoned for his effort. Congress pardoned him after Fujimori's resignation.

We tried to stay above the fray and focus on issues such as education, health care, unemployment, economic policy, and . . . terrorism. Humala supporters consistently attacked García because of the difficult economic times Peru suffered toward the end of his first presidency. García admitted his administration had made mistakes but said he had learned from them: He would be a more effective leader the second time around. Polls showed that the message resonated with voters.

I feared Humala's hatchet men in the media would attack me because of my legal problems after El Frontón. I shouldn't have been concerned: At the time of the elections Humala had been charged with torturing and killing campesinos during 1992–93.

Humala had other baggage. He was not up from poverty. He had been born into a fairly wealthy family that had disturbing social beliefs. His mother stated during his campaign, for instance, that all homosexuals should be shot. His father was a reverse racist who claimed dark-skinned people should rule Peru and subjugate whites. He believed that terrorist leaders Abimael Guzman and Victor Polay should be released, Peru should invade Chile, and politicians should be shot. He was anti-Semitic and denied the Holocaust. Humala's family was a cross for him to bear. He ordered his parents to keep their mouths shut during the campaign.

The same regions of the country that terrorists could exploit—with their grinding poverty and governmental neglect—fell under the spell of Humala: the southern Andes and the jungle. As I listened to his speeches, I was struck by their resemblance to the messianic ravings of Abimael Guzman. Humala's coup attempt revealed his contempt for democracy. His speeches had a subversive tint. Just as Guzman spoke of creating a "new order," Humala spoke of creating a "new republic" with a new Constitution that might well reflect his family "values."

As results came in for the first round of the election, Humala surged ahead, followed by Flores, and then García. Elections in Peru go slowly. We mostly cast and count our votes the old-fashioned way—by hand. No electronics. Weeks passed; the vote total crawled toward 100 percent. It became evident no candidate would receive a majority. A runoff was inevitable between the two leading vote getters.

Humala enjoyed an insurmountable lead of slightly more than 30 percent as the total count crept above 90 percent. Lourdes Flores held slightly more than a 1 percent lead over Alan García. The closer the vote total came to 100 percent, the slower the count became. Toward the end waiting for results was like watching paint dry.

Finally García overtook Flores and defeated her for second place: 24.3 percent of the vote to 23.8 percent. A close call. We would face Humala in a runoff.

During the final round we campaigned to the point of exhaustion and beyond. The election was nasty, brutish, and mercifully short. In Cuzco a pitched battle between armed García and Humala supporters raged through the city. Many people were injured, including several gunshot casualties. Luckily no one died.

Polls showed the candidates racing neck and neck. And then came a gift from God for APRA: Hugo Chávez weighed in on behalf of Humala. He called García "corrupt, a thief," and worse. The Venezuelan president threatened to take his oil and withdraw from the Andean Pact if Peru elected García president.

Peru no less than the United States and other democracies has little patience for outsiders who meddle in national elections. Chávez became for Peru what Citizen Genet and Osama bin Laden had been for the United States during its elections.

President Toledo, my fellow hostage for such a short time, recalled the nation's ambassador from Venezuela and filed a formal protest. Chávez was unfazed: He called Toledo and García "alligators from the same sewer." Chávez ridiculed García as President George W. Bush's "puppet" and "office boy." A democratic socialist the puppet of a neoconservative? A man from a party with a tradition of challenging "Yankee imperialism" the office boy of a US president? I think not. Many other Peruvians thought not, either.

After Chávez's meddling, the polls shifted dramatically in favor of García. An unfortunate incident while Humala and his wife were voting in their neighborhood revealed the depth of Peruvian discontent over the Venezuelan's attempt to influence our elections. Protestors temporarily trapped the pair in the polling place at Universidad Ricardo Palma in Lima. The protestors shouted, among other far nastier things, "You're the same as Chávez!"

When the count finally ended, we had defeated Humala 52.62 percent to 47.40 percent. Alan García would once more be president of Peru, and I would be his first vice president. Lourdes Mendoza, a deputy mayor from the southern city of Arequipa, would serve as second vice president. I won my congressional election and would represent Callao as an *aprista*. Imagine that.

Particularly gratifying were our victories in some Andean and jungle departments that had voted for Humala in the first round. The APRA message of national integration and unity was being heard and heeded in places where terrorism once flourished.

WHEN I SETTLED into the vice president's office, I prominently displayed photos of two navy admirals who had been my close friends: Juan Carlos Vega Llona and Carlos Ponce Canessa. Terrorists had murdered these men. I displayed their photos not only in homage, but also as reminders of what would happen to me if I were not ever-vigilant.

I also displayed a framed letter written by Lieutenant Colonel Juan Valer on the eve of his death during our rescue. It reads:

Dear *Compañeros:*

As you read these lines you'll know the rescue operation has cost me my life. I pray we achieved the objectives we trained for with such determination and for such a long, dangerous time. I regret some of us had to neglect duties at our beloved Command and General Staff College, but this was necessary to save Peru from terrorism, from the brutal acts of criminals.

Our victory will help end the terrible situation that has so harmed our peaceful nation. Ours will be part of the effort to once more put Peru on the path of sustained development and an improved standard of living for all citizens—particularly the children.

Many times I neglected my family. More than once I didn't go to the house of a *compañero* to study for the Staff College. But if we achieved our combat objectives—even if some of us fell in the effort—then our sacrifices were justified. We died in defense of *La Patria*. What greater glory.

Let this be my epitaph: "He died a soldier fulfilling his duty. He asks the world to remember him as Valer. Valer was our *compañero* and loyal friend."

May God Bless You,
Comandante Valer

Lest we forget.

ADMIRAL LUIS GIAMPIETRI ROJAS,
Peruvian navy (retired)

INDEX

ABOUT THE AUTHORS

LUIS GIAMPIETRI, a retired admiral, is now vice president of Peru. In a forty-year career he has been a deep-sea diver, a combat swimmer, commander of two warships, a naval attaché to Great Britain, and a field commander of special operations forces fighting terrorists and drug traffickers.

BILL SALISBURY is a retired navy commander and former US Navy SEAL who has written widely for the *San Diego Reader, Miami New Times,* and *Soldier of Fortune* magazine. He practices law in San Diego.

LORENA AUSEJO is a journalist who has written for leading Peruvian magazines and newspapers. She has published a book of her interviews with famous Peruvians, including former secretary general of the United Nations Javier Pérez de Cuéllar. She is currently the news director for a prime-time TV program about politics telecast by Peru's equivalent of CNN.

ABOUT THE TYPE

This book was set in Albertina, a typeface created by Dutch calligrapher and designer Chris Brand. His original drawings, based on calligraphic principles, were modified considerably to conform to the technological limitations of typesetting in the early 1960s. The development of digital technology later allowed Frank E. Blokland of the Dutch Type Library to restore the typeface to its creator's original intentions.